# "No One Helped"

*Kitty Genovese, New York City, and
the Myth of Urban Apathy*

Marcia M. Gallo

Cornell University Press
Ithaca and London

First published 2015 by Cornell University Press
First printing, Cornell Paperbacks, 2015

Printed in the United States of America

Library of Congress Cataloging-in-Publication Data

Gallo, Marcia M., author.
    No one helped : Kitty Genovese, New York City, and the myth of urban apathy / Marcia M. Gallo.
        pages cm
    Includes bibliographical references and index.
    ISBN 978-0-8014-5278-9 (cloth : alk. paper) —
    ISBN 978-0-8014-5664-0 (pbk. : alk. paper)
    1. Genovese, Catherine, –1964. 2. Murder in mass media. 3. Murder—New York (State)—New York. 4. Bystander effect—New York (State)—New York. I. Title.
    HV6534.N5G35    2015
    364.152'3092—dc23        2014039464

Cornell University Press strives to use environmentally responsible suppliers and materials to the fullest extent possible in the publishing of its books. Such materials include vegetable-based, low-VOC inks and acid-free papers that are recycled, totally chlorine-free, or partly composed of nonwood fibers. For further information, visit our website at www.cornellpress.cornell.edu.

Cloth printing          10 9 8 7 6 5 4 3 2 1
Paperback printing      10 9 8 7 6 5 4 3 2 1

To Spouse A, with love

# Contents

# Acknowledgments

Many people helped, in many ways, with the creation of this book. During the last seven-plus years, which have taken me from Wilmington, Delaware, to New York City to Las Vegas and back too many times to count, I received exceptional support and encouragement during a remarkable journey of discovery.

My first acknowledgments are to Mary Ann Zielonko and Angelo Lanzone for reliving painful moments, telling poignant stories, and providing intriguing insights into the woman they both loved. I also had the privilege of meeting and talking briefly with two of Kitty Genovese's brothers, William and Vincent, and I thank them for sharing their memories. I am indebted to Rob Snyder for his belief in this project from the start, his knowledge of New York City history, and his introduction to Michael J. McGandy at Cornell University Press, who is an exceptional editor and a joy to work with. At Cornell, Michael and an extremely competent team that includes Mahinder Kingra, Kitty Liu, Max Porter Richman, Ange Romeo-Hall, and Amanda Heller shaped a manuscript into a polished book. My thanks, too, to the University of Texas Press for permission to reprint parts of my May 2014 article in the *Journal of the History of Sexuality*, "The Parable of Kitty Genovese, the *New York Times*, and the Erasure of Lesbianism."

A cadre of people have followed the story of Kitty Genovese and the thirty-eight witnesses since 1964; they are researchers, writers, artists, academics, and activists, many of whom generously provided valuable information, research leads, and encouragement. My thanks in particular go to psychologist Bibb Latané; Kew Gardens historian and attorney Joseph De May; sociologist Andrew Karmen; writer and performer LuLu LoLo; former Queens reporter John Melia; writer Jim Rasenberger; feminist scholar Carrie Rentschler; screenwriter and director James Solomon; psychologist Harold Takooshian; and playwright J. R. Teeter.

Next up for special recognition are the librarians and archivists who have aided me in my research. Given that there is no "Kitty Genovese Collection" located in any repository, I am grateful to many of them, starting with Polly Thistlethwaite, chief librarian, City University of New York Graduate Center Mina Rees Library. Polly was predictably creative in helping me find materials at numerous sites early on in this project, and I appreciate her generosity and friendship. My thanks also go to archivist Jeff Roth at the *New York Times* and to the many women and men of the New York Public Library, Rare Books and Manuscripts Division, who aided me during semiannual research trips to Forty-second Street. For their extra efforts in helping me illustrate the impact of the Genovese crime on feminist organizing against rape, I thank the artist Marty Waters and Daria Hyde, Michigan Natural Features Inventory at Michigan State University, as well as Cecilia Malilwe, Digital and Multimedia Center and Peter Berg, Special Collections, Michigan State University Libraries. I also acknowledge Thomas Cleary, Civil Rights Archivist, Department of Special Collections and Archives, Queens College Libraries, CUNY for his assistance in providing the image of the flier announcing a civil rights protest on the opening day of the 1964–65 World's Fair. Last but not least, I thank the clerks at the Queens County Courthouse for providing case files and incisive commentary during my research trip there in 2011.

I was fortunate to have had a remarkable team of former and current UNLV students who provided research assistance. Marie Rowley not only tracked fiftieth-anniversary coverage of the Genovese story but also secured permissions for the images in the book. She and Angela Moor helped me create sane and sensible "back matter" as well. My thanks also go to Ian Baldwin, who compiled contemporary media coverage of the Genovese crime from Chicago, Los Angeles, and Washington, D.C., sources and discovered hard-to-find television shows and to Alexandre Léonard, who provided excellent French-English translation for an important source. In addition, in New York, the writer Lisa Reardon Seville helped me access Queens case files and provided valuable insight into crime beat reporting.

To those who have read all or parts of the manuscript, I give my deep appreciation, starting with Ann Cammett and extending to Mila De Guzman, Elaine Elinson, Adrian Jones, Mary Klein, LuLu LoLo, Leisa Meyer, Angela Moreno, Esta Soler, and Carmen Vázquez. Thank you all for astute observations and excellent suggestions.

In addition, the following colleagues and friends offered encouragement, comfort, critiques, good company, and/or copies of helpful materials: Yolanda Alvarez, Bonnie Anderson, Kelly Anderson, Amy Aronson, Marcella Bencivenni, Jennifer Brier, Raquel Casas, Chris Cleary, Blanche Wiesen Cook, Clare Coss, John Curry, Nancy Davis, John D'Emilio, Peter Diaz, Martin Duberman, Caryll Dziedziak, Alice Echols, Dorothy Ehrlich, Kathleen Feeley, Lynn Fonfa, Elizabeth Fraterrigo, Estelle Freedman, Andy Fry, Joanne Goodwin, Hilary Hallett, Greg Hise, Donna Hitchens, Sandy Holmes, Surina Khan, Colin Loader, Aleah Long, Laurie Lytel, Marta Meana, Dennis McBride, Gene Moehring, Debbie Palmer-Sutter, Yaniyah Pearson, Arlene Roach, Vicki Rosser, Tuan Samahon, Dean Savage, Amy Scholder, Sarah Schulman, David Tanenhaus, Jennifer Terry, Michelle Tusan, Mary Wammack, Susan Ware, Doris Watson, Jessica Weiss, Elspeth and Charles Whitney, Christolynn Williams, Tom Wright and Dina Titus, and Eli Zal. My apologies in advance to anyone I may have forgotten; please know that I appreciate your support.

This journey of discovery has led me to many unexpected places, but I really hit the jackpot at the University of Nevada, Las Vegas. In addition to the Rebels already mentioned, I thank UNLV's History Department faculty and staff, all of whom have been supportive and helpful as this project progressed over the years from job talk to publication. I thank our dean of the College of Liberal Arts, Christopher Hudgins, for summer research funding in 2011 and 2012. Colleagues Barb Brents, Lynn Comella and Anita Tijerina Revilla, and Ann McGinley and Jeanne Price provided guidance in early phases of this work. I relied on support from Claytee White and Barbara Tabach of the UNLV Oral History Research Center as well as the leaders and members of the Southwest Oral History Association. Current and former UNLV history students Denise Boutin, Summer Burke Cherland, Stefani Evans, Kendra Gage, and Emylia Terry all helped me think through the story I wanted to tell.

Finally, I am blessed with a remarkable assortment of people who make up my extended family. Each in her or his own way has contributed to this book and my ability to research and write it. I begin with the amazing Tara Dunion and thank her for her beauty, strength, and compassion; she continues to bring great joy into my life, as do Gary, Nate, and Kyle Guggolz. I celebrate my Brooklyn "roommate," the fabulous Mena Cammett, who I am so privileged to have watched become the remarkable woman that she is. I am grateful for the love and lessons bestowed by the indomitable Grace Elizabeth Maggitti, aka Mombo, as well as the fearless and best mother-in-law of all, Sandi Cooper. My gratitude extends to Mary Klein for fifty years of exceptional friendship as well as to the Maggitti clan: Mike, Shelley, Melissa, and Mark, with a shout-out to Matthew for lending me his copy of *Watchmen* and special thanks to Ed for help with research on 911 at a critical moment in the summer of 2013. Sue Catanzarite and Kailey Berman have enriched our clan as well. I remain proud to have as family Adrian Jones; Anita Jones; Melani Cammett; Angelo, Alex, Lena, and Nikos Manioudakis; Howard and Myrna Allen; Joanne Hansen; and Lisa Cammett and Dee Battistella. I miss Ed Maggitti Sr. and John Cammett and wish they were here to celebrate this book with us.

Above all, I am grateful to and for Ann Cammett, the one and only Spouse A. Her commitment to radical lawyering coexists with her love of the arts and her passion for humanity. Thank you, Anni, for consistently enriching my life and work. I owe you a Blue Note.

# PROLOGUE: A NEW YORK STORY

Since 1964 the story of Kitty Genovese has shaped our expectations of community. It has served as a powerful cautionary tale, especially but not exclusively for women, at a time when new possibilities for independence and involvement drew many young people to big cities. Specifically, it was deployed to alert New Yorkers to a problem that did not exist: that of apathy. Activism was in the air and on the streets in 1964, and many New Yorkers joined local, national, and international organizing campaigns. Far from being apathetic, they gave their time and money as individuals to build groups and campaigns that could press their demands for reform and revolution.

The infamous phrase "I didn't want to get involved" was quoted in a front-page *New York Times* report in March 1964 that blamed the killing of Kitty Genovese on more than three dozen people—thirty-eight witnesses to a heinous crime. Her neighbors were castigated for a failure of personal and collective responsibility. Almost immediately, the story of a young woman's death became a warning of the growing "sickness" of apathy.

The media promoted an epidemic of indifference at the precise moment when millions of Americans were organizing for social change. The myth that resulted is at the heart of the paradoxical story of Kitty Genovese.[1]

It is a myth that has inspired concrete social changes. In the decades since the shocking tale of uncaring neighbors first made headlines, it has become commonplace to call 911 in an emergency, but in 1964 that was not possible—the 911 system did not exist. The Genovese crime hastened its development as one solution to the perceived problem of apathy. Like another hallmark of the crime—psychological research into how and why people react when they see someone in trouble—the emphasis was on understanding responses to crime. But in part the research that resulted in the theory of "bystander syndrome" was based on the assumption that the witnesses in Kew Gardens, because they lived near one another, behaved as a group rather than as individuals when they heard a young woman's cries for help. Ultimately the studies exposed stark discrepancies between New Yorkers' expectations of personal responsibility and community involvement.

My own interest in Kitty Genovese began when I first saw her photograph. As a thirteen-year-old girl in Wilmington, Delaware, with dreams of living a grown-up life in New York City, I was riveted by the image of her pale heart-shaped face and piercing dark eyes. For me, she was a potent symbol of the horrible fate that could befall a woman bold enough to navigate the world on her own. Her story has haunted me ever since. As I finished high school, married, moved, divorced, moved again, came out, went back to school, and moved a few more times, Genovese's story, as the poet Maureen Doallas has said, "stayed with me." I could not shake her image from my mind nor forget the awful details that I remembered from newspaper accounts. Genovese was a reminder that, despite the changes brought about by 1960s social movements, freedom could have devastating consequences. From time to time over the years I caught references to her name and read articles about the bystanders who did not help her, but without learning much more about the woman she had been. That changed in 2004. In February, to commemorate the fortieth anniversary of Genovese's death, a powerful feature in the *New York Times* brought her to life for me. The cipher became a person, one who laughed and danced and was devoted to her family and friends, who included a female lover. As I sat at the computer at home in Brooklyn writing my dissertation on the first American lesbian rights organization, friends from all over the country brought the lengthy story in the Sunday *Times* to my attention. At that point I knew I had to learn more about Kitty Genovese.[2]

The more I learned, however, the more apparent it became that newspaper and other media accounts eliminated salient facts from the narrative. Also missing was any sense of the vivacious twenty-eight-year-old Italian American woman who drove a red Fiat around New York in the early 1960s. I realized that she had been flattened out, whitewashed, re-created as an ideal victim in service to the construction of a powerful parable of apathy. It seemed to me that Kitty Genovese's personhood had been taken from her, first by her murderer and then by the media, in order to serve a greater good. The erasure of the facts of her life ensured that she would not be the focus of the story. Instead, her twenty-eight years of existence were reduced to one sentence in most early news accounts, while the awful details of her death were transformed into an international saga of her neighbors' irresponsible behavior.

In the construction of the story of Kitty Genovese, neither Genovese the victim, nor the perpetrator, a twenty-nine-year-old African American man named Winston Moseley, nor the senselessness of the violent crime itself was ever at the heart of the matter. In the *Times*' telling of the tale, both Genovese and Moseley were overshadowed by the people who lived across the street from Kitty in Kew Gardens, a quiet neighborhood in Queens where such horrible things were not supposed to happen. The very scene of the crime was aberrant. It was not a place that was associated with violence. For many New Yorkers in 1964, the opposite was true: Kew Gardens was considered safe because it was largely middle class, almost all white, with well-maintained single-family homes and midrise apartment buildings on narrow tree-lined streets. Many residents of Kew Gardens knew their neighbors, spoke to them on the street when they passed, did their shopping and socializing in the stores and restaurants along Lefferts Boulevard and Austin Street, much as Genovese and her girlfriend Mary Ann Zielonko had done. But two weeks after the crime took place, the *New York Times* highlighted a story, initiated by local police complaints, that blamed her death on her neighbors. The women and men of Kew Gardens took center stage in the media drama that then unfolded, making them infamous as bystanders.

The story of Kitty Genovese as constructed by the *Times* generated social and political questions in a city divided along lines of race and class.
New Yorkers in 1964 were increasingly feeling the impact of rapid social
change, which was often equated with race, the deterioration of communities, and upheavals in gender and sexual norms, all of which spiked in the
last decades of the twentieth century. Historian Elaine Tyler May summarized the era: "The civil rights movement challenged racial hierarchies,
and women were challenging domesticity by entering careers and public
life. The counterculture, the antiwar movement, and the sexual revolution
added to the sense that the tight-knit fabric of the Cold War social order
was coming apart." The story of urban apathy was promoted at a time
when the intensifying war against crime dominated political discourse and
undercut debates about racial justice. The racialization of crime, based on
the increasing identification of wrongdoing with people of color, solidi-
fied a process that had been under way throughout the twentieth century
and fundamentally affected America's cities. "The idea of black criminal-
ity was crucial to the making of modern urban America," asserted historian Khalil Gibran Muhammad. "In nearly every sphere of life it impacted
how people defined fundamental differences between native whites, immigrants, and blacks."[3] It can be seen in media accounts as well as popular
culture, and the story of the Genovese crime and the political responses to
it fit within this context.

Furthermore, some people began to look inward and examine their
consciences on hearing about the Kew Gardens neighbors. They asked
themselves and one another: Who had we become if we could stand by
silently and ignore someone's cries for help? The answer took many forms:
condemnations of urban density and disconnectedness, the atomizing effect of popular culture, the growth of individualistic survival strategies in
a dog-eat-dog world, and the disintegration of community.[4] Tensions that
had escalated during two years of protests over the intransigence of racial
segregation in New York City education, housing, and employment, as
well as ongoing instances of police violence against blacks and Latinos,
exploded in the summer of 1964 at the same time that Moseley was being
tried and sentenced. Genovese's rape and murder took place near the start
of a meteoric rise in the crime rate in New York City, which led to growing
fears of victimization among residents and calls for shifts in policing strategies throughout the city. Changes in other public policies soon followed.

The political reactions to her death, informed by local as well as national discourses on race and crime, gender and sexuality, involved law enforcement, social scientists, activists, and community organizations.

## Apathy at Stabbing of Queens Woman

"For more than half an hour 38 respectable, law-abiding citizens in Queens watched a killer stalk and stab a woman in three separate attacks in Kew Gardens." With this sentence, on March 27, 1964, the *New York Times* introduced its account of one of the city's most notorious murders. While the headline of the front-page article caught readers' attention—"37 Who Saw Murder Didn't Call the Police"—it was its subhead that established the moral of the story: "Apathy at Stabbing of Queens Woman Shocks Inspector."[5] When the report first appeared, it was as if a bomb had been detonated in the middle of Manhattan. "Kitty Genovese" and "Kew Gardens" dominated conversations and captured the attention of the city, highlighting fears at a time of growing mistrust among residents and a sickening sense of the city in decline.

The story began when the life of Catherine S. Genovese ended early on Friday, March 13, 1964. She had done nothing out of the ordinary, nothing more than what she often did: drive home from work. According to bartender Victor Horan, who was the last person to speak to her before she died, Genovese said good night to him about 3:10 a.m. and headed home to her Kew Gardens apartment from Ev's Eleventh Hour, the tavern where they worked. Genovese was the manager of the small neighborhood bar in Hollis, Queens. Usually the drive from Hollis to Kew Gardens took her about fifteen or twenty minutes, depending on the time of day.

On this cold morning, as she made her way through the quiet streets, Winston Moseley spotted Genovese driving in her red Fiat and followed her. He saw her pull into the Long Island Rail Road station parking lot on Austin Street, the narrow tree-lined semi-commercial street where she lived in a second-story apartment, and park her car. He then stopped his car and left it parked at a bus stop next to the lot. Moseley later told police that Genovese saw him watching her as she got out and locked her car door. She ran from him, heading up Austin Street toward Lefferts Boulevard. Moseley caught up with her and stabbed her twice in the back.

She began screaming for help, which alerted at least one neighbor in the Mowbray Apartments, the midrise building directly across the street. The neighbor lifted his window and shouted at Moseley, "Hey! Get out of here!" Moseley said that he saw other apartment lights switch on and he ran back to his car.

Realizing that his white Corvair was visible under the streetlight, and fearful that someone in the neighborhood might be able to read his license plate, he got in, started the ignition, and backed his car into nearby 82nd Road. Then Moseley sat in his car and waited. After ten minutes, seeing no one approach, he changed from a knit hat to a fedora in order to disguise himself and returned to Austin Street to search for Genovese. She had picked herself up from the sidewalk and made her way toward her apartment building, which faced the walkway near the railroad tracks on the far side of the parking lot. She was bleeding from the stab wounds Moseley had inflicted but was able to open the door of the first apartment a few doors down from hers. She collapsed inside on the floor of its small entryway. At the same time, Moseley had looked for her inside the railroad station building, which was empty, and then went up the walkway next to the tracks, trying the doors of the apartments. He found Genovese inside the foyer at 82–62 Austin Street. When she saw him she cried out again. He stabbed her in the throat to keep her quiet and then continued stabbing her in the chest and stomach repeatedly. He told police that he thought he heard and glimpsed someone at the top of the stairs opening the door, but when he looked up, he saw no one there.

Moseley's description of his two attacks on Genovese included details of a sexual assault while she lay dying. He cut open her blouse and skirt, as well as her girdle and panties, removed her sanitary napkin, and attempted to rape her. Unable to penetrate her, he went through her pockets and then ran off with some of the personal items he found, leaving her bleeding profusely and now unable to speak or cry out.[6] Within minutes after Moseley left, Genovese's neighbor Sophie Farrar rushed to help her. She had received a telephone call from another neighbor telling her that Kitty had been attacked. Farrar rearranged Genovese's ripped clothing and held her in her arms while they waited for the police and the ambulance, both of which arrived within minutes. It was now about 4:00 a.m. Genovese died on the way to Queens Hospital.

Police officers then awakened Mary Ann Zielonko, who shared the apartment at 82–70 Austin Street with Genovese. They brought her to the hospital to identify Genovese's body. They also began knocking on the doors of the people who lived nearby, trying to piece together the details of what had happened. They interviewed the local milkman, Edward Fiesler, who provided information about the man he had seen walking on Austin Street that morning during his deliveries. Less successful were the police questionings of more than forty people throughout the rest of the day. The officers heard repeatedly from many of the neighbors that they had been awakened by screams but "saw nothing." Some neighbors refused to answer any questions; one couple admitted that they thought they had glimpsed or heard a "lovers' quarrel" and decided it was none of their business.[7]

Genovese's death quickly made the news. Local papers such as the *Long Island Press* put it on the front page the same day it happened, as did *Newsday*. The *Press* highlighted the story, running it on the front page under the headline "Woman, 28, Knifed to Death." They also helped publicize police requests for information from anyone who might have seen the murderer. The *New York Daily News* printed the details on page one the next morning; the *New York Times* treated the story as a relatively unimportant crime report and gave it four short paragraphs on page twenty-six on March 14.[8]

Five days later Moseley was captured in another part of Queens as a result of the quick action of suspicious homeowners who spotted him burglarizing a neighbor's house. The two men disabled his car to keep him from fleeing the scene and called police, who caught up with Moseley as he walked away from the Corona neighborhood. Realizing that he matched the description of the man wanted in the Kew Gardens case, Queens police questioned Moseley about Genovese. He readily confessed not only to her murder but also to two other deadly attacks on women in the previous year. He then told police about numerous sexual assaults and hundreds of burglaries.

It was because of his confession to one of the other murders that Moseley originally came to the attention of *Times* metropolitan editor A. M. Rosenthal, a Pulitzer Prize–winning foreign correspondent recently returned to New York to assume the editorship of the city desk in an effort to freshen the paper's appeal to New Yorkers and halt declining sales. In the midst of orienting himself again to the city of his youth, and alert to its many changes during the decade he had spent reporting from other countries, Rosenthal was struck by a growing sense of fear and alienation among New Yorkers that coincided with a rise in crime. The attention given the Kew Gardens killing by other papers awakened him to the realization that the Queens story might be bigger and more significant than just another homicide in an outer borough. After talking about it with the city's police commissioner, he decided to investigate. The result was the March 27 front-page story, written by Martin Gansberg, which blamed Genovese's death on the indifference of her neighbors. It quickly dominated all subsequent coverage and became the official version, especially when Rosenthal published a book about the case, titled *Thirty-Eight Witnesses*, less than three months later.[9]

In all of the accounts that have followed in the story's wake, what has rarely been noted is that there is only one actual eyewitness to Genovese's death. That person is her killer, Winston Moseley. It was his confession to Queens police that provided the singular account of the case. His crime brought him notoriety and a life spent in prison; it also placed him, and Kitty Genovese, in a triangulated relationship with one of the most powerful men in New York City and arguably the world, A. M. Rosenthal, who would go on to become executive editor of the *Times*. It was Rosenthal who made "the manner of her dying" into a morality tale despite the complex circumstances surrounding it.[10]

The *Times* story hit a nerve with New Yorkers. Neither the initial factual and interpretive errors, nor the sense among more seasoned crime reporters at the time that the story of apathetic neighbors did not "sit well," undermined the paper's version of the events in Kew Gardens. This likely was due to the fact that the *New York Times*, known as the "Gray Lady" for its stolid eminence, was internationally renowned for factual coverage and unbiased reporting. The *Times'* long-standing status as "the paper of record" provided it with immunity from overt criticism.[11] As one journalist wrote: "When Rosenthal joined the *New York Times* as a city reporter in 1944, that newspaper and others wrote the 'official record' in relatively objective fashion. At his retirement [in 1986], investigative reporting had blossomed, with newspapers going far beyond the official record; papers regularly devoted dozens of columns to stories probing the mores and morals as well as the misfeasances of society." The advent of television meant that newspapers were no longer the main source of news for most people, necessitating a shift toward interpretation beyond "the twenty-two minutes available on a network evening news broadcast."[12]

Just as significantly, media approaches to crime reporting were changing at this time. The media analyst Chris Greer points out that contemporary

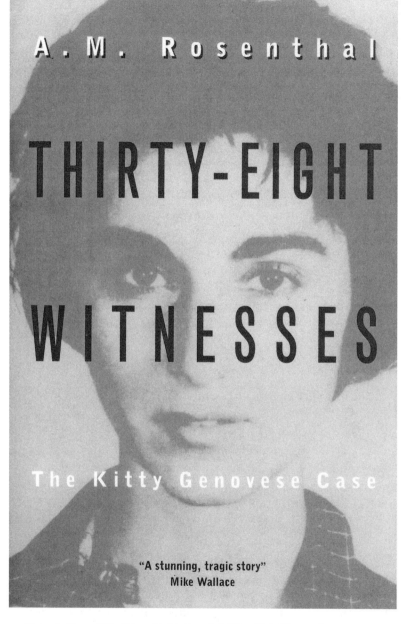

**Figure 1.** Cover, 1999 edition of A. M. Rosenthal, *Thirty-Eight Witnesses*. Image courtesy of University of California Press. Used with permission.

media highlight "the criminal victimization of strangers." Furthermore, Greer notes, "The foregrounding of crime victims in the media is one of the most significant qualitative changes in media representations of crime and control since the Second World War." Since the early 1960s, and in the decades since Genovese's death, "victims have taken on an unprecedented significance in the media and criminal justice discourses, in the development of crime policy, and in the popular imagination."[13]

The *New York Times'* coverage of the Genovese murder is a prime example of this shift. The media, across formats, tend to focus on the most egregious examples of crime and victimization, emphasizing images of violent and, frequently, sexual offenses. This is true despite the fact that property and drug crimes are the most common offenses. Yet these are given less attention, if not ignored altogether. The media's focus on violent crime is highly selective as well: not all crime victims receive equal attention.[14] Media resources are most often allocated to those victims who can be portrayed as "ideal." The "Ideal Victim" is the person or category of people who are socially normative and "vulnerable, defenseless, innocent, and worthy of sympathy and compassion."[15] The erasure of the non-normative details of Kitty Genovese's life enabled the media to present her as an Ideal Victim in telling the story of her death.[16]

## Outside of a Small Circle of Friends

The dramatic tensions inherent in city living, as represented by the story of unresponsive neighbors and the creation of the myth of urban apathy, have been transmitted vividly through popular culture. In addition to the multitude of newspaper accounts, feature stories, popular books and films, and scholarly articles, there are numerous fictionalized accounts of the Genovese crime, all of which share one basic trait: the tragic propensity of "good people" to remain passive in the face of evil. The story began its artistic circulation within weeks of the news of her death. "Kitty Genovese's screams were ignored in 1964, but she has been embraced as a pop culture icon ever since," wrote one scholar. "Musicians, playwrights, and filmmakers have all found meaning in the story of her murder and its 38 witnesses."[17]

The story also led both real-life and fictional heroes to act boldly in the face of danger, starting with Genovese's younger brother William, known as Bill, who volunteered for the U.S. Marine Corps two years after her death and lost his legs during a dangerous mission in Vietnam. It inspired many people, such as Associate Justice Sonia Sotomayor of the United States Supreme Court, who reported in her memoir that she won her first extemporaneous speech competition at her Bronx high school in the mid-1970s by selecting the Kitty Genovese story from among the topics available for student presentations. The US Airways pilot Captain Chesley Sullenberger mentioned the story as an important personal influence in interviews given after he safely landed a distressed commercial jetliner in the Hudson River off lower Manhattan in January 2009. But the emphasis on apathy also provided a dark rationale for vigilantism. For example, it was portrayed as the inspiration for the creation of Rorschach, the violent protagonist of the dystopian 1986 comic book *Watchmen*, as well as a real-life vigilante, Kew Gardens native Bernhard Goetz.[18]

Through the sensationalism of the story, Genovese's anonymous neighbors became larger than life. As she was stripped of substance, they were transformed into sobering symbols of the anomie of city life. The account of the death of Kitty Genovese that the *Times* created resulted in the demonization of a New York neighborhood and the suppression of the truths of one young woman's life. The emphasis on the neighbors' non-involvement, however, debuted during a time of increasing community mobilizations. The architect of the Genovese story, A. M. Rosenthal, used the crime as a clarion call for personal involvement and discounted what he termed "impersonal social action." The exclusive focus on apathy as the moral of the story disparaged those New Yorkers who challenged the status quo, from race relations to police accountability to gender and sexual norms.[19] Examining the story of Kitty Genovese from the vantage point of today provides an opportunity not only to look beyond the headlines of past decades but also to evaluate its legacy during the fiftieth-anniversary commemorations of the crime.

# "No One Helped"

1

# Urban Villages in the Big City

As the acclaimed essayist and children's novelist E. B. White wrote in 1949, "New York blends the gift of privacy with the excitement of participation; and better than most dense communities it succeeds in insulating the individual (if he wants it, and almost everybody wants or needs it) against all enormous and violent and wonderful events that are taking place every minute."[1] That particular urban blend of privacy and participation that White described also can be experienced as a tension between residents' expectations of solitude and the sense of accountability to one's neighbors, between individual responsibility and collective action. These are central themes in the story of Kitty Genovese and they fueled the creation of the myth of urban apathy.[2]

The story was shaped by the place where the crime was committed. Its geography coincided with the personal and professional obsessions of two men—one a sociopathic killer, the other a powerful newsman—and the tragic death of a young woman. Their paths collided in the neighborhood of Kew Gardens in the heart of Queens just when what would become known as The Sixties was taking off. Yet some people cannot recall exactly where or when the crime took place. Perhaps this is because the killing happened in a "good" neighborhood, defined as a safe, stable area, especially for those New Yorkers who were fleeing the changing demographics of the inner city.

Somehow the story seems more likely to have sprung from the mean streets of Manhattan, perhaps in the bleak bankrupt years of the late 1970s

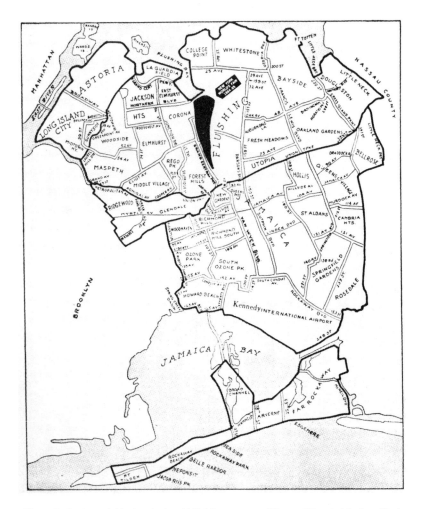

**Figure 2.** Queens neighborhoods circa 1964. Map courtesy of Queens Historical Society. Used with permission.

or the self-absorbed greed-is-good era of the 1980s, rather than emerging from a community in Queens in early 1964. Despite its proximity to Manhattan, Queens existed then as a land apart, even though events of momentous proportion were taking place in the borough that year. While many of the nation's teens and preteens were riveted by the televised arrival of a rock-and-roll group from Liverpool at the recently renamed John F. Kennedy International Airport in the southern part of the borough, activists were following news stories of civil rights protests at housing construction sites in Jamaica and at public schools throughout the borough, baseball fans were eagerly scanning sports pages for details of the completion of brand-new, ultramodern Shea Stadium, and families were planning spring and summer vacations at the bigger-and-better-than-ever World's Fair in Flushing Meadows, for many observers these events were viewed as taking place in "New York City"—meaning Manhattan—rather than in one of its outer boroughs. As the historian Kenneth Jackson has observed: "Queens is not really a place in the usual American sense. It is not politically independent, it does not have a distinctive personality, it does not have a single post office address, and its sports teams are known by another moniker—the New York Mets rather than the Queens Mets, for example." In the words of one local kid who made good—comedian Rodney Dangerfield, who grew up in Kew Gardens—it seemed that, like him, the city's largest borough and county "got no respect."[3] Yet in many ways Queens in the mid-1960s was representative of changes that were taking place throughout New York City.

## The Forgotten Borough

Named in 1683 in honor of Queen Catherine of Braganza, the Portuguese wife of the English king Charles II, by the time of the three-hundredth anniversary in 1964 of the British takeover of the city from the Dutch, Queens was bigger (110 square miles) and growing faster than any of the four other boroughs that make up America's largest city. Although sometimes referred to as "the forgotten borough" by New Yorkers, Queens has long been home to immigrants from throughout the world, who by the early 1960s were arriving by jet at one of the borough's two international airports rather than by boat at Ellis Island or train at Penn Station, joined by migrants from other parts of the city and the nation. The population of Queens County quickly multiplied in the twentieth century. Revolutionary changes in transportation helped facilitate its phenomenal growth.[4]

Increased access to and from Manhattan began in the first few years after 1900, when trains were electrified and extended through Queens. The opening of East River tunnels in 1910 meant that commuters could easily work in Manhattan while enjoying "country living" in the green and leafy borough. Furthermore, the completion of the Queensboro Bridge in 1909, and the construction of a system of roadways, including Queens Boulevard, meant that cars, trucks, buses, and other vehicles could travel farther east of the city more easily than ever before. When the New York City subway system expanded its reach into Queens in the mid-1910s, even more people could and did consider living and working there.

Explosive growth followed soon after World War I. Queens experienced a huge population surge of 130 percent during the 1920s, which was brought to a halt by the Great Depression of the 1930s. But the mid-to-late 1930s saw the completion of another new bridge, the Triborough, as well as the Grand Central Parkway to Kew Gardens in 1936, which continued to bring commuters in and out of the borough's many new neighborhoods. So too did the opening of Queens College in 1937 and LaGuardia Airport in 1939. "Even more critical was the World's Fair of 1939–1940," historians Vincent Seyfried and Jon Peterson have noted. The event "put the new borough on the national map for the first time." Memorialized by F. Scott Fitzgerald in *The Great Gatsby* as the "valley of ashes," the area north of Queens Boulevard was transformed from a massive garbage dump into a marvel of open space now named Flushing Meadows Park.[5]

After World War II the borough continued its growth, which did not level off again until the early 1960s. A massive new-housing boom was under way postwar, replacing former farmland, fields, and marshes with single-family homes and huge housing complexes. The rapid pace of construction meant homes for thousands of new residents. One housing complex in Fresh Meadows, built by the New York Life Insurance Company, was home to fourteen thousand people. As Seyfried and Peterson noted, "In the late 1950s and early 1960s, much of central Flushing, once celebrated for its country-squire atmosphere, was smothered with four- and five-story apartment buildings, which extended block after block along many streets."[6]

The people who filled these and other new apartments and homes often came from other parts of the city—from Brooklyn, the Bronx, and Manhattan—pursuing the jobs and the semi-suburban lifestyle that was being touted breathlessly by developers in local papers and advertised in national magazines in the 1950s reaching a range of readers. For example, *Ebony* magazine featured a neighborhood in St. Albans in promoting home ownership to its middle-class African American readers. Like Kew Gardens, Addisleigh Park featured handsome Tudor-style as well as colonial revival homes set among well-tended lawns and mature trees; it was described as a "swank suburban neighborhood . . . a suburban Sugar Hill" within New York City limits. The availability of home ownership in a safe and stable neighborhood for black families was underscored: the *Ebony* essay featured photographs of homes in the area belonging to such celebrities as Ella Fitzgerald, Roy Campanella, Billie Holiday, Jackie Robinson, and Count Basie but portrayed it as accessible and inclusive for average folks as well, "a suburban community, with its civic association, women's clubs, Boy Scout troops, and Saturday night pinochle games."[7]

Some of those who sought to settle in Queens had been displaced by the development of the very same new roads and bridges that enabled the borough to grow. New York power broker and development czar Robert Moses, nicknamed "The Grand Remover," combined "imagination and arrogance" to redefine New York from the mid-1930s to the late 1960s. Historian Joanne Reitano summarized his influence: "His imprint is everywhere—on 16 expressways that dissect the city and 16 parkways leading into the city, on 7 bridges, 660 playgrounds, and over 1,000 public housing buildings." She noted further that Moses also had been responsible for expanding the city's public recreation areas—beaches, parks, swimming pools—as well as major cultural and political landmarks like Lincoln Center and the UN.[8] His final triumph was the 1964–65 World's Fair, held again in Flushing Meadows.

Moses was known more for his devotion to cars and office buildings than to community development, running afoul of neighborhood activists such as Jane Jacobs. As scholars have noted, the spatial reordering of the city under his regime through urban renewal projects and the construction of public housing was also devastating to many neighborhoods as it also eliminated blue-collar jobs and increased segregation. Nevertheless, he had supported the construction of Rochdale Village, which opened in southeastern Queens in 1963. The largest integrated cooperative in the world, housing 25,000 women, men, and children, Rochdale was placed strategically in South Jamaica, which was the third-largest black neighborhood in the city.[9]

As many white families were leaving New York City for the tracts of Levittown and other new developments in adjacent Nassau County, housing opportunities opened up for nonwhites but exacerbated racial disparities. Given the strong connection between New Yorkers' housing patterns and their workplaces, the postwar growth of Queens was intimately tied to changes in employment throughout the city. As New York shed thousands of manufacturing jobs and welcomed the growing number of corporate offices in high-rise headquarters throughout Manhattan, working-class families were pushed farther and farther to the limits, inexorably changing the city's look and feel. Historian Joshua Freeman noted, "Slowly but relentlessly, the goods production and distribution sectors shrank. . . . [A]s factories migrated outward, so did workers." An example is the cosmetics titan Helena Rubinstein, who moved her main factory from Queens to Nassau County in 1952. The union representing the workers at her factory established a private bus system to help employees travel to the new plant; it lasted until enough of them had moved nearby or started driving to work. But in addition to causing transportation headaches for workers, the relocation of factories worsened racial segregation, as most of the suburban counties ringing the five boroughs of New York City did not welcome nonwhites and in fact enforced racial covenants to exclude them. For instance, Levittown, near the site of Nassau County's growing defense industry, had no African Americans among its more than eighty thousand residents in 1960.[10]

More changes came to Queens after the passage of the federal Immigration Act in 1965, which overturned much (but not all) of the restrictive legislation that had been in place for four decades. In 1998 the political scientist Michael Jones-Correa noted the significance of immigration to New York City in general and to Queens in particular: "In 1969, the city was about three-quarters white—now it's less than half. Much of this racial and ethnic change has taken place as the result of immigration. Just as white residents began moving out in the 1960s, immigrants were taking their place." He observed that new immigrants averaged 57,000 a year in the 1960s, a that rose rapidly over the next three decades. He paints a vivid portrait of what these changes meant to the neighborhoods in Queens: "Russians living next to Puerto Ricans living next to Koreans, who themselves are neighbors with Dominicans, Guyanese, or Argentines—the permutations in Queens are practically endless. . . . [T]he overall impression is of a mélange of new languages, cultures, experiences."[11]

## A Collection of Villages

The British journalist and commentator Alistair Cooke observed that the vastness and diversity of New York City seemed to engender a desire among its populace to create small-scale environments, with the result that New York was "the biggest collection of villages in the world." His statement captures a truth about the city that outsiders often cannot see; it is especially true in Queens, which started life as a collection of rural villages and townships which then developed into the fertile mix of urban and suburban that the borough had become by the mid-twentieth century. Despite the growth and expansion that took place, many Queens communities retained a commitment to a village orientation, from the unique names of neighborhoods to the importance of involvement in the community, as well as a hostility to "outsiders."

New Yorkers also are highly mobile, and "moving up"—in terms of both employment status and housing—was prized. The influx of southern blacks and Puerto Ricans during the 1950s prompted some white families to leave their neighborhoods in Manhattan, Brooklyn, and the Bronx in response to these changes. More than 1 million New Yorkers moved out of the city during the 1950s, with another half million leaving during the 1960s, "an outmigration on a scale associated in world history with forced departures or natural disasters." Although such relocations inevitably produced more segregated living conditions in many parts of the city, they also opened up some opportunities for racial minorities.[12] Northeastern Queens saw the greatest growth, offering the lure of a semi-suburban area that was easily accessible to other parts of the metropolis yet still provided, in the words of one promotional article from 1963, an affordable place to raise a family and enjoy "a swatch of land for growing roses or tomatoes."[13]

Queens attracted many city employees and brought together as neighbors people working in disparate positions, from managers and craftsmen to clerical workers. But it was not their occupational status that connected them. Some of the women and men who moved to these new communities were concerned with property and land use issues in their neighborhoods and were not necessarily welcoming to newcomers, particularly in areas like Howard Beach and South Ozone Park, home to many Irish and Italian families who had moved there after World War II. Many were fiercely protective of their investments in the local community, remaining alert to any perceived threats, including increased development, higher taxes, and especially racial integration.[14]

Such fears were inflamed in 1963, when civil rights demonstrations targeted Queens workplaces, schools, and even the World's Fair in Flushing Meadows. Hundreds of black and Latino activists and their white allies turned out to protest the exclusion of nonwhites from two lucrative city-supported construction projects, one in Brooklyn and the other in Queens. Historian Clarence Taylor has documented these large-scale organizing efforts, led largely by members of the Congress of Racial Equality (CORE): "In July of 1963, CORE forged an alliance with a group of Brooklyn ministers and led a huge protest at the construction site of the Downstate Medical Center where over 700 people were arrested, becoming 'jailbirds for freedom' in an attempt to force the state to hire blacks and Puerto Ricans as construction workers."[15] In addition, the building of Rochdale Village on the site of the former Jamaica Race Track ensured that Queens would receive a significant amount of attention from civil rights activists, labor unions, and the news media. Local chapters of CORE and the National Association for the Advancement of Colored People (NAACP) led protests over employment discrimination at the massive cooperative housing complex, and new neighborhood groups such as the Rochdale Movement also organized to fight racial discrimination in the area.

The mid-1960s saw a momentous change in New Yorkers' attitudes toward integration, and some of the most visible changes could be seen in Queens. From areas such as South Jamaica came detailed accounts of routine and fairly widespread racial discrimination, and soon the borough became a pivotal place for social action. But protests such as those mounted at building sites in 1963 not only failed to produce the desired number of jobs for blacks and Puerto Ricans but also caused deep disillusionment with liberal promises. The result was an increased militancy among activists. Some of the local civil rights leaders who engaged in negotiations with Governor Nelson Rockefeller to end the protests had agreed to drop demands for 25 percent of construction jobs in exchange for enforcement of existing antidiscrimination laws. Castigated as "sellouts" and "Uncle Toms" by coalition partners such as Brooklyn CORE when jobs did not materialize, civil rights leaders learned bitter lessons from their failure to secure concrete concessions as protesters had demanded. These lessons would shape all future organizing, especially when neighborhood schools were targeted for protests.

## Protests, Pickets, and Freedom Schools

Early in February 1964, just six weeks before the Genovese murder, the international civil rights activist Bayard Rustin, working in concert with a local leader, the Reverend Milton Galamison, and the Brooklyn chapter of CORE, highlighted the dismal state of segregation in New York City schools. They harnessed the energies generated by the successful August 1963 national March on Washington for Jobs and Freedom six months earlier. Rustin brought his expertise as lead organizer of the march, whose national headquarters were located in Harlem, to support local activism to draw attention to the severe lack of equality in the public schools of the nation's largest city.[16] The successful citywide protest made front-page news when nearly half a million children stayed away from their desks on February 3. Thousands of them joined the rallies at the city's Board of Education instead. The goal was simple: insist that the board come up with a plan and a timetable for integrating the school system. The demonstration highlighted northern racism at a time when the attention of most of the nation was focused on the South; it was so dramatic and prominent that it received positive notice from Dr. Martin Luther King Jr. Supported by a coalition of civil rights groups, the Citywide Committee for Integrated Schools, chaired by Galamison, had the active support of national leaders with roots in New York, such as Congressman Adam Clayton Powell Jr. of Harlem and minister Malcolm X, who lived with his family in Corona, Queens.

Galamison then urged a second action in March, owing to the continuing lack of an acceptable plan for desegregating the schools. The *Long Island Press,* a respected borough-oriented daily, reported on

**Figure 3.** The New York civil rights organizer Reverend Milton Galamison (left) joined by Congressman Adam Clayton Powell Jr. (center) and Malcolm X (right). Argenta images.

March 16: "A Board of Education integration plan was rejected by civil rights groups in January. The board proposed to join the enrollments of 30 of the 165 predominantly Negro and Puerto Rican schools with those of 30 predominantly white schools." The *Press,* which served a growing readership that matched the booming population of Queens, provided the best coverage of events taking place throughout the borough at that time. The article went on to say that while some activists had criticized the Board of Education's plan as being too limited and too slow in coming, not all of them supported a second boycott of the schools. Bayard Rustin, for one, accused Galamison of extremism and left the coalition, as did the national leadership of CORE and the NAACP. Galamison and his allies condemned their lack of support as capitulation to the white establishment, causing a public split among the most visible local leaders of the civil rights movement.[17]

"8 Queens Schools Target of Picket" read the headline in the *Press* just three days after Genovese's murder was prominently featured in the paper. The front-page story publicized the resumption of protests at schools throughout New York City, noting: "Pickets were slated to demonstrate in front of eight Queens schools today as part of the second school boycott. A double force of city police was called to duty, backed up by extra roving patrols to insure that the demonstrators remain orderly." The paper helpfully gave the location of the boycott sites: "CORE has scheduled boycott demonstrations at Andrew Jackson High School, Cambria Heights; Jamaica High School; P.S. 37, Jamaica; P.S. 118 and P.S. 134, both Hollis; P.S. 136 and P.S. 36, both St. Albans; and P.S. 38, Rosedale." The *Press* also reported that activists had arranged temporary educational sites for Queens children whose parents supported the boycott, modeled on Freedom Schools, the southern civil rights movement's celebrated alternatives to segregated, sub-par classrooms, at two Methodist churches in Springfield and St. Albans.[18]

But some Queens residents reacted negatively to what they perceived as potential threats to their homes and to the semi-suburban way of life they felt they had to protect from increasing demands for racial inclusion. Like their counterparts in southern towns and cities, these white northerners responded defensively to challenges to segregation that exposed the bubbling cauldron of race relations that was simmering in Queens, and throughout the nation, in 1964. One small example is a full-page "Open Letter" in the *Long Island Press* to three state legislators, "key members of the Rockefeller Administration's official family," from "parents of school children in the communities of South Ozone Park, Rosedale, Richmond Hill, Springfield Gardens, Hollis, Queens Village, Woodhaven, Laurelton, Cambria Heights, Ozone Park, and Jamaica." The large ad was prominently placed in the March 15 edition of the paper; it urged passage of a new state law to forbid the assignment of students to public schools "on the basis of race, creed, color, or national origin." Designed to stop any efforts at implementation of desegregation plans then being considered by the city's Board of Education, the ultimately unsuccessful legislation was supported largely by white families who did not want to see changes made in the racial composition of the student body in their local schools.[19]

The reason for the problem of segregated schools was segregated housing patterns throughout the city. The ad—and a lobbying visit to Albany by a group of Queens parents affiliated with the anti-integration Parents and Taxpayers (PAT)—was timed to coincide with the second civil rights boycott of New York's racially imbalanced public schools.[20] PAT, which claimed a membership of nearly half a million people in one hundred organizations, emerged as a strong force for maintaining the racial status quo throughout New York City and especially in Queens. The Board of Education finally implemented an integration plan which paired schools in mostly white areas with those in predominantly black and Latino neighborhoods. Historians have noted that the modified plan involved thirteen thousand students when it was implemented in September 1964. The groups affiliated with PAT not only organized their own boycotts and adopted other tactics of the civil rights movement to resist integration but also organized private schools in neighborhoods such as Jackson Heights to thwart racial balance in the borough.[21]

Not surprisingly, the diverse populations who lived in the many neighborhoods of Queens in the early and mid-1960s also held radically divergent views on the benefits and costs of racial equality. As Sylvie Murray asserted in her history of community activism in northeastern Queens, the residents in that part of the borough, though ideologically diverse, shared a "sense of obligation toward their residential community that was one of the key elements of Queens political culture." Although many Queens residents actively resisted integration at the time, Murray has suggested that one reason they did so was "an old refrain" in the borough: "Policy makers were ignorant of the reality of specific neighborhoods and disrespectful of grassroots opinion." This negative aspect of the urban village—a tendency toward parochialism and a skeptical attitude toward outsiders—may help explain some of the resentments generated in one Queens neighborhood by the media's depiction of its residents after the Genovese crime made headlines.

## One of the Better Neighborhoods

It was in Kew Gardens, one of the most bucolic areas of Queens, that the unthinkable occurred in the middle of March 1964. The story of an early-morning murder passively witnessed by neighbors shocked the city at a moment of increasing activism and debates over integration throughout the quickly polarizing neighborhoods of Queens. The headline of the short four-paragraph report of March 14 in the *New York Times* instantly identified the murdered "Queens woman" with the borough she lived in. The first sentence placed the murder even more precisely: "A 28-year-old Queens woman was stabbed to death yesterday morning outside her apartment house in Kew Gardens."[22]

The semi-suburban location of the crime was in itself news. Located almost exactly in the middle of the huge borough, at the intersection of a number of its main thoroughfares, Kew Gardens owes its name to England's well-known botanical gardens and its desirability to a livable scale, its proximity to Forest Park, and its neo-Tudor architecture. It was created as a result of the 1875 opening of Maple Grove Cemetery on sixty-five acres in the northeastern part of the neighborhood.[23] A Long Island Rail Road station, named Hopedale, was built nearby to serve visitors to the cemetery; its tracks cut through the Richmond Hill Golf Club, built by descendants of the Manhattan lawyer and land developer Albon Platt Man, who had created adjacent Richmond Hills. Albon's son Alrick Man and colleague Joel Fowler designed a new neighborhood on the grounds of the former golf club and named it Kew Gardens.[24]

Throughout the 1910s and 1920s, they and other developers built grand single-family homes as well as stately apartment buildings in the area. By 1936, with the creation of a new subway line along Queens Boulevard as well as paved parkways such as the Grand Central, the neighborhood enjoyed a reputation as a comfortable place to live, easily accessible to the city. Populated mostly by middle-class whites and a few black families, it had the look and feel of "an urban village in the Big City," according to the architectural historian and Kew Gardens native Barry Lewis. A number of celebrities made the neighborhood their home, such as the film legend Charlie Chaplin and Ralph Bunche, the pioneering black political scientist, diplomat, and winner of the 1950 Nobel Peace Prize.[25]

Although the neighborhood of Kew Gardens had had its share of tragedy—for example, two Long Island Rail Road trains collided in November 1950 during the evening rush hour, killing 78 people and injuring 363—it was viewed as a place of refuge for Jewish émigrés fleeing Nazi Germany as well as New Yorkers in search of a more suburban lifestyle within the city in the years after World War II. One of them, a Brooklyn-born Italian American woman named Catherine Genovese, known as Kitty to family and friends, moved to 82–70 Austin Street in 1963. Kitty Genovese had lived, worked, and played in a variety of Queens locales— among them Jamaica, Hollis, and South Ozone Park—during the years when she made the borough her home, but she was most delighted by her move to Kew Gardens with her girlfriend Mary Ann Zielonko in 1963. Like most New Yorkers, Genovese likely would have remained largely unknown and relatively unimportant to those beyond her intimate circles had she not encountered another Queens resident, Winston Moseley, early one morning in March 1964.

Later that year, A. M. Rosenthal wrote about reporter Martin Gansberg's initial response to the area during his investigation of the crime: "In the car to Kew Gardens, the detectives, as if mesmerized by the shock of the familiar become unrecognizable, kept saying what a nice neighborhood it was, how quiet, how respectable. Gansberg seemed impressed by the number of trees, which to him seemed to be a sign of solidity." Rosenthal quoted his colleague's expression of appreciation of the area: "The trees were bare, but there were so many of them, sycamores, Norway maples, silver maples, that you knew a good class of people lived around them." Gansberg noted the diversity of its residents as well: "There were some foreign accents to be heard in the streets and shops, because John F. Kennedy International Airport was nearby and many of the people in the neighborhood worked at the terminal." Ultimately, Gansberg decided, "the more I walked around the neighborhood, the more I felt I wouldn't mind living there. Looks like a suburb, not a section of a busy borough in a busy city." It is exactly this quality of suburb-within-the-city that made Genovese's murder shocking, regardless of whether anyone had come to her aid or not. The location was aberrant as a site of violence and apathy.[26]

Rosenthal described the surroundings with just a touch of Manhattan condescension: "There are private homes on the street, an apartment house with the fake-Tudor front that used to be the quintessence of swank in Queens, and neighborhood stores—a barbershop, a dry cleaner, coffee shop, a grocer—all quite cheerful except for the paint-covered window of the mail-order bookstore." Indeed, the borough of Queens "is probably the least exotic place in the city—great housing developments crowding out the private homes that were once the borough's pride, a place of shopping centers and baby carriages and sewer troubles and, to newspapermen, paralyzing ordinariness." Rosenthal confessed that the *Times*, "which has full-time staff correspondents in Karachi and Stockholm and Leopoldville and Algiers," had no one assigned to cover the borough, adding, "It can be shown statistically, I believe, that in the past few years *Times* reporters have spent more time in Antarctica than in Queens."[27]

In keeping with the paper's attitude toward the outer boroughs, which he shared, Rosenthal did not focus on the Genovese story initially. In 1999, he explained: "When the report of the murder of a woman on Austin Street came into the *Times* later the day she died, the *Times* gave it about the same amount of attention as it gave any murder in Queens those days—about four paragraphs. I was not even aware of the story; it was not important enough for my attention as metropolitan editor." He recognized this treatment of the item as underscoring the paper's dangerous disconnect from an area that housed a significant portion of its potential readership. But in 1964 he could still write, "Death took Miss Genovese in Queens, a borough of New York growing faster than any other place in the city, home for 1.8 million people, most of whom are like most reporters and editors, not particularly poor, not particularly rich, not particularly famous." At that time, it also was the scene of a series of sexual assaults on women, including the heinous rape and murder of a young black woman just two weeks before the attack on Kitty Genovese, as well as the murder of a teenager in the summer of 1963, crimes that often are barely included in the history of media coverage of the killing in Kew Gardens.[28]

It was readily apparent that neither Rosenthal nor the reporter he assigned to the Genovese story, Martin Gansberg, was familiar with Queens in general or Kew Gardens specifically. As a result, Gansberg's efforts to understand the link between the Genovese murder and Moseley's confessions to other crimes cost him precious investigative time. It also is significant that the only photographs to accompany the first front-page *Times* story of the killing were of the crime scene and its surroundings. Despite the fact that local newspapers already had featured photographs of the white female victim as well as the black male perpetrator, the *Times* offered only detailed reconstructions of the victim's purported route from her car to the places where Moseley assaulted her, mistakenly portraying three separate attacks rather than the two that actually took place. In addition to a bird's-eye view of Austin Street and the Long Island Rail Road parking lot, the images show narrow streets, shops, a seemingly livable environment, giving readers the impression that this was a quaint, almost countrified part of the city.

In his story Gansberg quoted Police Lieutenant Bernard Jacobs: "It is one of the better neighborhoods. There are few reports of crime. You only get the usual complaints about boys playing or garbage cans being turned over." The unspoken assumption throughout is that people who lived in this neighborhood belonged to a tight-knit community, a village where people knew and looked out for one another. A large part of the shock value of the Kitty Genovese story was the sudden realization that this assumption might not be true.[29]

## If You're Thinking of Living in Kew Gardens

In travel stories, local histories, and newspaper updates featuring Kew Gardens published in the last thirty years or so, Catherine Genovese is

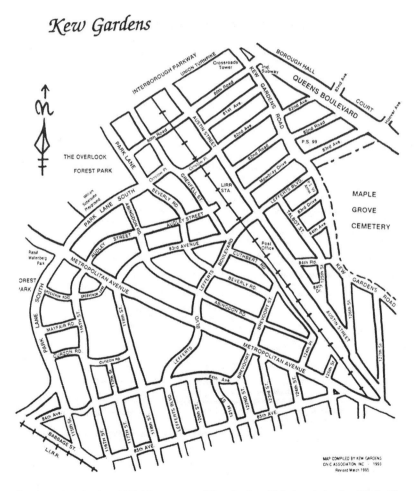

**Figure 4.**  Kew Gardens, 1993. Map courtesy of Kew Gardens Civic Association, Inc. Used with permission.

often mentioned—more so certainly than Queen Catherine, the royal consort for whom the borough of Queens is named. For example, a *New York Times* feature published in 1985, two decades after the crime, and titled "If You're Thinking of Living in Kew Gardens. . . ," dutifully emphasized the affordability of homes and apartments and then rhapsodized about the peaceful surroundings. Nearly midway through the article came the mention that "occasionally someone resurrects the story of Catherine (Kitty) Genovese, the woman murdered in 1964 on a Kew Gardens street while neighbors ignored her screams for help." Author Diana Shaman then added, "But many residents feel that the community is still a sanctuary in an urban battlefield." Twenty years later, in an article in the New York/ Region section of the *Times*, Jennifer Bleyer somewhat defensively began her feature, headlined "Café and Society," with a reference to Genovese's murder: "That the Bliss Café in Kew Gardens, Queens, is located in the same Tudor-style complex outside of which Kitty Genovese was killed in 1964 makes for a bit of a local twist. The notorious murder was blamed in part on neighborly disregard, but to the regulars at Bliss, the café is a paragon of neighborly connection."[30]

In 2007 Claudia Gryvatz Copquin included the story of Genovese's death in the Citizens Committee for New York City's reference work *The Neighborhoods of Queens,* writing: "The apartment building at 82–70 Austin Street became the focus of far different attention on March 13, 1964, when twenty-eight-year old Catherine (Kitty) Genovese was stabbed to death there, and it was widely reported that although she cried for help none of the thirty-eight residents purportedly within earshot came to her aid or even called police. The event sparked not only citywide but national and international outrage, stemming from deep concern over growing urban apathy."[31] By 2012, a writer for an informational website that featured Kew Gardens—which was referred to as "a gem of a neighborhood in central Queens"—would report dispassionately (and redundantly): "The murder of Kitty Genovese in 1964 brought negative notoriety to Kew Gardens. News reports at the time claimed that no neighbor responded to her pleas for help. Her story is used in textbooks as an example of anonymity and apathy in urban settings. Her story, however, is very much the exception to life in safe, neighborly Kew Gardens."[32]

The references to Kitty Genovese's death in promotional stories about the desirability of Kew Gardens as a place to live are ironic, to say the least. Yet some of those who lived in the area in the late 1960s had the idea of installing a plaque to mark the place where she died, though it never materialized. Instead, a few years later, they organized a block association. This was in keeping with community traditions. As noted by one writer in 2004, the impulse toward creating local organizations and neighborhood groups is a powerful one for both longtime residents and newcomers. It continued during the four decades of population growth in Queens starting in the late 1960s. "Writing more than 40 years ago in *The Death and Life of Great American Cities*, Jane Jacobs observed that cities work best when many small, unofficial self-governing bodies strive to make their own little neighborhoods more livable and prosperous," Steven Malanga noted in 2004. "She might have been describing Queens, which at the time she was writing boasted more than 200 civic associations, some of them vestiges of the borough's former town governments, others remnants of ethnic organizations that previous generations of Queens residents had brought with them or established." Such civic engagement continued as the population of Queens grew and diversified. "Queens's new arrivals learned to use this universe of community and civic associations, churches, small chambers of commerce, business districts, parent-teacher associations, and youth organizations and leagues as effectively as their predecessors."[33]

The story of more than three dozen apathetic neighbors in the midst of the tree-lined streets and winding roads of the "urban village in the Big City" has always seemed incongruous. Increasingly, it has also been revealed as an exaggeration. The myth of urban apathy created by the *Times* in its version of the events of March 13, 1964, relied on the elision of significant details about the people and the place where the crime took place. Like Kitty Genovese and the neighborhood and city she loved so much, the story is more complicated than it first appears.

2

# Hidden in Plain Sight

Catherine Susan Genovese had a powerful presence. As Mary Ann Zielonko told the world in 2004, "Kitty was the most wonderful person I've ever met." In an interview aired on National Public Radio, Zielonko helped revive the young woman who had been hidden in plain sight for forty years: "I still remember her face. I can see it in my mind: very Italian looking, very chiseled features, dark hair, like only about five feet tall. [A] very likeable person, very vibrant, where I'm very quiet, so we were complementary."[1] Zielonko's memories are reinforced by images in the Genovese family's home movies from the late 1950s and early 1960s. Despite the grainy quality of the film, now more than a half century old, Kitty commands the screen with her bright smile and playful vamping for the camera at a series of family gatherings. But for four decades after her death, this "vibrant" young woman, whose name became known worldwide, was reduced to a cipher, her personhood erased in service to the myth of urban apathy. Yet Kitty Genovese's life is representative of a newfound sense of possibilities available to young women in the late 1950s and early 1960s.

She joined the ranks of those urban working women who balanced freedom with engagement, independence with commitment. Making their own decisions about where they would work and with whom they would partner, some of them, like Kitty, also carefully maintained connections with their families.

## Kitty Worshipped Life in the City

She was the first of five children of Italian American parents, born on July 7, 1935, and raised in Brooklyn, New York. Her mother, Rachel, was a homemaker; father Vincent owned a successful restaurant linen supply store, the Bay Ridge Coat and Apron Supply Company. She had one sister, Susan, and three brothers—Vincent Junior, Francis (Frank), and William (Bill), her favorite among her siblings. As Bill has explained it, "She and I had a special affinity." He remembered how she would "sweep into New Canaan to visit the family in her Nash Rambler, or later in her red Fiat, fresh from the city and bubbling with new ambitions and ideas." He said that the two of them would "stay up late into the night" talking about subjects as esoteric as solipsism and Einstein's theory of relativity. Another brother told a reporter in the days after her death, "Kitty worshipped life in the city."[2]

Intelligent and inquisitive, lively and fun-loving, Kitty was known as the class "cutup" during her years at Prospect Heights High School. After graduating in 1953 and finding work in an office, she married an Italian man, Rocco Fazzolare, on Halloween 1954, with her brother Vincent witnessing the ceremony along with Fazzolare's sister. Four years her senior, Fazzolare was enlisted in the U.S. Army at the time of their marriage at St. Augustine Church in Brooklyn. He planned to become a doctor, and Genovese supported him while he attended medical school, even studying with him for his exams, but the marriage did not last. After a few months, the couple parted ways.[3]

There were other big changes happening for the Genovese family in 1954. Lifelong New Yorkers, Rachel and Vincent Genovese decided to leave the city and move the family to the suburbs after an incident at their home in the Park Slope neighborhood of Brooklyn. According to Bill Genovese, a bleeding man running from a confrontation with police on St. Johns Place had attempted to break into the basement of the four-story building where the family lived. Although he was captured without incident, the experience badly frightened Rachel, who witnessed it. It also served to confirm the parents' belief that it was time to relocate. Like many other white ethnic working- and middle-class people living in urban areas in the mid-1950s, the Genovese family moved rather than face the rising crime rate and changing demographics of the neighborhood they had called home since the 1940s. In their case, they chose New Canaan, Connecticut.[4]

In some ways their move was reflective of a desire for what one scholar has referred to as the "sanctuaries of the good life," suburban spaces where safety was guaranteed by class and racial homogeneity and the environment "struck a delicate balance between privacy and community." Such desires for safety also reflect an increasing conflation of race with rising crime in urban areas, especially among white city dwellers, fueling their escape to the suburbs. In the 1950s, as industries began to abandon the city's boroughs, taking good jobs and tax revenues with them to neighboring counties, increasing black and Puerto Rican migrations began to challenge the racial and ethnic makeup of many New York City neighborhoods. Population figures cited in a study of postwar New York youth gangs reveal the shift: the number of European Americans in the city in 1960 fell to 6.6 million, while the figures grew to 1.1 million for African Americans and approximately 612,000 for Puerto Ricans. At the same time that opportunities for education and secure employment were evaporating, except in service-based sectors largely closed to blacks and Puerto Ricans, urban decline was blamed on the newcomers and on those who were unable or unwilling to leave. Yet the desire for escape that fueled white flight was futile; the city and its suburbs were intimately connected. Certainly for the Genovese family, the presumed safety of life in the suburbs would not protect them from the tragic loss of their eldest child.[5]

Kitty, a true urbanite, would not trade the excitement of the city for the supposed safety of the suburbs, but she did leave Brooklyn for Queens. Kitty's brother Vincent recalled that his sister chose to live in New York rather than New Canaan because, as Kitty herself had said, she "never took to the town and the town never took to her." In fact "her world was just too big, too broad for New Canaan," he said. "She was interested in art, in politics, in all of the things, all of the culture she couldn't find in a small town." Kitty Genovese was determined to live her own life as she saw fit, but she also balanced her passion for independence with her love for her parents and siblings. She often traveled the sixty miles between New York City and New Canaan to visit them, and enjoyed daydreaming with her father about the two of them one day opening up their own restaurant.[6]

For a twenty-year-old Italian American woman in 1955, Genovese's successful completion of high school was an achievement she could be proud of, even if the career expectations before her were limited. It was acceptable for young women like her to work for a few years before getting married and starting a family. As one historian wrote of Italian working-class women in New York City at this time, "proper appearance, good character, good habits, 'a pleasing personality' . . . along with vocational skills, became important for a new generation of female workers."[7] Kitty Genovese's education and her office work afterward are in keeping with the choices made by many of her contemporaries. For them, the shift from domestic or manufacturing work to clerical positions, though still near the lower end of the spectrum in terms of pay and status, provided new opportunities. Corporate offices were cleaner than factories, working hours were shorter, and there were fewer worries about seasonal fluctuations.[8]

## Kitty Ran the Whole Thing

Genovese followed this path for a short time, but by 1960 she veered off in a different direction. Although she had fulfilled many of the traditional familial expectations, she ultimately chose a more unconventional life. By the time she was twenty-five she was living in Queens and working in a bar. It provided her with a sense of autonomy that she would not have found in an office. It also gave her not just the opportunity to learn the basics of operating a small business, and one that required charisma as well as management skills, but the chance to be her own boss.

Notwithstanding the widespread frustration and boredom experienced by college-educated housewives that Queens homemaker and journalist Betty Friedan described when she began interviewing her former Smith College classmates in 1957—research that led to the publication of her groundbreaking 1963 book *The Feminine Mystique*—Genovese and other working women were increasingly earning their own salaries and making independent decisions about their lives. Critiques of Friedan's findings decades later noted that the women's magazines that Friedan had condemned as responsible for the promotion of the "happy housewife" stereotype in fact did not valorize housework uniformly. They often printed articles supporting full- or part-time jobs for single as well as married women.[9]

Rather than apathy, a renewed activism for women's equality in the workplace also could be glimpsed in the early 1960s. In December 1961 President John F. Kennedy acceded to the demands of civic leaders and officials within the government, in unions, and in religious and civil rights groups as well as academia, and established the President's Commission on the Status of Women. Chaired by former first lady and U.S. delegate to the United Nations Eleanor Roosevelt until her death in 1962, the advisory commission examined issues of women's equality under the law, in education, and in employment; it especially documented widespread discrimination against women in the workplace. As Kennedy observed in his public statement on signing the executive order creating the commission: "The great majority of women now seek gainful employment at some period of their lives. The community should make it possible for them to make the best use of their talents and to function constructively, both through legislation and through necessary supportive services by private or public agencies."[10] Given two years to do its work, the commission dissolved in 1963 after the completion of an exhaustive report, which led to a historic piece of legislation. The Equal Pay Act of 1963 was a concrete result of the commission's recommendations. Signed by President Kennedy on June 10, 1963, it amended the Fair Labor Standards Act of 1938 to prohibit discrimination among employees on the basis of sex "for equal work on jobs the performance of which requires equal skill, effort, and responsibility, and which are performed under similar working conditions." Kennedy called it a "first step" toward wage equality.[11] Following the dissolution of the President's Commission, women's rights activists organized state and local commissions on the status of women throughout the nation to continue their research, education, and advocacy.

Despite such important political changes, however, contradictory messages about work and worth often meant that young ethnic women of Genovese's generation had to navigate carefully to determine which social norms could be defied and which ones must be followed. Although

Genovese's marriage did not last, her interest in medicine and curing common physical ailments did, although there is no evidence that she ever considered pursuing health care as a career. While she held a few jobs that were considered strictly "female" work in the mid- to late 1950s, by 1961 she was the manager of Ev's Eleventh Hour, a working-class tavern at 193–14 Jamaica Avenue in Hollis.

Angelo Lanzone met her at Ev's in 1961, shortly after she had started working at the bar. The patrons at Ev's were "more or less a blue-collar bunch," he said. His strongest memory of Genovese is that she was a good-natured and generous person who loved talking with customers, often lent money to bar regulars, which was rarely paid back, and always had a kind word, some advice about curing a minor malady, or a joke to share. She kept the jukebox stocked with jazz and popular hits, loved dancing and debating current events.[12]

She also enjoyed going to the horse races with Lanzone. "We used to go to Yonkers, Roosevelt Raceway. Once the parking lot there was a sea of mud. She had a car with a snow tire in the back and the others were regular tires, and we managed to get out of that mud hole. We spun and spun but she got us out of there." He liked betting on the horses and shared tips with Genovese. "She was never a big gambler, so when I won I would give her a few dollars," he recalled. He remembered that he could talk with her about anything. Her presence at Ev's was a big part of the charm of the place. She was at the center of the tiny, familiar world that the bar patrons created, and she helped foster an atmosphere of camaraderie and acceptance. She also took on many responsibilities, from serving drinks to tallying the day's receipts and delivering them to the bar owner, a woman named Evelyn Randolph, who, according to Lanzone, was married to a postal worker and never ventured into the bar that bore her name. "She was a blond-haired lady probably in her mid-fifties—she just owned the place, but Kitty ran the place. Kitty ran the whole thing."[13]

In the days before New York established off-track betting, her responsibilities in the bar business also sometimes included helping regulars make wagers on horse races. This last aspect of her job brought her to the attention of the police in the summer of 1961. Genovese was tending bar at the Queens Café and agreed to help her girlfriend at the time, Dolores "Dee" Guarnieri, by phoning in a bet for a customer who turned out to be an undercover cop. Genovese was arrested, charged with bookmaking

**Figure 5.** Kitty Genovese behind the bar at Ev's Eleventh Hour, circa 1963. New York Daily News/New York Daily News Archive/Getty Images. Used with permission.

and had her mug shot taken. She hired the local Queens attorney Sidney Sparrow to represent her. As Lanzone described the incident: "It was no big deal. They knew she was no bookie." But the arrest not only resulted in a fine but also cost Genovese her job; she soon found a new one at Ev's, where she worked for the next two and a half years. For much of that time she lived in an apartment building nearby, one block off Jamaica Avenue between 168th and 169th streets. Lanzone remembered that it was about twenty blocks from Ev's, "but it would take her five minutes and she had a lot of friends in that apartment house—doors were open, people going in and out all the time, very friendly. She probably should have stayed there." Genovese also had an active social life. She had ended her relationship with Dee Guarnieri well before she met Zielonko in March 1963 and they decided to move in together. Even though it was a bit farther from work, she was delighted when they found an apartment in Kew Gardens. "Maybe she thought it was safer," Lanzone said.[14]

## Just One Look

According to the reporter Jeff Pearlman, who interviewed Zielonko in 2004, her earliest memories of the woman with whom she would develop her first serious relationship remained strong even forty years later. "She is still standing there, in the Manhattan bar where the two first met on an early spring day in 1963, running a hand through her short brown hair while taking a drag from the end of a Camel cigarette. Genovese was a talkative woman with big brown eyes, an infectious giggle and a tiny gap at the tip of her two front teeth, and the 25-year-old Zielonko was smitten." Zielonko remembered that after Kitty told her "I'd like to see you again," she explained to her that she didn't have a phone. "I lived in a rooming house. I came home that night from work, and I found the note on the rooming house door. 'WILL CALL YOU AT THE STREET CORNER PHONE BOOTH AT 7.—KITTY G.' She found where I lived, and called me at the pay phone that night."[15] Zielonko was amazed that Genovese had been able to find her and locate the building she lived in—"in New York City!"—at 72nd and Broadway in Manhattan; she had not given her the address. They met again a few days later at the Seven Steps, a West Houston Street bar in Manhattan that was popular with lesbians. Soon they decided to find a place to live together.[16]

After a two-week stay in a Queens motel, they found a one-bedroom apartment and moved to 82–70 Austin Street in a row of two-story Tudor-style townhouses adjacent to the Long Island Rail Road station at Kew Gardens. Although their apartment was in a part of the neighborhood that was considered lower class and transient, both women were excited about moving into their new home. With a mix of older European immigrants and younger men and women, many of whom worked at one of the two nearby airports—giving the area the nickname "Crew Gardens"—Kew Gardens had a largely middle-class population that was more than 90 percent white.[17] When Genovese and Zielonko moved there in 1963, one of their neighbors, Anthony Corrado, who owned the upholstery store on the ground floor, helped them out by hoisting a heavy sofa into their new living room. Corrado assumed the roommates would be entertaining members of the opposite sex when he first met them. "I remember saying, boy, gonna be a lot of wild parties up there. I thought they were airline stewardesses, which we had a lot [of] coming in," he remembered. Years later he said of Genovese, "She was always a very cheerful girl . . . always a 'good morning,' very quiet." Other neighbors also remembered Kitty as someone who shared a friendly greeting whenever she passed by.[18]

Kew Gardens was changing. Younger newcomers—like Kitty and Mary Ann, as well as their neighbor across the hall, a young mother named Sophie Farrar, and Andrée Picq, a Frenchwoman who worked as a stewardess and lived across the street in the Mowbray Arms apartment building—were slowly shifting the neighborhood's demographics. The mix of old and new did not disrupt the village feeling of the area even if the increase in population sometimes meant that parking spaces along Austin Street were hard to come by. Most folks just used the Long Island Rail Road lot for their cars, especially at night.[19]

Although both women worked in the bar business—Zielonko as a bartender at Club Chris and Genovese at Ev's—on their nights off they often went out to clubs and restaurants. It was one of the things that made Kew Gardens so appealing; it was easily and quickly accessible by car or train to "the city," especially Greenwich Village. Genovese and Zielonko spent many nights at places such as Gerde's Folk City, where they would drink beer and listen to folk music. Their new neighborhood was perfectly located: not only did it offer proximity to the Village and the Queens bars where they worked, but also there were attractions closer to home. The two women enjoyed checking out the local talent at the Interlude—the coffee shop just a few steps away from their apartment on the corner near the LIRR station—which also featured folk singers. They often joined Lanzone on their Monday nights off for dinners at the Hofbrau, the German restaurant nearby, or went out for ice cream at Jahn's in the neighborhood. They had made a home together in Kew Gardens, felt comfortable, and counted friends among their neighbors. Among them was Karl Ross, a gay man who lived a few doors down from their apartment, at 82–62 Austin Street.[20]

But it was only at gay or lesbian bars in Greenwich Village, such as the Swing Rendezvous on MacDougal Street, that Genovese and Zielonko felt free to let their guard down, where they could drink and dance to their special song, Doris Troy's 1963 Top Forty hit "Just One Look," and enjoy being together as lovers. They were always cautious in public, and for good reason. Neither woman had yet announced their intimate involvement to family members or anyone else beyond a small circle of friends, and they could not jeopardize their jobs or their new home by revealing too much to the wrong people. Zielonko remembered that their relationship was built on a great deal of private intimacy. The socially demanded secrecy that was imposed on them at that time, which they accepted in exchange for inclusion and a sense of security, inevitably resulted in frustration and tension between them.[21]

Their first year together was not easy. Angelo Lanzone remembered their quarreling often, "usually over money." Their disputes sometimes spilled out into public settings: Lanzone recalled that one night about six months before her murder, after a particularly nasty argument with Zielonko at the Hofbrau, Genovese stormed out of the restaurant before their dinners were served. All three of them ended up "banned" from the restaurant when Lanzone and Zielonko, who remained and finished their meals, refused to pay for the dinner Genovese had ordered. But such upsets did not diminish their commitment to each other. Despite the tensions in their relationship, the two women persevered.[22]

The anxieties and caution that lesbians and gay men incorporated into their daily lives were understandable, given the stigma surrounding homosexuality in the early 1960s. Although it was more openly discussed by 1964, well over a decade after the first tiny groups of gay men and lesbians began to assert their status publicly as members of a minority group deserving equal rights, same-sex desire was regularly depicted as deviant and routinely demonized in popular culture. Yet some significant voices were openly questioning such limited and damaging representations. In 1962 the explosive African American writer James Baldwin published *Nobody Knows My Name: More Notes of a Native Son* following his return to Harlem after a self-imposed ten-year exile in Europe. In it he reprinted one essay, "The Male Prison," that originally had been published in 1954 and addressed the issue of sexual identity in the works of the French writer André Gide. By this time Baldwin had published five critically acclaimed essays and novels, including the best-selling and controversial novel *Giovanni's Room* (1955), one of the first to explore issues of same-sex relationships. In "The Male Prison" he took aim at the issue of deviance by questioning that which is considered "natural" by society. Baldwin asserted: "To ask whether or not homosexuality is natural is really like asking whether or not it was natural for Socrates to swallow hemlock, whether or not it was natural for St. Paul to suffer for the Gospel, whether or not it was natural for the Germans to send upwards of six million people to an extremely twentieth-century death. It does not seem to me that nature helps us very much when we need illumination in human affairs. I am certainly convinced that it is one of the greatest impulses of mankind to arrive at something higher than a natural state."[23]

The dominant attitude in the early 1960s equated homosexuality not only with "unnatural acts" but also with pathology. The *New York Times*, in particular, regularly printed articles by psychiatrists such as Irving Bieber who specialized in finding "cures" for sexual sickness. One of the very first feature stories in a mainstream American newspaper on the growing visibility of gay men (lesbians were not mentioned) in New York was printed in the *Times*, at A. M. Rosenthal's suggestion, just a few months before Genovese was murdered. On December 17, 1963, the front-page article, headlined "Growth of Overt Homosexuality in City Provokes Wide Concern," focused on Greenwich Village and debated whether the public was becoming more liberal in tolerating public displays of same-sex affection. Written by a seasoned *Times* reporter, Robert C. Doty, it purported to be an in-depth feature on the growing numbers of homosexuals who were "colonizing" parts of the city. Relying on the same medical and sociological theorists whom the newspaper had consulted in the past, the article related their theories regarding the whys and wherefores of the "sickness" of homosexuality. The one innovation in the 1963 feature may have been that it was the first to report on changing terminology: "There is a homosexual jargon once intelligible only to the initiate, but now part of New York slang. The word gay has been appropriated as the adjective for homosexual."[24] By 1963 "gay" was the preferred descriptive term among activists who sought to eliminate the clinical-sounding and psychologically tainted term "homosexual."

The article's focus on gay men caused the New York chapter of the Daughters of Bilitis (DOB), the only lesbian rights organization in the United States at that time, to complain angrily to the editors, but to no avail. When DOB held its biannual convention at a hotel near Central Park in June 1964, however, the *Times* sent someone to cover it. The next day the paper ran a five-paragraph report tucked away on a back page and head-lined "Homosexual Women Hear Experts." Again, the story emphasized the opinions of psychologists and psychiatrists about causes of and possible cures for homosexuality. This time the coverage also briefly described the DOB and provided details on the rest of the weekend conference, giving the group free publicity and signaling to any lesbian reading the paper that she was not alone. This brief notice marked the first time that the paper acknowledged the existence of a lesbian organization, although the DOB chapter in New York had been formed in 1958 and had been publicizing its meetings and events ever since. The group's reach far exceeded its small size; it had come to the attention of activists such as the playwright Lorraine Hansberry, author of the potent Broadway drama "A Raisin in the Sun," who wrote the organization a few letters in the late 1950s. The celebrated black artist declared, "I'm glad as heck that you exist!" to DOB's monthly magazine *The Ladder*, which in the early 1960s was available by mail sub-scription and sold at newsstands and a handful of bookstores, such as the internationally known Eighth Street Bookshop in Greenwich Village.

The *Times'* brief nod to the Daughters in June 1964, however, while appreciated by its members, was hardly an endorsement; it certainly did not translate into changes in the newspaper's coverage of the Genovese murder or lesbian/gay rights activism. The paper's coverage of gay issues in general in the 1960s was extremely negative; it would not use the word "gay" (unless it was placed in quotation marks) in its articles until 1987, after Rosenthal retired as executive editor. Lesbians were treated mostly as if they were nonexistent, and gay men often were blamed for nearly everything viewed as negatively affecting the city and the nation, from the decline of Times Square to the increase in spy scandals and spectacular murders. The emphasis on deviance and pathology was a given whenever the paper printed a story that mentioned homosexuality.[25]

Because of the cultural atmosphere created by the homophobic attitudes of nearly all American leaders and institutions at the time, two women like Genovese and Zielonko who wanted to go out in public together in 1964 had very few places where they could do so without fear of harassment or assault—or arrest. At a minimum, they risked unwanted publicity and loss of a job if they were in the wrong place at the wrong time and got trapped in a police raid. At worst, exposure for lesbians could mean the rejection of family and friends and, for mothers, loss of custody of their children. The lesbian writer and activist Joan Nestle noted the difficult search for social spaces in New York in which women could safely indulge their desires for one another in the late 1950s and early 1960s. "Public space for the pre-Stonewall working-class lesbian bore all the tensions of a stigmatized private self. The public bar was a privately coded place. Its awning and darkened street window never revealed its secret, yet going to the bar meant going out. Our exposure was enclosed, but the secrecy was also disclosure. The space was both a gift and a torment. It replicated the wonder of desire and the burden of its condemnation."[26]

Paradoxically, when homosexuality was "explored" in the popular media, lesbians often remained invisible. In June 1964 *Life* magazine, then the largest-circulation weekly magazine in the United States, devoted several pages to homosexuality, "its habits and locales, what science knows and seeks to know about it." The entirety of the ten-page article, complete with photographs, focused on white gay men. Only the briefest mention was made of women. It read: "There are also female homosexuals, of course, but the number is much smaller—by the estimate of the Institute for Sex Research, perhaps only a third or a quarter as high as the figure for men [2.3 million]. One reason, some analysts have suggested, is that it is far easier for a woman who is afraid of men to perform adequately in marriage than it is for a man who is afraid of women. At any rate, women homosexuals are not nearly so numerous, promiscuous or conspicuous as their male counterparts, and the various studies have largely ignored them."[27]

Surprisingly, the appraisal of *Life*'s article in *The Ladder* was upbeat. Some DOB members, including the journal's editor Barbara Gittings, believed that a relatively unbiased piece was preferable to the general coverage of homosexuality in major publications at that time. She wrote: "LIFE magazine finally did it! The June 26 issue features 14 pages of pictures and text on 'The Homosexual in America.'" Noting that, predictably, only the most furtive "bar and cruising scenes" were highlighted and "as always, those homosexuals who are quiet-living, constructive people get short shrift in the article," she shared her disappointment that no one from Daughters of Bilitis had been featured despite interviews with *Life*'s reporters at DOB's Manhattan office. Despite the feature's dismissive attitude toward lesbians, however, Gittings appreciated its "surprisingly objective" approach as well as its condemnation of a recent study issued by the New York Academy of Medicine that once again equated homosexuality with pathology.[28]

On the newsstands and in bookstores in 1964, popular representations of lesbianism yielded a decidedly mixed bag. There was a plethora of lesbian pulp fiction, novels that most often were written by men using female pseudonyms to sell same-sex eroticism with lurid covers and tragic endings. But it was possible to find some true gems among the imposters, such as paperbacks written by women with a personal knowledge of the intricacies of real-world lesbian life. Beginning with Maryjane Meaker, writing as Vin Packer, and the best-selling novelist Patricia Highsmith, writing as Claire Morgan, a handful of lesbian writers achieved commercial success in the immediate postwar period. Ann Bannon and Valerie Taylor produced works that enjoyed great popularity during the early 1960s while complicating the by then formulaic approach to lesbian love stories that too often depicted only disaster or disgrace for the women involved. They created memorable characters, including a few women of color, as well as white women who not only engaged in heart-pounding sex and passionate romance but also faced challenges due to alcoholism, violence, and racism. In addition, the lesbian novels of Artemis Smith during the late 1950s and early 1960s were known and appreciated—especially in reviews printed in *The Ladder*—for their pro–gay rights political sensibilities.[29]

Rarely, however, were positive portrayals of lesbianism found in nonfiction books or magazine articles. A few writers—including Meaker, a former lover of Highsmith's, who published four "tell all" books as Ann Aldrich in the 1950s through the mid-1960s—produced "investigative reports" that promised to bring an insider's perspective to explorations of lesbian life; her view was decidedly dim. Even the best of the nonfiction reports rarely countered prevailing stereotypes. "But you don't look like a lesbian!" the back cover of Jess Stearn's book *The Grapevine* announced. Promising a "report on the secret world of the lesbian" when it was published in 1964, *The Grapevine* enjoyed widespread popularity. It captured the perspectives of many men and women toward lesbianism in the early 1960s, and while its tone was somewhat less condemnatory than in other popular writings about homosexuality, it also equated same-sex desire with emotional illness.[30]

A follow-up to *The Sixth Man*, his best-selling 1961 book on homosexuality, Stearn's foray into lesbianism was presented as his effort to understand how "female homosexuals" communicated and networked with one another. Stearn's depiction of lesbians was of an almost alien species of sexual body snatchers invading America from within. Despite the fact that it was based on interviews he conducted in 1962 and 1963 with women in New York, San Francisco, and other major metropolitan areas of the United States, as well as his conversations with participants at the 1962 DOB convention in Los Angeles, at which he was an invited speaker, what is most revealing throughout the book is the extent of his acceptance of popular myths about lesbians that were in circulation at that time. The author's incredulous realization that "normal"-appearing women could not be attracted to men is reiterated on nearly every page. So too are the largely unhappy portrayals he presents of the women he met. Stearns emphasized what he saw as the stealth quality of lesbianism, an expansion of the notion expressed briefly in the *Life* magazine "special report": the ways in which lesbians, unlike gay men, fit into society and live undetected by the general population, especially those female couples who are not obviously butch or femme in their self-presentation.

While *The Grapevine* relied on interviews with lesbian activists and generally spoke positively about the efforts of the Daughters of Bilitis, it nevertheless emphasized the hopelessness of such relationships. Stearn had to conclude, though, that not even the prospect of misery could dampen same-sex desire: "The fact that she is so often unhappy did nothing to deter the lesbian from lesbianism. With all the lesbian's idiosyncrasies, complexities, and mysteries, lesbianism was not only here to stay but, on a tidal wave of new feminine self-appreciation, might one day be openly professed by the countless who lurk in the shadows of a clandestine world." We can only imagine what Genovese and Zielonko—neither of whom "looked like" a lesbian—thought about such portrayals, if they paid any attention to them at all. But they would not be able to experience together the "tidal wave of new feminine self-appreciation" that Stearn prophesied and that lesbian activists worked to achieve. Instead, their relationship was cut short early on the morning of their first anniversary. [31]

## Footloose and Fancy Free

After working her shift at Ev's on the night of March 12, 1964, Genovese went out to dinner with a male friend, Jack Timmons; she returned to the bar after midnight and, after closing, drove the few miles home to the apartment she shared with Zielonko. She never reached it. Mary Ann later said that she had gone bowling with their friend Gloria Hominick that night and then went home and fell asleep. Instead of Kitty, it was the police who awakened her. She accompanied them to Queens County Hospital, where she identified Genovese's body. Afterward, they questioned her for eight to ten hours at the Queens precinct. With bitterness in her voice, Zielonko remembered that they wanted to know what lesbians did in bed. In shock, stunned by the horror of Kitty's death, she told them. "I was young then . . . and they got off on it." Many of their friends, including Lanzone, also were brought in for questioning by detectives. Lanzone said that the police treated him as if he were a suspect. He had been at work the night of the murder and was unaware of what had happened to Kitty until the next day. He called her at her home, where a neighbor answered and told him that she had been stabbed. She also told him that the police were looking for him and he should go immediately to Ev's. When he arrived, he had to push his way through a crowd of people. When bystanders recognized him they shouted, "There he is! There he is!" He not only was taken in for hours of questioning at the precinct but also was escorted by police around the Kew Gardens neighborhood while they asked people in the area if he was the man they had seen assaulting Genovese. He remembers being taken to the apartments of about a dozen different neighbors and "only a couple of them would answer." Lanzone told the police he would take a lie detector test to prove his innocence, but apparently satisfied that he had not been involved in the murder, they released him.[32]

That day, March 14, the *Long Island Press* put Genovese's picture on the front page. She is shown leaning on the counter at Ev's, her arms folded behind a half-filled glass, a pack of Marlboro cigarettes in front of her, looking into the camera with a smile. The headline was one of the few that appeared that day, and in the weeks and months that followed, which emphasized the person she had been. It read, "Kitty Worshipped Life in the City, and Died in Its Lonely Streets." The article began: "Kitty was footloose and fancy free, and the small Connecticut town where her family lived crowded in on her. . . . 'I feel free here,' she used to tell her friends. 'I can breathe. I'm alive.' They remembered this yesterday as they walked into Ev's Eleventh Hour Tavern at 193–14 Jamaica Ave., Hollis." The reporter, Edward Weiland, thus provided one of the very few portrayals of Kitty Genovese that tried to capture the fullness of the person she had been rather than the emptiness of too many of the stories, which rhetorically reduced her to the chalk outline left on the sidewalk at a crime scene after a body has been removed.[33]

Despite a few errors in the details of the crime—understandable, given that police were still trying to piece together what had happened—the article is powerfully evocative. "It was early in the day," Weiland wrote, "but the bar was busy. The air was filled with the cacophony of voices and tinkling glass, with the odor of tobacco and beer. The customers came in and they asked: 'Is it true?' Other customers nodded. It was true. Kitty Genovese had been stabbed to death shortly before 4 a.m. yesterday as she walked down the street to her apartment at 82–70 Austin St., Kew Gardens." Weiland captured the sorrow of the people who had been Kitty's customers and friends, as well as the shock of her family. "We haven't turned on a radio or the television," her brother Vincent Genovese Jr. told him. "We haven't read a newspaper. The grief of Kitty's death is enough. Reading about it, listening to it, would only make it worse." Weiland asked the patrons in Ev's that day what Kitty was like. "She was tiny, but everybody respected her," one woman said, adding that "when Kitty was behind the bar, 'Everybody talked about politics and art and history. Because these were the things Kitty was interested in.'" The article reiterated that "what Kitty was most interested in was politics and she didn't mind arguing her firm conviction with the best of them. 'She liked Johnson,' said Mrs. Elie Mason of Hollis. 'She thought he was a good President.'" The article continued: "But Kitty seldom talked about herself. Few knew where she had come from or what she did after she left the tavern each day about 6 p.m. The customers would see her get into her snappy red Fiat and speed away. 'She was always so happy,' Mrs. Anderson said. 'She'd always make us laugh. And when I'd watch her leave in that little red car, a phrase always came to my mind. "Footloose and fancy free." That's what it was. That's what Kitty was.'"[34]

A few days later, Angelo Lanzone and Mary Ann Zielonko attended Genovese's funeral in New Canaan. The family acknowledged their presence but could not acknowledge Mary Ann's intimate relationship with Kitty; despite whatever suspicions any of them might have had, at that time they knew only that the two women were close friends and roommates. The enforced secrecy surrounding their love served to deepen the trauma of the tragedy for Zielonko. To this day she berates herself for not having heard something, or been able to do something, to save her friend and lover in the early hours of March 13, 1964. In the days and months that followed, Zielonko refused to talk to the media and instead turned to friends—and alcohol—for support and solace. Lanzone remembered that he and a few others moved into the apartment for short periods of time so that Mary Ann would not be there alone. She too blamed the neighbors after the *New York Times* reported that more than three dozen of them had seen or heard Moseley attacking Genovese and done nothing to help her. Some of her friends were too afraid of the police to talk to her on the phone. Zielonko called one of them, who lived in Brooklyn, for support; the friend refused to speak to her because of fear that "her phones were tapped."[35]

But the most painful truth of the Genovese story is that the one neighbor who perhaps could have saved Kitty was their friend Karl Ross. As Zielonko recalled in 2004, after she identified Genovese's body at the hospital, she began drinking with him at his apartment. She discovered later that he likely was the final witness to her lover's death. "I went to the neighbor's, a man who could have saved her life. I went there and I drank with him all day not knowing that he was the last person to see her alive and she cried to him and he wouldn't open his door." In his confession, Moseley told police that he thought someone in the apartment at the top of the stairs opened the door while he was stabbing Genovese in the vestibule. Whether it was Ross he saw or another man is unclear, but Ross later told investigators that he panicked and called a friend to ask for advice about what to do. He then crawled out over the flat part of the roof to another neighbor's window and alerted her; she contacted Sophie Farrar, who immediately went to help Genovese. Ross finally called the police at about 3:55 a.m. But by then it was too late.[36]

Zielonko's anguish over their friend's failure to rescue her lover was palpable even forty years later. "I knew him. I knew he was afraid of everything, even to leave his house, but that doesn't excuse him. That's what I'm saying. Maybe people need to open doors. When someone reaches out for help, open your door, take a chance." During the eight months following Genovese's death, she "retreated from the world and into a bottle." She told one reporter: "I carried a sense of blame for years afterward. 'I kept asking myself if I could have saved her. I know if I'd known, I would have done something. But I couldn't have known, I didn't know until later, but still I felt that way,' she said. 'I felt helpless. I haven't resolved the helplessness.'"[37]

Her deep sense of loss and guilt still haunted her decades later despite her efforts to heal and construct a new life once again. She had already known her share of challenges before meeting Genovese. Born in New York on June 22, 1938, Mary Ann Zielonko lived the first four years of her life in an orphanage, the New York Foundling Home. Four years later her mother and father married, claimed her, and moved the family to Vermont, where her grandfather owned a store. They then moved again, to upstate New York, where her father found work at an arsenal during World War II. At a fairly young age, Zielonko was influenced by a relative of hers who had never married, and she decided that she, too, would "not put up with" a traditional heterosexual relationship. In 1953, at age fifteen, she moved alone to New York and spent a year in what she referred to as a "continuation school." She then worked in an office and found her own place to live, which consisted of a couple of rooms at 44 West 69th Street, on Central Park West. During her many years in New York afterward, she also lived in the Bronx and in Brooklyn. Her favorite apartment was in Manhattan, on Eldridge Street at Delancey on the Lower East Side, a fifth-floor walk up. She also lived in Far Rockaway, in southern Queens, and remembered walking on the beach there.[38]

In the years after losing Kitty, Zielonko went back to school at Queensborough Community College, then earned a master's degree and began to date again. Though she appreciated the efforts of earlier gay activists, it was the gay liberation movement of the late 1960s that really got her involved. She attended Gay Activist Alliance meetings in Manhattan and met Martha Shelley, one of the most visible lesbian feminist activists in New York at that time. "She wanted to be a big judo queen and teach all the women self-defense . . . yeah, right, in twenty minutes," Zielonko recalled. She also attended gatherings at a Unitarian church on Sunday nights with other activists such as Karla Jay and Allan Young. A few years later, she left New York and moved around throughout the Northeast, eventually settling down at a job at the Electric Boat plant in Groton, Connecticut, where she worked for almost nineteen years building submarines. Zielonko "did everything from ship fitter to computer work" there, one among many other women workers. Despite the blue-collar manufacturing environment, she said that her employers "didn't discriminate—the women there wouldn't put up with it." After Kitty's murder, she "never talked" about it again until 2004. (Zielonko first interviewed with Jim Rasenberger of the *Times*, then NPR, and finally local media.) Once her memories of their relationship exploded in the media, the carefully protected private life the two women had constructed became extraordinarily public. Asked by the reporter why she had finally decided to speak out after forty years of silence, Zielonko replied, "I agreed to talk because I think it's important for this area to know what happened, to know about the apathy of people."[39]

Despite her willingness to discuss her relationship with Genovese after so many decades, Zielonko remained skittish about being in the public eye. When she spoke to the media in 2004, she admitted that she was fearful of possible repercussions. She has good reason for caution: Zielonko had been beaten up twice for being gay, once on a subway in New York and again when she was assaulted in Connecticut. Now that she is known as the lesbian lover of one of America's most famous crime victims, and her recorded memories as well as her photograph are readily available online, she has had to work even harder to protect herself, her family, and their privacy.[40]

## I Witnessed Her Love

Despite her fierce desire for privacy, in 2004 Zielonko collaborated with New York writer and performer LuLu LoLo (Lois Pascale Evans) on a one-woman show centered on the story of her relationship with Kitty Genovese and the impact of Genovese's murder. The play began as part of a scene from a theater piece titled *Deviant Women*, which premiered at the Gay and Lesbian Theater Festival in Columbus, Ohio, in 2004. In October 2006 LuLu LoLo expanded it into a one-act play based on Zielonko's

**Figure 6.** LuLu LoLo (left) and Mary Ann Zielonko (right), New York City, 2009. Photo courtesy of Mary Ann Zielonko. Used with permission.

memories of Genovese and performed it in Provincetown, Massachusetts, as part of Women's Week at the Provincetown Fringe Festival. She continued developing the play during a Field Artist in Residence program in New York the following year. By 2009 an expanded production with a supporting cast of dancers from the Jody Oberfelder Dance Projects had been developed; it premiered at the New York International Fringe Festival in August. In *38 Witnessed Her Death, I Witnessed Her Love: The Lonely Secret of Mary Ann Zielonko (Kitty Genovese Story)*, LuLu LoLo presented a four-part three-character drama; she performed in it as *New York Times* metropolitan editor A. M. Rosenthal, murderer Winston Moseley, and Zielonko. As she noted, the play is based on interviews she conducted with Zielonko, who was present at the New York City performance in 2009 with her partner. One reviewer wrote, "I never heard that Genovese had been part of a loving lesbian partnership and left her lover not only bereft but totally shut out by Genovese's family."[41]

The reenactment not only underscores Zielonko's love for Genovese and the horrible loss she experienced but also emphasizes the cautionary nature of the Genovese story. For lesbians, and for all independent women, safety cannot be assured. The media's attention since the murder focused on the bystanders to the crime: the neighbors who reportedly witnessed Winston Moseley's attacks on Kitty Genovese yet did not intervene or call the police. No one publicly explored the life of the complicated young woman who had been killed. Instead, she was defined most often simply as "the Queens barmaid." But as the local detectives investigating her murder learned immediately after her death, Genovese's life in Kew Gardens and at work at Ev's in Hollis was full of friends as well as a female lover.

There was one account of the case that didn't hide the truth about Genovese's life. In 1974, ten years after the crime, NYPD Chief of Detectives Albert Seedman published some of the journals he had kept throughout his thirty years on the force. In his recollection of the Genovese murder, he and his co-author, Peter Hellman, wrote: "A sensitive fact about Kitty Genovese emerged as soon as the investigation turned to the people in her own life: she was a lesbian. You might think that doesn't have a thing to do with a case like this, but it does." Seedman went on to report, "The detectives rounded up all the women Kitty had known, just as they would have picked up all the men if she had been 'straight.'" He provided substantive information about Genovese's life, such as her brief marriage after

LuLu LoLo as A.M. Rosenthal

LuLu LoLo as Winston Moseley

**38 WITNESSED HER DEATH, I WITNESSED HER LOVE:**

THE LONELY SECRET OF MARY ANN ZIELONKO (Kitty Genovese Story)

Written and Performed by **LuLu LoLo**
based on interviews with **Mary Ann Zielonko**

**LULU LOLO° PRODUCTIONS**
lulululo@rcn.com
www.lululolo.com
Tel/Fax 212.426.3775

LuLu LoLo as Mary Ann Zielonkol

Photos: Paul Takeuchi www.paultakeuchi.com

**Figure 7.** LuLu LoLo, *38 Witnessed Her Death, I Witnessed Her Love: The Lonely Secret of Mary Ann Zielonko (Kitty Genovese Story)*. Photographed by Paul Takeuchi. Courtesy of LuLu LoLo. Used with permission.

her graduation from high school, the handful of office jobs she had held before managing Ev's, her "good business head."[42] In 1975 *New York Magazine* published an article by Seedman and Hellman; in a pullout quote, the editors highlighted her lesbianism. In response, they received a vehement letter from Julie Lee of Fanwood, New Jersey, a therapist and leader of the local Daughters of Bilitis. As a feminist, Lee was mindful of challenging still-prevalent stereotypes about women's same-sex relationships. Her letter to the magazine reflected a common response at the time to the outing of Kitty Genovese: her sexuality was part of the story of her private life but it had nothing to do with her death.[43]

Nevertheless, the publication of some of the details of Genovese's life, including her intimate relationships with women, barely caused a ripple in the flood of recriminations against her neighbors. The emphasis on urban apathy took precedence whenever the story of Kitty Genovese was referred to, and this remained largely unchanged for decades. It was not until Mary Ann Zielonko first candidly discussed their relationship in media interviews in 2004 that it became possible to fill in some of the blanks, to animate the bare outline of the figure on the sidewalk. As lesbian journalist Euan Bear wrote in Vermont's gay newspaper *Out in the Mountains*: "Genovese's name was always a cautionary tale—about being a woman alone in the city at night, about the need to care and take action in the face of assault. But now it's also somehow more about me as a lesbian, about our denied and undiscovered herstory, about the dangers we faced then—and now."[44]

In the early years of the twenty-first century, Kitty Genovese's death took on expanded significance not only because of her gender and the dangers facing "a woman alone in the city at night," but also because her sexuality was now part of the story, available for commentary and speculation. When Mary Ann Zielonko revealed their intimate relationship, the official version of the crime was infused with new details. "We were lovers together," Zielonko told the writer Jim Rasenberger. "Everybody tried to hush that up." Her memories of the lively young woman she had met in 1963 inspired news stories, blogs, and cultural productions nationally and internationally. Her coming out also made Genovese a queer icon and linked her to other tales of women and men whose sexual transgressions put them at risk of harm.[45]

For example, in the editorial she wrote after learning the story of Zielonko and Genovese's relationship, Euan Bear alluded to the infamous and brutal 1998 murder of a young gay man in Wyoming that mobilized queer and allied communities throughout the nation, captured widespread media attention, and made visible the prevalence of violence against lesbians, gay men, transgender people, and those who are perceived as such. Bear asserted that Kitty Genovese now would be mourned not just as a woman who had been raped and murdered but as a lesbian Matthew Shepard. The reconsideration of Genovese's death heightened speculation, especially in queer communities, about the often submerged deadly assaults on sexual minorities that had taken place decades before hate crimes were identified and prosecuted.[46]

For many people, the sudden attention that the mainstream media were giving to Genovese's sexuality generated new questions about the crime. Was she killed because she was a lesbian? Did her neighbors not come to her aid because of active or latent homophobia? Uncritical acceptance of the Genovese story as constructed by the *New York Times* still focused most people's attention on the reported thirty-eight witnesses. The news of Genovese's intimate involvement with a woman helped fuel suspicions that negative attitudes about her sexuality might have been the reason for her neighbors' reported inaction. Such understandable fears circulated widely despite the fact that Genovese and Zielonko had lived a relatively private life together. Outside their group of friends, they had shared their apartment in Kew Gardens without publicly advertising their relationship.

Zielonko's memories of her lover also reinvigorated the victim, whose name was famous worldwide but whose life had been reduced to its tragic ending. Kitty Genovese's personal choices—to love another woman, to live independently and work as manager of a sports bar in Queens, to resist the demands of tradition and dream of opening her own business—were atypical for a young Italian American woman in 1964. This likely was the reason why the purveyors of the story—from the *New York Times* to the police and prosecutors in Queens—suppressed them. Whether it was out of a sense of chivalry or a desire to protect her privacy, perhaps a sign of respect for her family's feelings at a time of overwhelming grief, or the power of the homophobia that went unquestioned at the time and at the *Times*, one thing is certain. If the facts of her life had been revealed in 1964, Kitty Genovese would have been the focus of the story; after a few days, it is likely that it, and she, would have faded from view.

As feminist scholar Jennifer Wood wrote in her analysis of crime victim policy, "It is clearly understood but never explicitly stated that 'good' victims are also 'good' mothers, 'good' girls, and 'good' women."[47] "Good" was not an adjective paired with "lesbian" in 1964. Both female and male same-sex desire and relationships were portrayed as sick, sinful, and criminal by all but a relative handful of courageous women and men. It would take another ten years for officialdom to remove the pathology label from same-sex desire, and even longer for some basic human and civil rights to be gained by sexual minorities through the efforts of a growing movement for change, in New York and throughout the nation. But in 1964, the erasure of her life ensured that Kitty Genovese could be portrayed as an ideal victim in the media. It also meant that for the next fifty years the focus of the story would be the presumed apathy of her neighbors.

3

# Thirty-Eight Witnesses

The first time that mention of "Miss Catherine Genovese" appeared in the *New York Times* was in a brief crime report on page twenty-six the day after she was killed. It gave only her age and occupation—twenty-eight-year-old bar manager—as well as her home address. The short five-sentence story, however, immediately introduced her neighbors and provided three quotes from local police. It also got some of the basic details of the crime wrong. The details are significant because the errors contained in this initial report were repeated, amplified, and treated as gospel over the next few months and for decades to come: "Neighbors who were awakened by her screams found the woman, Miss Catherine Genovese of 82–70 Austin Street, shortly after 3 A.M. in front of a building three doors from her home." In fact Genovese's neighbor Sophie Farrar had rushed to help her at about 3:40 a.m. after being alerted by another neighbor. Farrar found her lying on the floor inside the small vestibule of the apartment at 82–62 Austin Street, bleeding profusely from the second, and fatal, attack. Despite the discrepancies, within two weeks' time Genovese's death was providing an unprecedented opportunity for the media to examine individual as well as collective responsibility, in Kew Gardens and throughout the nation. The emphasis on apathy immediately unleashed a torrent of private accusations and public soul-searching, all centered on the perceived growing dangers of city living during a time of social upheaval.

The *Times* came a day late to the story. Its notice of her death followed more informative articles in other New York papers such as the *Long Island Press*, which was one of the first to report the crime. The *Press* continued to give prominence to the details of the police investigation as it unfolded, including a request for help in catching the killer, which ran on March 17. In an urgent appeal to those who lived nearby, readers were asked to call "a special telephone set up in the Richmond Hill police station" if they could provide any information that might lead to the arrest of Genovese's assailant.[1] Two days later the *Press* featured another article on the murder of Kitty Genovese, again on the front page directly below the paper's masthead, after Genovese's attacker had been arrested. This time the report included a mention of Winston Moseley's other murder victim, Anna Mae Johnson; the headline read "Suspect Held as Killer of 2 LI Women." A large photograph of a handcuffed Moseley, his head bent down as he was led into custody, accompanied the article. It began: "A 29-year-old South Ozone Park man was booked early today on two charges of homicide. Police said he admitted stabbing two women to death on the past two Fridays under what he said was an 'uncontrollable urge to kill.'"[2]

Moseley's photograph on the front page of the *Press* delivered two messages, one overt and the other symbolic. The picture of the light-complexioned African American man in handcuffs heralded the capture of a confessed killer, thus promising a return to safety and normalcy for some residents of the borough. It also invoked "the banality of evil," in the words of Hannah Arendt, a phrase that had become popularized since it first appeared in her 1963 writings from Israel on the trial of former Nazi Adolf Eichmann. A slender young black man with delicate features, in his photographs Moseley appeared nonthreatening. Yet he had admitted to several horrifying acts. Photographs of the young Italian American woman he had stabbed and raped were soon paired with Moseley's in the *Press* and other papers, but not in the *New York Times*. No photos of Moseley appeared in the *Times* until his sentencing in June 1964. According to Rosenthal, writing in 1999, "He [Moseley] was black, a fact we did not

NXP141/472(FILE)-3/18/68-BUFFALO,N.Y.: Winston Mosely (shown in a 1964 file photo), 36, convicted of the 1964 murder of Kitty Genovese on a Queens borough street, escaped 3/18 from a Buffalo hospital after overpowering a guard. Buffalo authorities said Mosely, who fled in his gray prison clothing, was not armed. But they described him as "very dangerous." UPI TELEPHOTO/FILE   RP

**Figure 8.** Winston Moseley at the time of his arrest, March 18, 1964. The typewritten caption was added in 1968 after he escaped from Attica State Prison. Photo courtesy of the *New York Times*. Used with permission.

print after he was arrested. Some white readers sent us nasty letters about that. *Times* policy is not to print that information in crime stories unless it is specifically pertinent to the crime or part of the description when police search for a wanted person." Yet other local papers ran photographs of the victim and the perpetrator and thus informed the public in no uncertain terms that this crime was not only brutal and senseless but also racialized. It contributed to the climate of fear rising throughout the city, especially in white neighborhoods. Significantly, no photographs of Moseley's earlier victim, Anna Mae Johnson, a young black woman, ever appeared. Within weeks she would fade from most popular versions of the story, as would her killer. So, too, in all but name would the young "bar manager" Catherine Genovese. Instead, the *Times* would focus everyone's attention on the awful indifference of the neighbors in Kew Gardens.[3]

## He Loved Dogs and Only Liked People

A fastidious man of medium height, Winston Moseley was an enigma. To his family and fellow workers, he was dependable and conscientious, if somewhat reserved and, increasingly, remote. Born in Harlem on March 2, 1935, just four months before Kitty Genovese's birth in Brooklyn, he was described as a "quiet child" by his mother. His early home life with her and Alphonso Moseley had been extremely volatile. At one point Alphonso Moseley, whom Winston learned at age seventeen was not his biological father, accused Winston's mother of infidelity and threatened her with a gun. Their arguments escalated even further until, when he was nine years old, his parents separated and Winston was sent to Detroit to live with his grandparents. In an autobiography written a few years later, at age thirteen, Moseley revealed himself as an intelligent, literate, and extremely self-aware boy who took time to document youthful adventures and mis-adventures. In this account of his life, which he titled "The Years Flew By," he wrote about his parents and extended family, his classmates and friends, and recorded his move from New York to Detroit. He described the schools he attended in both cities, noted his pride in being placed in a higher grade when he moved to Detroit, and detailed his growing fascina-tion with animals and insects. He wrote about playing with or constructing weapons—a BB gun, knives. He also recorded his desire to attend college and become either a scientist or an agent with the Federal Bureau of Inves-tigation, though he acknowledged his difficulties succeeding academically as he advanced to ninth grade. Despite this, he hoped to do well in school and, under "Future Plans," added, "Some day I might even be famous." After leaving Detroit, he lived for a time with an aunt in Pittsburgh, where he completed high school, and then returned to New York City.[4]

He married his first wife, Pauline, in 1952 and began working at Ray-gram Corporation in Mount Vernon, New York, in 1954 as a business ma-chine operator. He also purchased a home at 133–19 Sutter Avenue, South Ozone Park, in Queens. His marriage to Pauline ended badly, however; they divorced after he found out that she had been having an affair. As his father had done to his mother, he threatened her with a rifle. In 1961 he married a woman named Elizabeth (nicknamed Betty), and they had a son together; their family included another child, a young boy who was in Betty's care. Moseley had a good work record at Raygram and was making a salary of $100 per week by 1964. He had never been in any legal trouble, was not a big drinker, and rarely socialized. But despite his detached de-meanor, his obsession with his ant farms, and his extraordinary attachment to his German shepherd dogs, especially one particularly violent female who was affectionate only with him, he appeared to be as normal as anyone else. Betty said of him, "He loved dogs and only liked people." No one knew about his secret life until his arrest for the murder of Kitty Genovese on March 18 after an attempted daytime home burglary in Corona, Queens.[5]

On March 20, Moseley again appeared in the *New York Times*, which continued to trail the local papers in its coverage of the Kew Gardens crime. The paper printed a report on page twenty-one headed "Queens Man Seized in Death of 2 Women," which noted, "A 29-year-old man who told the police that he gave in to urges to kill and rape was arraigned in Queens yesterday for the knife slaying of two women within two weeks." Listing his occupation and home address, the brief item mentioned Moseley's multiple confessions: "The police said he re-enacted the crimes after detectives found that he fit the description of a man being sought for the murder of Catherine Genovese, 28, a barmaid who was stabbed to death near her apartment at 82–70 Austin Street, Kew Gardens, early last Friday." It added that Moseley also had confessed to the February 29 murder of "Anne [*sic*] Mae Johnson," a "24-year-old housewife" who lived in Ozone Park. Moseley had stalked, stabbed, and sexually assaulted the young black woman and set fire to her home to cover up the crime just two weeks before he attacked Genovese.[6]

The *Times* article also alluded to the continuing search for the killer of Janice Wylie and Emily Hoffert, which had happened on August 29 in Manhattan the previous year. The news of the Wylie-Hoffert (or "Career Girl") murders of two young white women in an affluent Upper West Side neighborhood was among the high-profile stories of 1963 because of the elite status of the victims and the media connections of the Wylie family. Moseley was questioned about the deaths but cleared when police checked the records of his employer and found proof that he had been at work on the morning when the two young women were slain.[7]

On March 22, the *New York Daily News*—at that time New York City's largest-circulation tabloid—scooped the *Times* with the story of Moseley's confession to yet another gruesome murder in Queens, that of teenager Barbara Kralik in Springfield Gardens in July 1963. In addition, the *Daily News* reported that at the time Moseley confessed to killing Kralik, the police already had a suspect, Alvin Mitchell, in custody for the crime. The confusion caused by the dual confessions was a potential embarrassment not just for the Queens detectives but for the entire New York Police Department. In early 1964 the NYPD was under scrutiny for its failure to solve a number of crimes that were plaguing an increasingly fearful city, including the still unsolved "Career Girl" murders of the previous summer. The *Daily News* story caught the attention of recently named *Times* metropolitan editor A. M. Rosenthal. "I was upset not for any moral reason at all but simply because we had not had the story ourselves," he wrote later that year. He did not like being bested by a competitor.[8]

## He Kept the Paper Straight

When he returned to New York in 1963 to take on the task of increasing the volume and vitality of the paper's reporting throughout the city, state, and region, Rosenthal was determined, according to his deputy metropolitan editor Arthur Gelb, "to shape the most comprehensive and imaginative city report ever produced." Gelb remembered, "When we took over the city staff, Abe and I made it our first priority to free reporters of their perceived writing restrictions, encouraging them to try new approaches, to experiment with their own styles the way we both had tried to do."[9] It would be during Rosenthal's long tenure at the *New York Times*—he went on to become managing editor in 1970 and executive editor in 1977— that the paper, a mainstay of well-educated New Yorkers since the early twentieth century, greatly expanded its influence. In 1988 Joseph Goulden wrote of its preeminence among American newspapers: "The public perception of events, as reported in the *Times*, is now accepted as the 'official version.' . . . Attention by the *Times* can both create and legitimize an issue as being suitable for the national agenda."[10] In his 2006 obituary of Rosenthal, *Times* writer Robert McFadden summed up Rosenthal's role in solidifying the paper's position: "He was tigerish in defense of high standards of reporting and editing, which called for fairness, objectivity, and good taste in news columns free of editorial content, causes, political agendas, innuendo and unattributed pejorative quotations." McFadden also noted that, at the same time that he safeguarded the paper's values, Rosenthal "presided over more changes than any editor in the paper's history."[11]

Famous for his reportorial skills as well as his explosive temper, Rosenthal also was known for his increasingly conservative politics. "Again and

again, he would say he was making crooked *Times* coverage 'straight,'"
wrote John Shafer upon Rosenthal's death in 2006. "For most of his 17
years at the helm, Rosenthal battled what he considered the left-liberal ten-
dencies of many of his reporters." Proud of his efforts to combat possible
bias in the paper's coverage, he asked that his epitaph read "He Kept the
Paper Straight," and so it was inscribed on his tombstone. For the closeted
gay reporters who worked under his supervision at the *Times* during the
1960s, 1970s, and 1980s and were acutely aware of his overtly homophobic
attitudes, the double entendre is especially fitting.[12]

Abraham Michael Rosenthal was born May 2, 1922, in Sault Ste. Marie,
Ontario, the only son among six children born to Russian Jewish parents
who relocated to the Bronx when he was a boy. By the early 1930s, a series
of deaths had shattered the family. The first tragedy was the loss of his
beloved sister Pauline, nicknamed Bess. Another sister, Ruth, eleven years
his senior, who had inspired him politically with her unapologetic communist activism, died suddenly when she was twenty-four. His father then
succumbed to complications from a workplace injury, and Rosenthal lost
two other sisters to illness. Of these tragedies, Rosenthal said, "I learned
at an early age that death was real, that it wasn't something that just happened to other people." In his early teens Rosenthal also developed osteo-
myelitis, an acute infection of the bone marrow. He underwent difficult
treatments and feared being disabled for life until an operation at the Mayo
Clinic, though excruciatingly painful, enabled him to walk again. Despite
the success of the eighteen-hour surgery, which required several weeks of
immobilization, for the rest of his life he had an uneven gait and suffered
chronic pain in his legs. His disease also cost him a year of schooling; but
Rosenthal persevered, graduated, and was admitted to the City College of
New York (CCNY) in 1941, an exceptional accomplishment. As he later
wrote of his classmates in an unpublished memoir: "We young, eager,
bright Jews were formed politically by Franklin D. Roosevelt, Adolf Hitler, and Josef Stalin. We were their creatures and could never escape from
them. . . . All of us at City College had those political genes in common.
How we reacted to them, however, varied, quite considerably within a ra-
dius. Some became radical and stayed radical. Most were radical freshmen
and liberal sophomores."[13]

At CCNY his friend Richard Cohen encouraged him to join the staff of
the college newspaper his first semester there. He did so and soon moved

up the hierarchy of *The Campus*; within two years he had become the paper's representative on the student council as well as news editor. A mentor at CCNY suggested him for the job of campus stringer for the *New York Times*, and he landed a full-time job on the paper in the spring of 1944.[14] Although his initial assignments, like those of all new hires, were not glamorous, the one thing Rosenthal largely was spared was the police beat. During that time, however, he learned that the vaunted power of the press could be stifled quickly when met with intransigence on the part of law enforcement officials. "Four eyes, I don't care if you drop dead," Rosenthal remembered a detective telling him when, as a bespectacled young reporter, he arrived at a crime scene eager to interview police and view the body. He later wrote that, at that moment, he learned "it was not the ordained, patriotic duty of every American to answer every reporter's question." The experience undoubtedly influenced his understanding of the power of the police in providing crucial information as well as interpretations of events. During his early years at the *Times*, he also was being instructed on which crimes were considered important enough to merit the paper's attention. Those that occurred in black neighborhoods were at the bottom of the list. As Rosenthal put it in 1964, "In twenty years in the newspaper business, I have spent only four nights covering police news, but I remember quite distinctly a police reporter of some experience telling me then of the relationship of color and geography to crime news—'Above 125th Street, if there's a killing don't bother phoning the desk; it happens too often.'"[15]

In addition, the young reporter had to come to terms with anti-Semitism at the paper. According to Joseph Goulden: "As his assignments bettered, Rosenthal realized he eventually must face another problem, that of his byline. Despite *Times* ownership by a Jewish family, the news operation was dominated by Protestants. . . . To many persons the *Times* went out of its way to avoid 'looking Jewish.' This meant that 'Jewish bylines' were anathema." Thus Abraham Michael Rosenthal became A. M. Rosenthal.[16] He earned a spot reporting from the new United Nations, which in 1946 met at what was then the satellite campus of Hunter College in the Bronx (now Lehman College). Rosenthal took advantage of all opportunities to learn from the people around him. The cachet of his UN post helped in his personal life; he met and then married a young Irish American woman, *Times* colleague Ann Burke, in 1949. For the next six years he continued to push for a foreign assignment, for that was "the cream of the paper." But anti-Semitism reared its ugly head again. Rumors of a "Jewish quota" enforced by the managing editor Turner Catledge and president and publisher Adolph Ochs Sulzberger meant that Rosenthal was unlikely to be considered. "The staff contained so many Jewish reporters that Catledge feared criticism if the *Times* had to mobilize for coverage of renewed war in the Middle East," wrote Goulden. Rosenthal's volatile temper also reportedly caused him to run afoul of an important member of the *Times* family and delayed his assignment to a foreign post.[17]

Finally, in 1955, after years of repeated requests, he was assigned to India. He moved his family, which by then included two young sons (a third would be born in India), to New Delhi in 1956, just after India's successful independence struggle with Great Britain. But after a year of witnessing extreme violence administered by what he termed the "ferocious dictatorship" then in control, he requested reassignment in 1957. "I was sent to Poland to cover what was then Communist Eastern Europe," he wrote in 1999. In Warsaw he would write about the remnants of the horrors of Nazism.[18]


## There Is No News from Auschwitz

One of the attributes that helped Rosenthal's climb up the ladder at the *Times* was the tone of his writing, which was described as "disarmingly personal: it was as if he had written a letter home to a friend." His 1958 essay for the *New York Times Magazine* titled "There Is No News from Auschwitz" is the best example of his evocative, emotional style. Based on his visit to the Nazi death camp, which offered guided tours of the facilities to visitors in 1958, it presages his writings about the Kitty Genovese crime. Rosenthal evoked the significance of place and the duty of witnessing in the face of horror:

> The most terrible thing of all, somehow, was that at Brzezinka the sun was bright and warm, the rows of graceful poplars were lovely to look upon and on the grass near the gates children played.
>
> It all seemed frighteningly wrong, as in a nightmare, that at Brzezinka the sun should ever shine or that there should be light and greenness and the

sound of young laughter. It would be fitting if at Brzezinka the sun never shone and the grass withered, because this is a place of unutterable terror.

And yet, every day, from all over the world, people come to Brzezinka, quite possibly the most grisly tourist center on earth. They come for a variety of reasons—to see if it could really have been true, to remind themselves not to forget, to pay homage to the dead by the simple act of looking upon their place of suffering.

Rosenthal noted that Brzezinka was part of "that minutely organized factory of torture and death that the Nazis called Konzentrationalager Auschwitz." The power of his writing, in addition to its ability to transport the reader instantly to the "grisly tourist center," also helped ensure that the women, men, and children who died there would not be forgotten. Toward the end of the essay, he focused particularly on one young woman:

> A long corridor where rows of faces stare from the walls. Thousands of pictures, the photographs of prisoners. They are all dead now, the men and women who stood before the cameras, and they all knew they were to die.
>
> They all stare blank-faced, but one picture, in the middle of a row, seizes the eye and wrenches the mind. A girl, 22 years old, plumply pretty, blonde.
>
> She is smiling gently, as at a sweet, treasured thought. What was the thought that passed through her young mind and is now her memorial on the wall of the dead at Auschwitz?

"There is nothing new to report about Auschwitz," he repeated at his conclusion. "There is merely the compulsion to write something about it, a compulsion that grows out of a restless feeling that to have visited Auschwitz and then turned away without having said or written anything would somehow be a most grievous act of discourtesy to those who died here."[19] The response to the essay from *Times* readers was immediate, as if a floodgate of emotion had been opened. One letter writer quoted the Russian novelist Aleksandr Kuprin: "The horror of it was that there was no horror."[20]

Rosenthal had established his reputation as a creative, powerful writer and was a rising star at the *Times*. Although he was expelled from Poland in 1959 after calling the country's leader "moody and irascible," Rosenthal had the last laugh: in 1960 he won the Pulitzer Prize for distinguished foreign reporting. He then was sent to Geneva and spent time in Africa—the

Congo, Mali, and Sudan—before being assigned to Tokyo.[21] He loved his assignments abroad. As he remembered in 1964, "For almost a decade, reality to myself, my wife, and our three sons was not the Grand Concourse in the Bronx or Broadway in Manhattan but Nizamuddin in New Delhi or Chodkiewicze Street in Warsaw."[22]

But by 1962, with the paper's circulation declining, *Times* managing editor Catledge was determined to counter the downward trend by making news stories more accessible and interesting to the majority of readers. He also wanted a metropolitan editor who would expand the paper's coverage of New York City and the surrounding region. He turned to Rosenthal to institute the necessary changes. "When the paper asked me to return from Japan to New York in 1962 and become metropolitan editor," Rosenthal recalled, "I did not relish the idea at all. The Khyber Pass was my kind of story, I said, not the Bronx. But New York wanted to try me out as an editor and I submitted, figuring that after two or three years I would either get the London bureau as the reward for my sacrifice or run off again. I remained an editor, but always in my mind still king of the Khyber Pass."[23]

In addition to preferring foreign locales, Rosenthal was also concerned about his ability to direct city coverage for the *Times* after being out of town, and out of touch, for nearly a decade. He searched for ways to reconnect, in the newsroom and beyond. He quickly asked his friend and colleague Arthur Gelb, then a deputy editor as well as a successful cultural writer and co-author of a biography on Eugene O'Neill, to join him as his deputy. Gelb wrote in 2003 that Rosenthal turned to him because "he wasn't familiar with the dramatic changes taking place in the city, colored by the Vietnam War and the civil rights protests in the South. He added that my familiarity with City Hall, [Mayor Robert F.] Wagner, [Robert] Moses, [Congressman and later Mayor John] Lindsay, the police and the municipal departments would be invaluable. Most tempting of all, he said he was sure that I would succeed him one day as metropolitan editor, as he had set his sights on higher goals."[24]

In those years after he first returned to New York, Rosenthal had a seemingly insatiable curiosity about the city. "Waiting for the elevator one evening he noticed the pristine white sand in the ashtrays in the lobby. Where does this sand come from? he asked another man," one writer noted. "Several days later the *Times* had a feature article answering the questions Rosenthal raised." He approached New York with the seasoned

**Figure 9.** A. M. Rosenthal (left) and Arthur Gelb (right), 1967. Photo courtesy of the *New York Times*. Used with permission.

eyes of a foreign correspondent in a new environment and took advantage of his friend's knowledge of the city's many venues. Gelb wrote in 2003: "As a kind of introduction to our taking over the metropolitan coverage on September 17, 1963, I suggested Abe join me on a tour of topical cabarets to get a feel of what satirical comics were saying about our government. After watching Dick Gregory's act at Basin Street East, Abe said he'd like to meet him." According to Gelb, Gregory, a black comedian who also was a civil rights activist, "dropped his comic mask" and became deadly serious. "Negroes are fed up and there's going to be a revolution," Gregory told them. "The top of the keg is going to blow off here in New York." Gelb noted that the comedian was not joking. "In less than a year, his prediction came true, with the explosion of the riots in Harlem."[25]

Gelb also remembered exploring with Rosenthal neighborhoods throughout the boroughs, "where Abe, having been so long away, saw potential stories on every block." He noticed the sharp increase in public visibility of New York's gay community. As one account noted, Rosenthal asked at a meeting, "Where did all these . . . *these queers* come from?" The result of his query was a December 1963 front-page story announcing "Problem of Homosexuality in City Provokes Wide Concern," written by Robert C. Doty, a former *Times* Paris bureau chief. As noted in chapter 2, the prominently placed feature urged New Yorkers to pay attention to troubling signs of overt sexual deviance and sickness in their midst. According to Gelb, Doty was "as fair-minded a reporter as existed on any mainstream newspaper" and spent several weeks "frequenting homosexual haunts" as well as talking to psychiatrists, police, and religious leaders. Writing forty years later, Gelb noted, "Some of its conclusions sound pitifully naïve today, but at the time the article was deemed an earnest effort to explain that homosexuality was 'the city's most sensitive open secret [and signaled] the presence of what is probably the greatest homosexual population in the world.' "[26] Rosenthal also assigned pieces on interracial marriage and other topics not usually pursued by *Times* reporters. A classic example would be the March 27, 1964, story of Kitty Genovese and the thirty-eight witnesses, a tale that "rocked the city to its core." It also secured Rosenthal's successful editorial tenure in the process.[27]

## Queens Story One for the Books

On returning to New York to assume his new post, wrote Rosenthal years later, "I set about doing what I would have done in any new foreign assignment: find out who ran the place and get to know them." A routine lunch on March 23 with Michael J. Murphy, New York's police commissioner, at Emil's, a restaurant near City Hall, gave him the opportunity to learn more about the police perspective on crime in New York's fastest-growing borough. He had come to lunch with some questions for Murphy about the recent double confessions in the case of young Barbara Kralik, killed in Springfield Gardens, Queens, the previous summer, as reported by the *Daily News*. But Murphy did not want to discuss Winston Moseley's surprise confession to the crime; he also did not want to talk about the man then in custody for Kralik's murder, Alvin Mitchell. Mitchell later told the press that he had been brutalized into giving a false confession. As the *Times* reported in 1965, Mitchell testified in court that he had been beaten by Queens police. The reporter quoted him as saying, "When I complained to Captain Dowd, I got a black eye," and noted that Mitchell "never complained again because, 'I knew what would happen to me.'" Rather than comment to the *Times* editor about any aspects of the double confessions, Murphy instead diverted their conversation to the frustrations generated by the police investigations into the Kitty Genovese case. "Brother, that Queens story is one for the books," Murphy said to Rosenthal. He proceeded to tell him about the crime in Kew Gardens.[28]

The two men had previously discussed the problems the city's police had had with uncooperative residents, and Murphy now zeroed in on the unwillingness of the neighbors to speak with local officers in the bitterly cold days after the Genovese killing, when officers went door-to-door and tried to interview more than three dozen people who lived near the crime scene. He emphasized the bewilderment of the police at the reasons some of the neighbors gave in explaining why they hadn't called the local precinct when they first heard Genovese's cries or glimpsed an attack. "We heard screams but saw nothing," one neighbor told them. "My husband saw a man and woman fighting on the street and yelled at them to stop," said another.[29]

Rosenthal was well aware that Murphy was redirecting their conversation, but he went along with it. "I told the Commissioner that this seemed to be a story, and since our talk was entirely off the record up to then, asked his agreement to my assigning a reporter to look into it. He agreed," Rosenthal later wrote. The suggestion that dozens of people heard a young woman scream for help and did nothing struck him as something that should be investigated. Later that day he asked Martin Gansberg, a veteran *Times* editor, to see what he could learn about what was going on in Queens. While this might seem an odd choice of personnel, given the availability of *Times* reporters such as Homer Bigart and Gay Talese—both of whom had had experience covering the 1963 "Career Girl" murders—Rosenthal said that it was because Gansberg happened to be in his line of vision when he went back to his desk that evening. But the selection of Gansberg also enabled Rosenthal to assign a longtime staffer who was eager to do some reporting and would be willing to travel out to Queens to gather the details without complaint. He also most likely would not challenge his editor's control over the final product.[30]

Gansberg made calls and walked the streets of Kew Gardens with police, knocking on the same doors and asking to interview the same neighbors police had questioned ten days earlier. By this time Winston Moseley was under psychiatric observation at Kings County Hospital. After being apprehended on March 18, he was taken to the 102nd Precinct in Queens and questioned by detectives, who asked him specifically about the Genovese crime. Not only did he readily admit to the murder of Kitty Genovese, but also he confessed to several rapes, attempted rapes, acts of sodomy, and burglaries in addition to the Johnson and Kralik murders.

While Queens detectives worked to untangle the details of his confessions, Moseley was indicted for the murder of Kitty Genovese by a Queens County grand jury on March 23. He first appeared in the Supreme Court of Queens County, just a few blocks from the murder scene, on March 24 and was asked if he could afford an attorney. When he said that he could not, the court appointed counsel for him. The next day a team of Queens lawyers led by Sidney Sparrow, with Julius Lipitz and Martha Zelman, were assigned to represent Moseley despite the fact that Sparrow had a personal connection to the victim, signaling a possible conflict of interest: he had represented Kitty Genovese in disposing of the gambling charges against her in 1961. Although Sparrow revealed this connection to the court, it was not deemed worthy of concern by the presiding judge, Irving Shapiro, and so Sparrow, Lipitz, and Zelman, as well as Sparrow's son Robert, proceeded to work on Moseley's behalf. Sparrow's previous involvement as counsel to Genovese was not noted in any media accounts. Instead, in a short March 26 article headlined "Suspect Committed in Slaying of Two," the *New York Times* caught up with what the *Daily News* had reported four days earlier. The piece identified Moseley simply as having "allegedly made a statement implicating himself in a slaying for which another man is being held." His involvement in "the fatal stabbing of Catherine Genovese, a barmaid," was reduced to one sentence.[31]

## 37 Who Saw Murder Didn't Call Police

The next day, Friday, March 27, the *Times* came out in full force with an original story of its own. It focused not on the victim, nor on the perpetrator and his series of attacks on Queens women, but rather on the victim's neighbors. The paper ran a front-page article with a headline that was guaranteed to grab readers' attention: "37 Who Saw Murder Didn't Call the Police." The story's subhead emphasized the main point—"Apathy at Stabbing of Queens Woman Shocks Inspector"—and the reported details ensured outrage. The first paragraph read:

> For more than half an hour, 38 respectable, law-abiding citizens in Queens watched a killer stalk and stab a woman in three separate attacks in Kew Gardens. Twice the sound of their voices and the sudden glare of their bedroom lights interrupted him and frightened him off. Each time he returned, sought her out and stabbed her again. Not one person telephoned the police during the assault; one witness called after the woman was dead.

The long article extended over four columns, with a large photograph of the crime scene complete with numbered locations of the purported three attacks. It continued on page thirty-eight for three more columns and included two additional photographs: one, again numbered, showed the front of the two-story apartment building where Moseley attacked Genovese inside the entryway; it also identified the doorway to her apartment nearby. The last photograph showed a uniformed police officer at the local precinct call box at the corner of Austin Street and Lefferts Boulevard. The caption read: "When first attacked, Miss Genovese was trying to get to the telephone box, at which policeman stands, on Lefferts Boulevard at Austin Street. She was nervous about man she saw after parking her car in lot at the railroad. Block of houses where she lived fronts on Austin Street."[32]

Toward the end of the article, some of the unnamed "witnesses" are quoted. Two responded that they "didn't want to get involved," a phrase that soon would become ubiquitous, especially because the article quoted police as saying that they were able to "piece together what happened—and capture the suspect—because the residents furnished all the information when detectives rang doorbells during the days following the slaying." One woman, identified as "a housewife," said that she and her husband "thought it was a lover's quarrel." Another couple simply said that they were afraid. None of their reasons adequately explained their failure to act. Suddenly, the story of the murder of the Queens barmaid shifted to one of cowardice and apathy on the part of "38 respectable, law-abiding citizens."[33] The number of witnesses to the crime became the sole focus of the story, despite contradictory statements as to how many people actually had been involved. Rosenthal later attempted to explain the discrepancies in the number of witnesses reported by the *Times*: "We kept confusing readers by shifting between thirty-seven and thirty-eight; the reason was that thirty-eight had witnessed the crime or heard it, but that one man finally did put through a call after it was too late."[34]

The existence of more than three dozen eyewitnesses to the crime never was verified. According to former Queens assistant district attorney Charles Skoller, who prosecuted the case against Moseley, the paper was in error about the number of attacks and the number of neighbors who saw them. Nevertheless, as Skoller later said, "the article did vividly describe Kitty's screams during the first attack and the indifference of her neighbors." He also succinctly identified what the *Times* account had accomplished: "Overnight, Kew Gardens became dirty words, and Kitty's neighbors were excoriated for their inhuman response to her tragedy." [35]

The detectives' reports from neighborhood interviews immediately after the crime detailed the responses of a number of people who reported hearing screams but observing little or nothing else.[36] Bailey's, the bar at Austin Street and Lefferts Avenue, is likely the place where Kitty Genovese was headed when she realized that Moseley was coming after her—not the police call box, as reported in the *Times'* version of events—but it had been closed that night at midnight because of fighting. A number of the Kew Gardens neighbors interviewed who had heard screams mistakenly thought that it was drunken brawlers who were awakening them yet again. In direct contradiction to the *Times* story, two Austin Street residents actually did call the police the night of the assault, but to no avail.[37] Despite the factual inaccuracies, however, the first paragraphs set the tone for future reporting of the case. The article quickly galvanized public outrage over the seemingly callous behavior of Genovese's neighbors. Once the tale of witnesses who hadn't wanted to get involved was created and publicized, the issue of urban apathy became the central point.

## Apathy Is Puzzle in Queens Killing

The *Times* ensured its interpretive dominance over the story by repeating the apathetic witnesses theme continually for the next six weeks in news articles, editorials, and features. The initial March 27 story was followed

two days later by another well-placed article headlined "Apathy Is Puzzle in Queens Killing." Written by Charles Mohr, the follow-up piece
quoted "behavioral specialists" (lawyers, clergy, psychiatrists, sociologists,
and a theologian—who, without a trace of irony, requested, "Don't quote
me. . .") on the reasons why the witnesses to Genovese's murder failed to
contact the police. What became clear was the inability of any of them to
make sense of what supposedly had happened in Kew Gardens. Blaming passivity on everything from "the megalopolis in which we live" to
the tendency of New Yorkers to feel that "you might get hurt if you act,"
the experts interviewed by the *Times* reflected their own puzzlement at
what one called an "atypical" incident. Not everyone quoted automatically
accepted that indifference was a necessary consequence of big-city living.
Some had concrete plans to respond. "Leo Zimmerman, vice president of
the Queens Bar Association, called the incident 'outrageous' and said he
was 'profoundly shocked.' . . . Mr. Zimmerman is organizing a 'Law Day
U.S.' program to be held May 1 at the World's Fair Pavilion in response to
a proclamation by President Johnson requesting that such ceremonies be
held throughout the nation. Mr. Zimmerman said the Kew Gardens case
showed the need for such programs to 'indoctrinate' the public with their
responsibility and to 'fight this tendency to look the other way.'"[38]

On March 31, a second article by Gansberg, which featured three civil-
ians honored by New York Police Department officials for their efforts to
help thwart criminals, again referred to the attacks on Genovese and the
cowardice of the Kew Gardens community. Under the headline "Police to
Honor 3 Who Gave Help," the bold subhead declared, "38 Watched Murder." The article went on to repeat the errors of the March 27 story: "In
that case, 38 persons in nearby apartment houses and homes watched the
killer stab the victim in three separate attacks in a 35-minute period. One
of the witnesses called the police after the killer fled and Miss Genovese
was dead."[39]

In early April, Gansberg followed up his March 31 story with a prominent page-one article focusing on the need for changes to New York's
dysfunctional system for reporting emergencies. He quoted Commissioner
Murphy admitting that "there had been many complaints about delays in
getting responses to calls" to police; Murphy said that a study was under
way to determine how best to establish one citywide emergency number.[40]
At that time there was no simple, direct way to contact the police in New

York City. Instead, as Rosenthal wrote in June 1964, "a New Yorker who needs the help of the police can dial the operator or call the department number in his borough. But the borough numbers sometimes pose a problem. For example, the telephone number for Staten Island is SAint George 7-1200. Yet the Police Department Official Roster issued last January 3 gives the exchange as ST George. Persons who dial ST to reach the police on Staten Island find they are in touch with a business concern in Manhattan." Even when callers did connect with the appropriate department, it was routine procedure to be asked to give their name, address, and reason for calling; sometimes the response on the other end of the line was a suggestion to the caller to "mind your own business." Many New Yorkers felt that it was difficult to contact police in an emergency even if they had the best intentions and no prior bad experiences with law enforcement. But rather than probing the reasons for residents' reluctance to engage the police, the *Times'* emphasis on the thirty-eight witnesses compelled a local as well as a national response of condemning the Kew Gardens neighbors.[41]

## The Dying Girl That No One Helped

Soon the neighbors became symbols of a city in decline. Less than one month after the Genovese murder, Loudon Wainwright devoted one of his first essays in *Life* magazine to "The Dying Girl That No One Helped." In his April 10, 1964, column "The View From Here," published two weeks after the *Times'* front-page story, he wrote: "To judge from the recent, bitter example given us by the good folks of a respectable New York residential area, Samaritans are very scarce these days. In fact, if the reactions of the 38 heedless witnesses to the murder of Catherine Genovese provide any true reflection of a national attitude toward our neighbors, we are becoming a callous, chicken-hearted and immoral people."[42]

Wainwright's essay has proved to be one of the most durable, oft-quoted responses to the *Times'* front-page exposé of the Kew Gardens community's inaction. He was a longtime staffer at *Life*, founded by Henry Luce in 1936 and published in New York City. Best known for its powerful photographic essays, in 1964 it enjoyed the widest circulation of any American weekly. Wainwright had provided potent verbal portraits of famous as well as lesser-known people for the magazine for many years, including a tribute to the Reverend Martin Luther King Jr. during the first of the lunch counter sit-ins that swept the South, and then the nation, in 1960. Writing about the murder of Genovese in 1964, Wainwright not only criticized the Kew Gardens neighbors but also established the moral imperative of examining one's own conscience for signs of apathy: "Psychiatrists, poking around in the ruins of character at the scene of the crime, have already come up with some generous, culture-blaming excuses for this grotesque piece of bad fellowship. But the matter calls for something more than sheer indignation. An examination of the pitiful facts of Miss Genovese's terminal experience makes very necessary the ugly personal question each of us must ask: What would *I* have done?" Wainwright quoted one of the so-called witnesses, concluding: "His comments—agonized, contradictory, guilt-ridden, self-excusing—indicate the price in bad conscience he and his neighbors are now paying. 'I feel terrible about it,' he said. 'The thing keeps coming back in my mind.'" In a phrase that would soon come to define—and condemn—the people who lived near the crime scene, Wainwright noted that one of them said: "You just don't want to get involved. They might have picked me up as a suspect if I'd bounced right out there. I was getting ready, but my wife stopped me. She didn't want to be a hero's widow."[43]

Wainwright reported the same neighbor's attempt to deflect criticism, remarking: "He was plainly depressed and disappointed at his own failure. 'Every time I look out here now,' he said, 'it's like looking out at a nightmare. How could so many of us have had the same idea that we didn't need to do anything? But that's not all that's wrong.' Now he sounded betrayed and he told what was really eating him. Those 38 witnesses had, at least, talked to the police after the murder. The man pointed to a nearby building. 'There are people over there who saw everything,' he said. 'And there hasn't been a peep out of them yet. Not one peep.'"[44]

At the same time that Wainwright's commentary appeared, but at the other end of the cultural spectrum, small groups of theatergoers on New York's Lower East Side experienced a visceral portrayal of the immorality of neighborly indifference. Playwright Jean-Claude van Itallie was inspired by the *Times'* front-page story in one of his first collaborations with Joseph Chaikin and the actors, musicians, and artists who were members of the legendary experimental Open Theater in Manhattan. Less than one month after reading about the crime, van Itallie created *The Murdered Woman*, subtitled *A Play for a Group, Inspired by a News Article on the Murder in Brooklyn, N.Y. of Katherine Genovese, Winter, 1964.* While he misidentified the location of the crime and also misspelled the victim's first name, as some early newspaper accounts had also done, he powerfully portrayed the self-absorption of modern life as represented by people like Genovese's neighbors. His play also graphically represented one of the most compelling aspects of the story of Kitty Genovese and the thirty-eight witnesses: the failure of community.

The play was staged simply: the set consisted of four structures representing separate yet contiguous houses, each with small groups of people inside. As the people in one "house" spoke to one another, they were spotlighted; the other houses fell silent. Van Itallie's notes for the play described his intentions: "One of the houses is a man and a woman. Slowly the situation of the man and the woman becomes serious and the man is driven to wanting to murder the woman. The woman, frantic, errs in the streets and goes from house to house begging help . . . but in the other houses they only relate to her for their own needs—they draw her, or try to draw her into their own situations, or, if she gets too obstreperous they ignore her, turn their backs on her. The murderer moves slowly, ritualistically, and stabs the woman every once in a while. Finally all the houses have their backs turned and the woman is killed completely. The houses continue to bicker or chatter with parts of phrases."[45] As the dance historian Sally Banes wrote of the performances, "The Open Theater made the issue of community—of family and neighborhood—a crucial topic."[46]

Some of van Itallie's short works were later incorporated into his successful 1966 off-Broadway production *America Hurrah*, which brought him critical notice and acclaim. As he put it in 1983, "Previous to *America Hurrah* the media would have cared less what we were doing."[47] This certainly was true of the critical silence that greeted *The Murdered Woman* in 1964. But its performance is yet another example of the impact of the *Times'* front-page story. Mass-circulation essays like Wainwright's and small experimental theater productions such as the one presented by van Itallie and the Open Theater show the extent of the cultural outrage generated in the immediate aftermath of the crime by the news of the seemingly callous behavior of the reported thirty-eight witnesses. Although these two responses may have reached very different audiences, both of them posed the difficult question of individual responsibility in crisis situations, exactly as Rosenthal and the *New York Times* intended.

By early May the paper's coverage had spread beyond Queens to another borough and an assault on another young woman. "Rape Victim's Screams Draw 40, but No One Acts," reported by Thomas Buckley, immediately alluded to the Genovese case, extending the epidemic of indifference. This time the crime "took place in broad daylight" and happened "on one of the busiest streets in the Bronx." An eighteen-year-old Puerto Rican woman, the switchboard operator at a small business, was found at the bottom of a flight of stairs leading up to her office, nearly naked and badly bruised, by police who had heard her screams. They also found a man standing over her, whom she accused of assaulting her. "It recalled the fatal stabbing of Miss Catherine Genovese on March 13 in Kew Gardens, Queens," wrote Buckley. "Detectives found later than 38 persons had seen the attack on Miss Genovese, which took place over a 30-minute period, without going to her aid or calling the police."[48]

Shortly thereafter, a woman who had been harassed by obscene telephone calls in Manhattan was featured in a lengthy page-one article in which she was reported to have worked with police to trap the caller. Gloria Palter, a thirty-three-year-old public relations consultant living in Gramercy Park, contacted the *New York Times* "after reading accounts of recent crimes that were committed in the presence of citizens who refused to raise a hand." She agreed to engage her harasser in conversations so that she could lure him to her apartment. The ruse worked, and police arrested the man. The story, however, noted her displeasure with the results: "Her tormenter is serving a 90-day jail term. But Miss Palter insists this will do no good. She believes that for his sake and society's the man should have been committed for psychiatric help." Her disenchantment led her to state that, faced with a similar situation again, she would refuse to contact police. "She said she would take the attitude of the 38 Queens residents who witnessed the murder of Miss Catherine Genovese on March 14 [*sic*] and did nothing to help her."[49]

The apathy narrative encouraged public examination of other pressing issues. A letter to the editor of the *Times*, for example, drew parallels between the supposed apathy of Genovese's neighbors and the irritation some white New Yorkers felt "when others' sufferings and demands threaten to impinge upon their daily lives, as in the civil rights movement."

An editorial in one of the nation's leading black newspapers, the *New York Amsterdam News*, used the Genovese case to take aim at recent comments from FBI director J. Edgar Hoover. In July 1964 Hoover had visited New York and claimed that racial violence in the American South was "no worse" than violence in the North. At this time activists, politicians, and newsmakers alike were focused on the spate of racist reactions to the increasing mobilizations for civil rights that were erupting throughout the nation, and especially in the South. The editors of the *Amsterdam News* replied to Hoover's remark with pointed questions:

> Certainly here in New York we have our Kitty Genovese murders and others which shake the conscience of our city. But the man charged with the murder of Kitty Genovese is already in jail awaiting his fate. . . .
>
> We would ask Mr. Hoover: Where are the murderers of Emmett Till? Where are the murderers of Medgar Evers? Why haven't the persons who bombed to death four little Negro girls in Sunday School been apprehended? Who killed Col. Lemuel A. Penn? Where are the three civil rights fighters who disappeared into thin air in Philadelphia, Mississippi? All these unsolved crimes have been in the South.[50]

The *Times'* shocking story of the thirty-eight witnesses also encouraged renewed debate about weapons and self-protection among its readers. For example, in a letter to the editor, one reader argued for a repeal of New York's 1911 Sullivan Law, likely the nation's first to require licenses for small weapons and make carrying an unlicensed concealed weapon a felony. The writer urged: "Here a vicious circle is created when there is no home protection. People are timid about 'getting involved' for fear of retaliation when life or limb is threatened in their area." Another letter writer argued two days later that "it is not difficult to understand why no one came forward to protect her. Probably no one had the most suitable weapon to protect himself or the woman, and anyone who appeared on the street with a suitable weapon would be hauled off to jail for violation of the Sullivan Law. Instance upon instance can be cited of would-be heroes arrested for using a weapon to suppress a crime."[51]

A potent example illustrating exactly that situation was reported in the *Times* shortly thereafter. Under the headline "A Defensive Arm May Be Illegal," the paper described the experience of Arlene Del Fava, a twenty-seven-year-old Forest Hills secretary who defended herself with a knife against a man who tried to rape her as she walked home from the World's Fair one summer night. When told by Queens police that she would be arrested for violating New York's Sullivan Law, Del Fava replied, "That's better than being killed." The *Times'* story noted: "Miss Del Fava told police that she had bought the knife after the Kew Gardens murder of Catherine Genovese last March. She added that she carried the knife whenever she was out late." As Del Fava said, "I didn't want to be another Kitty Genovese." The story also noted that the charges against her were dropped a few days later. But Del Fava made it clear that she would continue to defend herself: "When I have to go out again, I'm going to try not to stay out late alone. But if I am, I'll be carrying a hatpin—one like grandmother used to carry."[52]

Genovese's murder reverberated throughout New York and the nation as a cautionary tale and a locus for debate. News reporters as well as radio and television crews descended on Kew Gardens, interviewing anyone who would speak about the crime. Commentators throughout the country weighed in on the costs and consequences of citizen inaction and, as in a headline from the *Los Angeles Times*, discussed the "other side of non-involvement." Millions of people asked themselves what they would have done in a similar situation and questioned whether the crime on Austin Street—"a classic example of public indifference"—could happen in any city, anywhere.[53]

# 4

# The Metropolitan Brand of Apathy

"I wish to thank you for publishing the story of a woman's murder while 37 citizens watched but did nothing. It is a disturbing, shocking story. Such apathy and lack of concern is apparently endemic in our society today," wrote Sarah M. Johnson to the *New York Times*. Under the headline "Commitment to Others," the paper printed her letter on March 31, 1964. "It rather forcibly reminds one of those many German citizens who "didn't know" of, and "didn't want to get involved" in, the political events of the Nazi regime," she asserted. "Perhaps this seems like a harsh comparison, but injustices and crimes such as this one are based on a person's lack of involvement with and commitment to another person. The public airing of such an event is a public service; it is terribly important that such apathy not be accepted as normal behavior." Letters from readers like Johnson began to appear immediately after the first front-page story of the Genovese murder was printed on March 27. Some writers drew immediate connections between the issues of apathy associated with Nazism, such as Rosenthal had vividly expressed in his essay on Auschwitz, and the reports of the Kew Gardens neighbors' failure to help Kitty Genovese.[1]

Another *Times* reader went even further: he connected both issues to the legacy of slavery in the United States and growing racial unrest throughout the nation. Under the headline "Apathy to Crime Discussed: Moral Issues Examined in Failure of Witnesses to Intervene," the paper printed David Singleton's thoughts:

> "I was tired. I went back to bed." That was the excuse of one man and essentially that of 36 others, as reported in the Times on March 27, who failed to intervene when one of their neighbors was being stabbed. This points up the disturbing lesson that it is not necessary for a group actively to wield the weapon to participate in a crime; they merely need to stand idly by.
>
> Twenty-five years ago whole nations were "tired and went back to bed" with the result that millions died under a program of planned murder. In our own country the vast majority of citizens have apathetically ignored the oppression of a racial minority for over three hundred years with disastrous consequences for the entire society.
>
> Regardless of the nature of a crime, if one is aware of the moral problem, he cannot refuse to commit himself, because by doing so he shares responsibility for the results.
>
> The truth of this has been shown too often and it does not speak well for us that we must constantly be reminded. What so clearly occurred elsewhere can and does occur in our own society.[2]

A few days later, Milton M. Goldman commented on a March 28 editorial on apathy that the *Times* had printed. He noted that it should have asked "What Kind of Society Are We Living In?" The writer asserted that "when 37 law-abiding Americans so grievously fail another human being," all of society should be concerned about their behavior and seek to find answers to explain it. He continued, "Is the individual becoming a displaced person in our society, which is characterized by population pressures, giantism in business, labor and government, nagging domestic and foreign crises, all increasingly beyond the capacity of the individual citizen?" He concluded that such modern developments likely were weakening "the traditional values of independence, decency and morality, relegating the individual to a role of a passive bystander."[3]

The passionate responses of these and many other *Times* readers to the troubling questions of individual and community responsibility raised by media coverage of the Genovese crime caught the paper's metropolitan editor by surprise. Rosenthal wrote early that summer, "I became intensely interested in the reaction of people who wrote letters to the paper about the story, and the fact that people talked so often about it, could not seem to let it go."[4] Recognizing the power of the story he and Gansberg had constructed, still a topic of intense conversation six weeks after Genovese's murder and in the midst of wide-ranging debates about the behavior of the now infamous thirty-eight witnesses, Rosenthal published a lengthy essay in the May 3 issue of the *New York Times* Sunday magazine which provided the capstone for the story of Kitty Genovese. Using sickness as his trope and the *Times* as his lectern, Rosenthal instructed his readers on the pathology of what he defined as "the metropolitan brand of apathy" by defending the New York Police Department, questioning the sincerity of civil rights advocates, and arguing for personal responsibility rather than "impersonal social action." Rosenthal presented the essay, titled "Study of the Sickness Called Apathy," as a highly idiosyncratic and contradictory treatise on solving social problems. He linked the neighbors' lack of involvement in the Genovese crime to other forms of apathy—racial, ethnic, global—that permeated the cold war era. Echoing themes he had explored in his essay on Auschwitz, Rosenthal expanded them to accuse unconcerned citizens of culpability for criminal activity. His emphasis on individualism, however, denied the pressing need for institutional reform and community engagement. Rosenthal dismissed the impact of organizing then under way in New York to address segregation in employment, education, housing, and the provision of essential services in the city. He completely ignored problems of police violence against New York residents. Instead, "Study of the Sickness Called Apathy" focused on individual responses to wrongdoing and discounted or disparaged the power of government, organizations, and the media in working toward, or thwarting, social change.[5]

He began by dramatically highlighting the sudden impact of the Genovese crime: "It happens from time to time in New York that the life of the city is frozen by an instant of shock. In that instant the people of the city are seized by the paralyzing realization that they are one, that each man is in some way a mirror of every other man. They stare at each other—or, really, into themselves—and a look quite like a flush of embarrassment passes over the face of the city. Then the instant passes and the beat resumes and the people turn away and try to explain what they have seen, or try to deny it." He repeated the *Times'* version of the story, starting with the "choking fact" that no one in "entirely respectable" Kew Gardens came to Genovese's aid when she was attacked. He emphasized that the victim herself was not the point of the story. "It was not her life or her dying that froze the city, but the witnessing of her murder." This slant was necessary in part because her life, if fully revealed, might have rendered her unsympathetic to the paper's readers. So instead, Rosenthal focused on the cowardice of the Kew Gardens neighbors and underscored the thesis that he and Gansberg had promoted in their March 27 front-page story, the significance of the number of reported witnesses to the crime: "'Thirty-eight!' people said over and over. 'Thirty-eight!' It was as if the number itself had some special meaning, and in a way, of course, it did." He then reinforced his main point: "One person or two or even three or four witnessing a murder passively would have been the unnoticed symptom of the disease in the city's body and again would have passed unnoticed. But 38—it was like a man with a running low fever suddenly beginning to cough blood; his friends could no longer ignore his illness, nor could he turn away from himself."[6]

Rosenthal went on to recount New Yorkers' reactions to their newly diagnosed sickness: shared guilt, followed by "a rash of metropolitan masochism," a finding supported by experts who spoke of "alienation of the individual from the group," the impact of "megalopolitan societies," "the disaster syndrome." He asked rhetorically, "What the devil do you expect in a town, a jungle, like this?" and quoted one woman whose response had been, "Dear God, what have we come to?" He answered her: "In that instant of shock, the mirror showed quite clearly what was wrong, that the face of mankind was spotted with the disease of apathy—all mankind. But this was too frightening a thought to live with and soon the beholders began to set boundaries for the illness, to search frantically for causes that were external and to look for the carrier." He concluded that the problem was not with "them"; it was "us." No one was immune. "People who came from small towns said it could never happen back home," he declared. Although he challenged the idea that villages and small towns were safer than cities, his essay zeroed in on the problems of urban living, especially what he termed a lack of "person-to-person responsibility."[7]

## Echoes of Nazism

Rosenthal used the story of Kitty Genovese and the thirty-eight witnesses to make the powerful point that a particularly urban version of apathy was threatening the health of the body politic. He asserted that "apathy" was the most consistent characterization of the witnesses' behaviors that he heard in the days after the story's promotion on the front pages of the *Times*. It was a logical point to make for the sociologists, psychologists, theologians, and others whom the paper's reporters contacted, as concerns about apathy were very much in the public consciousness in the early 1960s. Articles had appeared in American newspapers, popular magazines, and scholarly journals throughout the postwar period, harkening back to the complicity of many peoples and nations with Nazism. As noted in chapter 3, the controversial writings of Hannah Arendt for the *New Yorker* magazine on the lessons of the 1961 trial of former Nazi Adolf Eichmann in Jerusalem were published as a book in 1963. Arendt argued that one of the lessons of Nazism was that evil wore many faces, not just those of demonic monsters but also those of "banal" bureaucrats. According to Amos Elon, Arendt's findings showed that "in the Third Reich evil lost its distinctive characteristic by which most people had until then recognized it. The Nazis redefined it as a civil norm. . . . In matters of elementary morality, Arendt warned, what had been thought of as decent instincts were no longer to be taken for granted."[8]

Although *Times* readers needed little prompting to quickly draw connections between the complicity of many Germans with Nazism and the seeming failure of the "decent instincts" of the thirty-eight witnesses in Kew Gardens, one letter writer wrote in protest to the paper to express what, for him, were the obvious distinctions between the two situations:

> The Austin Street people ran no risk, they had only to phone the police, and their maximum of inconvenience would have been a few days in court as witness.
>
> The German people, on the other hand, had no police to phone—the police would have arrested them and not helped the victims of the Nazi terror—and any act of assistance (performed, nevertheless, by quite a number of Germans) exposed them to the danger of concentration camp, if not to a worse fate.

> Or does Mr. Rosenthal equate the Austin Street people's failure to phone
> the police with the German people's failure to revolt unarmed against the
> S.A. and S.S., or to storm Auschwitz?

In response, Rosenthal insisted that he had not intended to equate Genovese's neighbors with Germans; rather he wanted only to show the prevalence and variability of apathy. Nevertheless, he added, "since the question
has been raised, I think the German people might have shown rather more
reaction than they did (to put it politely) to the evil portended by Hitler
when he first began to climb to power. It seems that most of them welcomed him to power and then excused their inaction on the basis of the
power they had given to him."[9]

His warnings of apathy in early 1964 in part reflected his keen awareness, born of his years in eastern Europe, that "echoes of Nazism" still were
seen and heard. Student groups in Germany at that time were speaking
out, fearing that the lessons learned only twenty years earlier were already
in danger of being forgotten and that the German people were once again
becoming complacent and apathetic. An article in the *Times* from February 1963 reported that George Binder, chairman of the National Student
Association in the German Democratic Republic, had warned his country-
men and women in a memorial speech that "people who bore the responsibility then—and not only in minor positions—are again clothed with
official office. We, the survivors of the catastrophe, act as if nothing had
happened."[10]

As counterpoint to the very real lessons of Nazism, in the early to mid-
1960s, concerns about apathy were invoked as useful shorthand to describe
almost every ill that plagued society. The problem of apathy was invoked
in the *Times* with regard to the dwindling number of voluntary donors to
blood banks in New York City; the lack of interest among voters toward
the revision of the City charter; a psychiatrist's report on "sex, drugs, and
psychoses" among American college students; and in the business and fi-
nance pages of the paper to describe Detroit automakers' concerns about
lagging new car sales and Wall Street stockbrokers' need for new investors.
But most often, apathy was depicted as the enemy of civic participation.[11]

At the same time that Rosenthal was warning of the "sickness" of apathy, however, activists were promoting the idea and practice of partici-
patory democracy to challenge the status quo. Whether in the South, the

North, the East, or the West, students, teachers, community organizers, labor and religious leaders, and people from all walks of life engaged in campaigns for change, including efforts to increase voter registration during a heated presidential election season. In the midst of the summer of 1964, for example, civil rights organizers mounted a massive effort to involve blacks in the electoral process. The *Times* reported on national as well as local activism. "The success or failure of the campaign, which is being put on in about 350 cities, is not yet known. But the men and women who are trying to register the voters say that they have discovered that apathy is their greatest obstacle. 'In the South it is fear that keeps people from registering,' said one worker. 'Here in the North, we find it's apathy.'" The stakes were high, given the nomination of Barry Goldwater for president at the Republican National Convention that summer. The paper highlighted specific efforts then under way in the New York area, reporting: "One example may be found in Mount Vernon, N.Y., a city of about 61,000 whites and 15,000 Negroes. The traditionally Republican city has 34,000 registered voters. Miss Toni Potter, a 17-year-old Negro, assembled seven other young people last week at Grace Baptist Church in Mount Vernon and equipped them with voter-registration materials." The article noted the lack of interest in the presidential election that the young people encountered as they went door-to-door and talked with potential voters.[12]

Rosenthal's deployment of the apathy trope also coincided with well-publicized upheavals in the nation's largest city. A series of organized as well as spontaneous demonstrations over stark educational and other racially based inequities disrupted "business as usual" in New York throughout 1963 and into the first four months of 1964. The outpourings of rage against systemic racial violence on the part of law enforcement which had plagued residents and communities for decades would explode in Harlem and Bedford-Stuyvesant early in the summer of 1964. But Rosenthal asserted in his May 3 Sunday magazine essay that one of the main causes of apathy might be New Yorkers' attitudes toward law enforcement. "Guilt turned into masochism," he wrote about the days after the Genovese tragedy, "and masochism, as it often does, became a sadistic search for a target. Quite soon, the target became the police." He then offered some reasons for people's distrust of law enforcement, but from a distinctly privileged viewpoint. "There is no doubt whatsoever," he wrote, "that the police in New York have failed, to put it politely, to instill a feeling of total confidence in the population. There are great areas in this city—fine parks as well as slums—where no person in his right mind would wander of an evening or an early morning." He then turned to the lack of a unitary emergency response system: "There is no central emergency point to receive calls for help. And a small river of letters from citizens to this newspaper testifies to the fact that patrols are often late in answering calls and that policemen on desk duty often give the bitter edge of their tongues to citizens calling for succor." Yet in the next paragraph he asserted without hesitation and with considerable vitriol: "The police of this city are more efficient, more restrained and more responsive to public demands than any others the writer has encountered in a decade of traveling the world. Their faults are either mechanical or a reflection of a city where almost every act of police self-protection is assumed to be an act of police brutality, and where a night-club comedian can, as one did the other night, stand on a stage for an hour and a half and vilify the police as brutes, thieves, homosexuals, illiterates and 'Gestapo agents' while the audience howls in laughter as it drinks Scotch from bootleg bottles hidden under the tables."[13]

After this damning portrayal of those who would criticize police misconduct, Rosenthal pivoted to the story of the Kew Gardens neighborhood in which Catherine Genovese lived and died, again spending more time and attention on the semi-suburban locale than on the victim. He summarized the details of the crime, supplied by Winston Moseley to Queens police after his arrest. Rosenthal also gave the murderer himself short shrift, never mentioning, for instance, that he was African American. Instead, Moseley was treated as if he were a bit player in the story. Rosenthal dispensed with him in two sentences: "Not much is said or heard or thought in the city about Winston Moseley. In this drama, as far as the city is concerned, he appeared briefly, acted his piece, exited into the wings."

In addition to dismissing the significance of the murderer, Rosenthal reiterated some of the factual errors that had appeared in the *Times'* March 27 front-page story: "The first attack came at 3:15. The first call to the police came at 3:50. Police arrived within two minutes, they say. Miss Genovese was dead." In actuality, one witness, retired New York Police Department officer Michael Hoffman, was a teenager at the time of the crime. He lived in the Mowbray Apartments on Austin Street, and he heard Genovese's screams, yelled from his bedroom window at whoever was making the noise, and glimpsed what he thought was a fight between a man and a woman. He then alerted his father, who called the police after the first attack at 3:20 a.m. Hoffman's father did not realize the seriousness of the attack when he spoke to the dispatcher, and by then, Moseley had run away. The call did not result in police being sent from the precinct. Police did respond to a second call placed by a neighbor and arrived at the apartment two doors down from Genovese's at 3:50, after the second attack inside the entrance of 82–62 Austin, when Genovese was still alive. She died at 4:10 a.m. in the ambulance on the way to Queens County Hospital.[14]

What is also striking is that in his essay Rosenthal never explained where the count of "thirty-eight" Kew Gardens neighbors that he and Gansberg kept repeating had originated. He wrote only: "That night and the next morning the police combed the neighborhood looking for witnesses. They found them, 38." Queens detectives took statements from the neighbors and made them available to prosecutors at the time and to researchers since. Their records indicate that forty or more people who lived in the two apartment buildings that overlooked the parking lot of the LIRR station, where Genovese parked her car, and Austin Street, where Moseley first stabbed her, were interviewed within the first twenty-four hours after the crime. Four people described hearing her cries for help and seeing "a woman" on the sidewalk with Moseley, either kneeling or lying on the ground. One person saw him striking her. Robert Mozer, who lived on an upper floor of the Mowbray Apartments, heard something that sounded like a cry, got up, and went to his window. He raised it and yelled down at Moseley, who ran away. Genovese stood up and made her way around to the alleyway, out of public view of all but two of the people who had been awakened, and into the foyer of one of the apartment entrances nearest the railroad tracks. Two neighbors saw Moseley return but did not see his final assault. Although this does not excuse their actions or explain why police were not notified immediately, it does complicate the reports that dominated the news about the crime. One of the four neighbors has said that she did pick up her telephone to call but was so upset she could not even speak to the operator. Yet the clear impression given in the *Times'* coverage of the crime and Rosenthal's expanded writings about it was that a large number of her neighbors passively watched Kitty Genovese die.[15]

As Rosenthal wrote in his May 3 essay: "Two weeks later, when this newspaper heard of the story, a reporter went knocking, door to door, asking why, why. Through half-opened doors, they told him. Most of them were neither defiant nor terribly embarrassed nor particularly ashamed. The underlying attitude, or explanation, seemed to be fear of involvement—any kind of involvement." Rosenthal also recorded the neighbors' reactions a week after the March 27 front-page story appeared, quoting Frank Facciola, a local merchant, who said: "I resent the way these newspaper and television people have hurt us. We have wonderful people here. What happened could have happened any place. There is no question in my mind that people here now would rush out to help anyone being attacked on the street." Facciola asked rhetorically: "The same thing happens in other sections every day. Why make such a fuss when it happens in Kew Gardens? We are trying to forget it happened here."

Rosenthal again returned to the unique symptoms of metropolitan apathy: "It seems to this writer that what happened in the apartments and houses on Austin Street was a symptom of a terrible reality in the human condition—that only under certain situations and only in response to certain reflexes or certain beliefs will a man step out of his shell toward his brother." He repeated his defense of New York law enforcement: "Certainly police procedures must be improved—although in the story of Miss Genovese all indications were that, once called into action, the police machine behaved perfectly. As far as is known, not one witness has said that he remained silent because he had had any unpleasant experience with the police." This of course neglects to ask why people who are afraid of the police or have had negative experiences would admit their fears to them or to newspaper reporters. By focusing on the neighbors, Rosenthal also ignored the glaring failure of "the police machine" in Queens to solve the series of sexual assaults on women that Winston Moseley had committed for months before he spotted Kitty Genovese driving home on the morning of March 13, 1964. Her life might have been spared if local law enforcement had apprehended him after he tortured Anna Mae Johnson on February 29, 1964. But instead the focus became the motivations of the witnesses.

Rosenthal continued to insist that the larger culprit was the city itself: "Nobody can say why the 38 did not lift the phone while Miss Genovese was being attacked, since they cannot say themselves. It can be assumed, however, that their apathy was indeed of a big-city variety." He described such metropolitan apathy as "almost a matter of psychological survival," interjecting his own experience: "Indifference to one's neighbor and his troubles is a conditioned reflex of life in New York as it is in other big cities. In every major city in which I have lived—in Tokyo and Warsaw, Vienna and Bombay—I have seen, over and over again, people walk away from accident victims. I have walked away myself." Here Rosenthal agreed with unnamed others who asserted that a particular kind of apathy was associated with urban living: "Out-of-towners, and sometimes New Yorkers themselves, like to think that there is something special about New York's metropolitan apathy. It is special in that there are more people here than any place else in the country—and therefore more people to turn away from each other."

In addition to generalized problems of surviving in the city, Rosenthal also offered his views on race and reaction: "For decades, New York turned away from the truth that is Harlem or Bedford-Stuyvesant in Brooklyn. Everybody knew that in the Negro ghettos, men, women and children lived in filth and degradation. But the city, as a city, turned away with the metropolitan brand of apathy. This, most simply, consists of drowning the person-to-person responsibility in a wave of impersonal social action." Dismissing the effectiveness of community and political organizing, he took aim at the "committees" that were formed, the "speeches made," and the "budgets passed" to address the "filth and degradation" of the ghettos. He derided such efforts and criticized them as having diminished those living in poor black communities, the "individual people who ache and suffer in the loss of their individual prides."

He then proceeded to demonize a particular category of middle-class women, the "housewives who contributed to the N.A.A.C.P. [but] saw nothing wrong in going down to the daily shape-up of domestic workers in the Bronx and selecting a maid for the day after looking over the coffle to see which 'girl' among the Negro matrons looked huskiest." The demeaning tone of this description of liberal "housewives" is surprising, as it seems to come out of nowhere, referencing no one in particular. But the *Times* had printed many stories about integration with comments from women such as "Mrs. Ellen Lurie," a white New Yorker who had dedicated her life to community activism and participation in civic affairs and was particularly involved in the struggles over racial integration of the city's schools. In the first six months of 1964, she was prominently featured in a number of *Times* articles on the public events and protests designed to force the Board of Education to implement a desegregation plan. For example, a June 1964 article was headlined "White Liberals Here Extend

Fight for Integration." Lurie was profiled as "a 33-year-old, 5-foot-2-inch, green-eyed, blond housewife" who was "experienced at using resources. She worked from 1952 until 1962 as a community organizer in East Harlem." At the time Lurie was chair of a parents' group, EQUAL, which worked closely with black activists such as Thelma Johnson of the Harlem Parents Committee and the Reverend Milton Galamison of the Citywide Committee for Integrated Schools. She was a spokeswoman for white involvement in the civil rights struggle and thus for collective responses to social problems. She also may have been an example of the kind of woman engaged in the "impersonal social action" that Rosenthal used his essay to condemn.[16]

Equating anti-racist activism with "impersonal social action," Rosenthal asserted: "Now there is an acute awareness of the problems of the Negroes in New York. But, again, it is an impersonal awareness, and more and more it is tinged with irritation at the thought that the integration movement will impinge on the daily personal life of the city." He then extended his charges of insensitivity and indifference to black activists and communities as well: "Nor are Negroes in the city immune from apathy—toward one another or toward whites. They are apathetic toward one another's right to believe and act as they please; one man's concept of proper action is labeled with the group epithet 'Uncle Tom.' And, until the recent upsurge of the integration movement, there was less action taken within the Negro community to improve conditions in Harlem than there was in the all-white sections of the East Side." Rosenthal went on to insist that what he was calling urban apathy was color-blind. He recounted a story of "an aspiring Negro politician, a most decent man, [who] talked of how the Jewish shopkeepers exploited the Negroes, how he wished Negroes could 'save a dollar like the Jews,' totally apathetic toward the fact that Jews at the table might be as hurt as he would be if they talked in clichés of the happy-go-lucky Stepin Fetchit Negro." In equating apathy with ignorance and prejudice, Rosenthal not only expanded its definition but also extended the accusation to all New Yorkers; now it was not only the Kew Gardens neighbors but also pro-integration whites and black activists who were charged with infecting the body politic.

As if to share the blame for the illness of indifference, but without acknowledging his power as metropolitan editor of the nation's leading newspaper, Rosenthal included himself in the indictment: "Since the

Genovese case, New Yorkers have sought explanations of their apathy to-ward individuals. Fear, some say—fear of involvement, fear of reprisal from goons, fear of becoming 'mixed up' with the police. This, it seems to this writer, is simply rationalization." His refusal to explore, much less acknowledge, what were valid fears of involvement with law enforcement on the part of many New Yorkers at this time is masked by an appeal to conscience. Rosenthal recalled his own experiences in faraway places: "I think I would have called the police to save Miss Genovese but I know that I did not save a beggar in Calcutta. Was my failing really so much smaller than that of the people who watched from their windows on Aus-tin Street?" He then compared the story with recent international atroci-ties: "And what was the apathy of the people of Austin Street compared, let's say, with the apathy of non-Nazi Germans toward Jews? Geography is a factor of apathy. Indians reacted to Portuguese imprisoning Goans, but not to Russians killing Hungarians. Color is a factor. Ghanaians reacted toward Frenchmen killing Algerians, not toward Congolese killing white missionaries. Strangeness is a factor. Americans react to the extermination of Jews but not to the extermination of Watusis."

His attempt to distinguish between individual conscience and compli-cated geopolitical choices was particularly resonant in mid-1964 as debate over expanded American involvement in the civil war in Vietnam was in-creasing. Yet he continually brushed aside the role of institutions as he argued for individual responsibility. The *Times* had printed an editorial on February 27, 1964, that asserted, "What the United States must seek [in Vietnam] is not a plan to fight or a plan to negotiate." Instead the pa-per's editors argued for both: "What must be sought is a policy that will permit the United States and its South Vietnamese allies to fight and to negotiate at the same time." In May, using the Genovese case, Rosenthal came down on the side of intervention: "The 'mind-your-own-business' attitude is despised among individuals, and clucked at by sociologists, but glorified as pragmatic national policy among nations." He called for a reas-sessment and redirection of American policies abroad: "Only in scattered moments, and then in halting embarrassment, does the United States, the most involved nation in the world, get down to hard cases about the na-ture of governments with which it deals, and how they treat their subject citizens. People who believe that a free government should react to oppres-sion of people in the mass by other governments are regarded as fanatics or romantics by the same diplomats who would react in horror to the oppression of one single individual in Washington. Between apathy, regarded as a moral disease, and national policy, the line is often hard to find."[17]

Rosenthal concluded his essay by underscoring the theme of individual responsibility, again without mentioning the significance of institutional power or the effectiveness of collective action. He asserted that there were only two possible responses to the killing of Kitty Genovese: "One is the way of the neighbor on Austin Street [who says,] 'Let's forget the whole thing.' The other is to recognize that the bell tolls even on each man's individual island, to recognize that every man must fear the witness in himself who whispers to close the window." He saw in Genovese's murder the opportunity to sound a warning for the inhabitants of a city becoming increasingly divided and distrustful—a city that was not only the nation's most populous and most diverse but also the center of its news media, financial institutions, and, with the establishment of the United Nations enclave on Manhattan's East Side, international human rights discourse.

His advocacy of individual responsibility to combat apathy generated widespread debate. Rosenthal described writing the May 3 essay as a necessary catharsis: "When the *Times Magazine* asked me to write a piece about the story, I wanted to eagerly, more eagerly than almost any other article I have written," he wrote in June of that year. He provided his readers with some explanation of his motivations: "In the back of my mind, perhaps— I am not sure—was the feeling that there was, that there must be some connection between the story of the witnesses silent in the face of greater crimes—the degradation of a race, children hungering. I am not sure, but I think there is. But in any case, I do know that I did not want to write the article to make any great political points." Yet he used his essay on urban apathy against people who were anything but apathetic, particularly those New Yorkers who were challenging the intransigence of racial inequality.[18]

## Stop Singing and Start Swinging: Civil Rights in the Early 1960s

Demoralized by the failure of white liberal leaders in the city to implement integration despite years of promises, and in disagreement over the most effective strategies to highlight ongoing race discrimination in education, housing, and employment throughout the five boroughs as well as nationally, some New York–based black leaders aired their frustrations with the city and with one another in the media in the spring of 1964. Among other issues, intense debates had been going on for several months between the Brooklyn activists of CORE (Congress of Racial Equality) and other local and national chapters of the group, as well as the NAACP and other civil rights organizations, about the timing and tone of demonstrations planned for the April 22 opening day of the 1964–65 World's Fair in Queens. Ultimately, many of the groups simply agreed to disagree, and a number of them organized separate actions, some of which were more effective than others.

A leaflet distributed by CORE activists during the fair's opening day festivities provides a contrast to Rosenthal's warnings of urban apathy. Their leaflet challenged the fair's celebration of progress, given the sorry state of civil rights in the nation, and highlighted the significance of the racial justice movement's acts of witnessing:

> From all over the nation—from Mississippi, from Louisiana, from California, from Maryland, from Florida, from Illinois, from Missouri, from New York and Massachusetts CORE chapters have brought their grievances to the World's Fair.
>
> We contrast the real world of discrimination and brutality experienced by Negroes, North and South, with the fantasy world of progress and abundance shown in the official pavilions.
>
> For every new car, we submit a cattle prod, for every chromium-plated decoration we submit the charred remains of an Alabama church and for the great steel Unisphere we submit our bodies—from all over this country—as witnesses to the tragedy of the Northern ghetto, as witnesses to the horror of Southern inhumanity and legalized brutality.[19]

Their emphasis on witnessing was part of a collective action in pursuit of social change. It assumed a conscious and shared commitment to speak out against injustice, the opposite of apathy. CORE and other groups that showed up at the entrance despite the foul opening day weather made it abundantly clear that the fair's theme of "Peace Through Understanding" was as much an invention as the color television, Bel-Gem waffles, and Futurama exhibited within the gates. Their peaceful protest received no understanding from fair organizers. As one scholar noted, Robert Moses

# HOW CORE VIEWS THE FAIR:

# SYMBOL OF AMERICAN HYPOCRISY

From all over the nation—from Mississippi, from Louisiana, from California, from Maryland, from Florida, from Illinois, from Missouri, from New York and Massachusetts CORE chapters have brought their grievances to the World's Fair. We contrast the **real world** of discrimination and brutality experienced by Negroes, North and South, with the **fantasy world** of progress and abundance shown in the official pavillions. For every new car we submit a cattle prod, for every chromium-plated decoration we submit the charred remains of an Alabama church and for the great steel Unisphere we submit our bodies—from all over this country—as witnesses to the tragedy of the Northern ghetto, as witnesses to the horror of Southern inhumanity and legalized brutality.

**CORE DEMANDS FROM:**

**MISSISSIPPI**—An end to killing, an end to brutality, the simple right to vote for disenfranchised Negroes, equal representation at the National political conventions . . . in two words, FREEDOM—NOW!

**MARYLAND**—A new public accommodations law that does **not** endorse segregation in public bars and restaurants that do more than 51% of their business in liquor. NEGROES CAN BE SERVED HERE AT THE WORLD'S FAIR—BUT NOT IN THE STATE OF MARYLAND.

**NEW YORK STATE**—A $1.50 minimum wage, integrated low-cost urban renewal, an end to hiring discrimination in public utilities, state-wide rent control, state-wide quality integrated education, state-wide civilian police review boards.

**LOUISIANA**—The right to vote, the right to live without fear, the right to eat, live and breathe where we please. An end to police brutality, an end to cattle prods, pistol-whippings and murder. AN END TO SLAVERY!

**ILLINOIS**—An end to Chicago's rat-strewn ghetto schools, jobs for everyone without regard to color, integrated low-

cost, well-constructed new housing—and an end to police brutality THAT WALKS THE GHETTO STREETS BOTH DAY AND NIGHT.

**FLORIDA**—The right to vote, an end to outright segregation and exclusion in public accommodations. A FLORIDA "PARADISE" FOR ALL.

**NEW ENGLAND**—Fair housing in Boston! Fair employment throughout New England! A viable plan for the creation of a quality, integrated school system.

**MISSOURI**—A state-wide fair employment and public accommodations law. Our people have been arrested, publically denounced and subjected to fantastically excessive sentences in St. Louis. THIS PAVILLION SYMBOLIZES A LACK OF FREEDOM IN THE MIDDLE WEST.

**SCHAEFER BEER**—The Schaefer Beer Company is being boycotted in protest of their flagrant discrimination in hiring. BOYCOTT THEIR PAVILLION IN SYMPATHY WITH HUNDREDS OF THOUSANDS WHO WON'T DRINK JIM CROW SCHAEFER BEER.

**GENERAL MOTORS AND FORD**—An end to employment discrimination at Ford and General Motors plants and showrooms away from the city of Detroit.

THE UGLY SPECTRE OF BIGOTRY AND DISCRIMINATION THROUGHOUT THIS NATION MAKES THIS WORLD'S FAIR BOTH LUDICROUS AND HYPOCRITICAL. THE MILLIONS OF DOLLARS IT COST MUST BE MEASURED AGAINST THE 22 MILLION AMERICAN NEGROES LIVING IN THE AGONY OF FIFTH-CLASS CITIZENSHIP BOTH NORTH AND SOUTH.

CORE (Congress of Racial Equality) 38 Park Row, New York, N. Y. 10038 ● CO 7-6270 ● James Farmer, National Director

**Figure 10.** Leaflet distributed by members of CORE at the 1964 World's Fair in Queens. Flier courtesy of Civil Rights Movement Archives, Queens College, City University of New York. Used with permission.

and the World's Fair Corporation "adeptly used the law and, when that failed, good old muscle to keep protestors at bay." But the growing visibility of activism throughout the city on local, national, and international issues could not be ignored.[20]

The summer of 1964 brought sobering wake-up calls that underscored the depths of resistance to the cause of racial justice. In June the news that two white New Yorkers, Andrew Goodman and Michael Schwerner, were missing in Mississippi along with a young black man, James Earl Chaney from Meridian, brought home the horrifying reality of white racist violence. All three of the men were participating in Freedom Summer mobilizations. Goodman, a student at Queens College, had received permission from his parents to join the voter registration project; he was teamed with CORE activists Chaney and Schwerner. They were en route to investigate the burning of a church that had housed a Freedom Summer school when members of the Ku Klux Klan and local law enforcement ambushed their car. The racist mob shot all three of them at close range and set their car on fire. The bodies of the three young men were not discovered for nearly two months.[21]

In the midst of terrifying headlines about southern violence, black residents of Harlem and the Bedford-Stuyvesant neighborhood of Brooklyn erupted in furious anger against the most recent incident of deadly police violence in New York. The catalyst was the July shooting of a fifteen-year-old black summer school student, James Powell, in the Yorkville neighborhood of Manhattan by an off-duty police lieutenant named Thomas Gilligan. Historian Marilynn Johnson described the contradictory assessments of those at the scene: "Some witnesses (mainly white adults) said Powell had a knife and lunged repeatedly at Gilligan. Others (mainly black teenagers) said they saw no knife and that Powell had not advanced on the officer. In any event, Gilligan fired three shots that killed Powell. Before long, an angry crowd of three hundred black teenagers began throwing bottles and cans at Gilligan and other police who arrived on the scene, yelling 'This is worse than Mississippi' and 'Come on, shoot another nigger.'"[22]

Almost immediately, New York's most active civil rights groups, CORE and the NAACP, demanded an investigation into the shooting; on July 17 CORE organized a march through the Upper East Side neighborhood where Powell and his friends had attended summer school, across the street from where the shooting took place. The next night an even larger crowd gathered in Harlem to demand that Gilligan be suspended and arrested. They were met with a show of resistance and then physical force. Johnson wrote: "As the marchers converged on the police station,

officers attempted to move them behind barricades across the street. Scuf-
fles broke out, with police using their batons and protesters hurling bricks
and bottles. CORE organizers' pleas to remain nonviolent were ignored,
and the first major ghetto uprising of the 1960s was underway."[23] The upheavals that followed spread to Brooklyn, lasting six days and resulting in
465 arrests, one death, over one hundred injuries, and extensive loss of services and property. Among the worst in American history, they heralded
the beginning of five consecutive years of summertime eruptions of racial
rage in the mid- to late 1960s in cities throughout the country. All at once
the nation's attention turned again to its large urban centers, starting with
New York. Despite the media focus on the South, New York City was a
significant site of civil rights ideology, organizing, and publicity. The 1964
riots highlighted the deep disillusionment with the promises of liberalism.
Johnson noted, "As in the 1930s and 1940s, local cases of police abuse took
on an ominous significance in a national context of racial repression and
violence."[24] They also served as precursors to the expression of increasingly
deep frustration, on the part of activists and average folks alike, with the
glacial pace of racial justice.

Decrying decades of peaceful efforts at desegregation, in April 1964
minister Malcolm X had voiced the frustrations of many when he fa-
mously declared, "It's time to stop singing and start swinging."[25] From the
immediate post–World War II period to the spring of Genovese's murder
in 1964, New Yorkers' optimism over the possibilities for significant social
change without violence declined as a result of the impact of rapid shifts
in the nation as a whole and in the city in particular. Neither was immune
from the political and economic contractions of the 1950s and 1960s, including increasing conservatism, the rise in housing segregation, and the
debilitating effects of deindustrialization. It seemed to a growing number
of activists that past efforts to repair a century of so-called de facto racial discrimination in all of its manifestations had proven ineffective: new
strategies were required. Apathy was not on the agenda.

Eight months earlier, an article in the *Times* had captured the mood in
its headline: "New York's Racial Unrest: Negroes' Anger Mounting." The
prominent feature story began with a telling anecdote: "Nailed over the
door of the Church of God and True Holiness on Harlem's 135th Street
is a freshly painted sign that reads: 'Protest Meeting Every Monday—
8:30 P.M.' A Negro lawyer, waving his hand at the sign as he passed it the

other day, declared: 'See that? See that? That thing expresses my sentiments exactly. Only I would change it to read 'Protest Meeting Every Monday, Tuesday, Wednesday, Thursday, Friday, Saturday and Sunday.'" Written by Layhmond Robinson, one of the first black reporters at the *New York Times,* the detailed article appeared on page one on August 12, 1963— three weeks before the March on Washington for Jobs and Freedom—and announced "Years of Resentment Find Outlet in Wave of Protests." Robinson wrote: "The resentment among the 1,500,000 black residents in the city and its suburbs, long built-up, has found an outlet. Negroes and their supporters have taken to the streets in an assault on racial segregation and discrimination." For anyone paying attention, the message was loud and clear. In the words of the subhead for Robinson's article, "'Now or Never' Feeling Is Sweeping Moderation Aside."[26]

New York had been a leader in enacting legislation to provide its residents equal access to the city's resources. "The first civil rights laws since Reconstruction were passed in New York City and state, including the first fair housing, employment, and education laws," historian Martha Biondi has noted. Yet extreme discrimination persisted and activists continued to fight against police brutality and for defendants' rights; for equal access to services, housing, and education, including African American teachers and black history classes in the city's schools; and to elect blacks to office, including statewide office.[27] As noted in chapter 1, scholars of New York City's legacy of civil rights struggles such as historian Clarence Taylor have focused on the increasing challenges to liberal leaders and institutions posed by local civil rights groups in the early 1960s. "While [some] New York politicians, union officials, and policy makers worked to eliminate racial discrimination in education, housing, and employment, they were unwilling to adopt a more vigorous agenda that would assure blacks and Latinos a greater share of public services, jobs, and resources," Taylor noted. According to Biondi, "The continued racial oppression of the Black population in the urban North produced urban upheaval and violence in the 1960s, just as Congress passed major civil rights laws. New York State had passed antidiscrimination laws years before Congress had, but they were not solving the growing crisis of Black unemployment or reversing the spread of residential segregation. . . . Defeats in housing, police reform, and employment struggles in the postwar years set the stage for the escalation of conflict in the 1960s and beyond."[28]

By blaming the tragic death of Kitty Genovese on the failure of individuals and discounting what he termed "impersonal social action" in his discussion of civil rights, Rosenthal not only diverted his readers' attention from an examination of the conditions that governed many New Yorkers' lives, starting with fear of law enforcement, but also gave credence to growing dissatisfactions with the changing tempo and tone of organizing for social change. The previous summer of 1963 had been a key moment in the city for civil rights demonstrations, which built on the successful 1962 "Operation Clean Sweep" campaigns by Brooklyn CORE activists to draw attention to the criminally inadequate sanitation services in the predominantly black Bedford-Stuyvesant neighborhood.[29] The following year saw mass protests against discrimination in the building trades unions and the city's schools, including a "silent march" on the New York City Board of Education by two thousand women, men, and children organized by the National Association for Puerto Rican Civil Rights early in March 1964. The frustrations created by the seeming indifference of the city's powers that be in the face of continuing racial discrimination were ones that Rosenthal capitalized on in his discussion of urban apathy.[30]

Just as he followed the lead of Police Commissioner Michael J. Murphy and condemned the Kew Gardens neighbors instead of questioning why Queens police had allowed a serial rapist and murderer to roam the borough for more than two months, Rosenthal led his readers away from demanding that the city's institutions fulfill their promises to its residents or face the consequences. The increasing tensions between law enforcement leaders such as Murphy and outspoken civil rights advocates like Malcolm X over changing race relations in the city may have influenced his construction of the Genovese story as one of a failure of "individual responsibility."

After leaving the Nation of Islam early in March 1964 and forming the Organization of Afro-American Unity that summer, Malcolm X had been increasingly outspoken with his support for challenging racism in all its manifestations. He had publicly endorsed the second boycott of the city's segregated public schools despite his criticisms of integration campaigns as undesirable and doomed to fail, calling instead for a new commitment to black self-sufficiency and self-defense. In an extraordinary response on March 15, Murphy denounced him in front of 6,200 cheering police officers and threw down the gauntlet of law and order. As the *Long Island*

*Press* reported, "Police Commissioner Michael Murphy angrily denounced 'irresponsible' civil rights leaders yesterday and vowed to keep them from turning New York City into a 'battleground.'" Speaking at a Holy Name Society Communion breakfast at the Hilton Hotel in Manhattan, Murphy took aim at Malcolm X, who, the *Press* reported, lived in Corona, Queens. It noted that Malcolm X "last week urged Negroes to band together with rifles to defend themselves against 'oppressors'" and then reported the commissioner's incendiary remarks: Murphy had described Malcolm X as a "self-proclaimed leader" who "openly advocates violence, bloodshed and armed revolt, and sneers at the sincere efforts of reasonable men to resolve the problem of equal rights by proper, peaceful, and legitimate means." He accused Malcolm X of being "cynically and coldly unmoved by the possible serious consequences of his words." Although Murphy also acknowledged that most civil rights leaders were "men of intelligence, stature and good judgement," he emphasized that some had a "lust for power" and other "sinister motives." He then issued a serious challenge: "But no matter what occurs, nobody will be allowed to turn New York City into a battleground. No one will be allowed to turn neighbor against neighbor." Speaking directly to any perceived troublemakers, Murphy warned, "The peace of this city will be preserved by the decency and intelligence of the people themselves, supported in full strength by their police." When he was told later of the speech, Malcolm X said he regarded Murphy's charges as a "compliment." He added that it was the "irresponsible Negro leaders" who made society change. "The responsible Negroes are those who are controlled by downtown." Malcolm X defended his call to arms, saying it was necessary because "the government has failed to protect the Negro."[31]

The next month, in speeches delivered in Cleveland and Detroit titled "The Ballot or the Bullet," Malcolm X explained to his audiences what it meant to be a Black Muslim: "It doesn't mean that we're anti-white, but it does mean we're anti-exploitation, we're anti-degradation, we're anti-oppression. And if the white man doesn't want us to be anti-him, let him stop oppressing and exploiting and degrading us." He warned white Americans that if they failed to accept the demands of civil rights activists, African Americans would use other means to secure their liberties. "If we don't do something real soon," he declared, "I think you'll have to agree that we're going to be forced either to use the ballot or the bullet. It's one or the other in 1964." Anything but apathetic, his warnings that "time has run out!" were meant to signal that activists would only increase the intensity of their resistance to racism.[32]

Echoing the warnings voiced by comedian Dick Gregory to Rosenthal and Gelb six months earlier, Malcolm X also predicted impending racial upheavals. Just days after breaking from the Nation of Islam, he was quoted in the *New York Times* on Friday, March 13, as saying that "there would be more violence than ever" in the United States in 1964. Headlined "Malcolm X Sees Rise in Violence," with the subhead "Says Negroes Are Ready to Act in Self-Defense," the article by M. S. Handler reported on a press conference at which Malcolm X had announced a new "broadly based, politically oriented black-nationalist movement composed of Muslims, Christians, and nonbelievers who were intellectually and emotionally ready to follow the black nationalist banner." The reporter noted the significance of both the new movement and its tactics as he quoted Malcolm X, "We should be peaceful, law-abiding. But the time has come for the American Negro to fight back in self-defense whenever and wherever he is being unjustly and unlawfully attacked," who added, "If the Government thinks I am wrong for saying this, then let the Government start doing its job."[33]

His announcement marked a radical departure from the calls for nonviolent strategies of resistance that were still being advocated by most of the local and national civil rights organizations at that time. In the paper the very next day was the first brief notice of the killing of Kitty Genovese. Rosenthal tangentially connected these unrelated events in the small book that he wrote about the crime, *Thirty-Eight Witnesses*, published by McGraw-Hill three months later.

## Thirty-Eight Witnesses

In his book Rosenthal reprinted Martin Gansberg's March 27 front-page story on the Genovese crime along with his own May 3 essay "Study of the Sickness Called Apathy," and added commentary and additional details, including his experiences of returning to New York after living abroad. *Times* publisher Arthur Ochs Sulzberger contributed the introduction, in which he reiterated the paper's commitment to New York City. Acknowledging that the *Times* "has come to be regarded as a newspaper that pays minute attention to all matters of foreign and national significance," he noted: "We are above all a community newspaper. We print for a specific community and although we search for readership beyond it, that community is our bread and butter, and its members the real basis of our existence."[34]

In his opening pages, Rosenthal acknowledged his relative distance from Kitty Genovese and from Kew Gardens: "So Catherine Genovese died in Queens and I assume I read the story in the paper the next day. I do not remember. I do remember that the first time her story came directly into my consciousness it was with a sense of irritation and professional annoyance." He then recounted his lunch with Commissioner Murphy: "Murphy did not have a murder on his mind that day; he rarely does. In the spring of 1964, what was usually on the mind of the Police Commissioner of New York—as it was of most policemen and politicians—was the haunting fear that someday blood would flow in the streets of New York because of the tensions of the civil rights movement." Rosenthal further emphasized his point: "He lives with fear of a fire from a match carelessly or deliberately thrown away igniting in the ready, dry kindling wood of Harlem. His talk was of integration movements and civil rights and civil rights leaders and civil rights laws, not of detectives and precincts and stabbings." However focused Murphy may have been on civil rights, he nevertheless consciously and effectively steered Rosenthal in the direction of Kew Gardens.[35]

The same month that *Thirty-Eight Witnesses* was published, the black man accused of the crime went to trial just a few blocks from the mostly white, semi-suburban New York neighborhood where it took place. Moseley's trial was held in early June at the Queens County Courthouse in Kew Gardens. The courtroom and the hallways and streets surrounding it overflowed with people from the area and others who traveled there by car, bus, and subway from throughout the city and region. Only four of Genovese's neighbors, not thirty-eight, were called to testify as witnesses to the crime; the more than three dozen people who the police claimed did nothing and whom the *Times* blamed for the crime were not a visible part of the government's case against Moseley. Queens County Assistant District Attorney Charles Skoller, who along with Assistant District Attorney Frank Cacciatore prosecuted Moseley, later charged, "The media descended on Kew Gardens in a mad frenzy, interviewing neighbors without any concern that their actions might compromise the prosecution."[36]

The prosecutors were concerned that the continuing drama over apathetic neighbors would overwhelm the case. "Reporters knocked on every door in the two apartment buildings," Skoller recalled in his memoir of the case. "The response, however, was disappointing. Many of the neighbors, either too ashamed to speak or hoping to avoid notoriety had become close-mouthed about the events of March 13." Skoller wrote that in preparing the case against Moseley, he and Cacciatore could not allow themselves to be swept up in the story of the thirty-eight witnesses as constructed by the *New York Times* and now accepted as fact. The initial front-page indictment of the neighborhood, bolstered not just by repeated references in the media but also by a prominent Sunday magazine article, was now further reinforced by Rosenthal's just-published book. "We also understood," Skoller wrote, "that jurors might transfer some of the hostility they felt toward Moseley to any neighbors who testified. We wanted their hostility reserved for Moseley alone, since we were pursuing the death penalty for him." He and Cacciatore carefully interviewed all possible witnesses, including the one man who actually had seen Moseley stab Genovese on Austin Street, Joseph Fink, the night elevator operator at the Mowbray Apartments. They decided not to call him to testify "in the interest of keeping the jurors' minds concentrated on Moseley's vicious attack" rather than the "inhumanity of the witness." They made the same decision about Karl Ross.[37]

Skoller later wrote, "I personally read every police report of the questioning of the neighbors and I interviewed no less that 25 in preparing the case for trial. . . .[N]o more than six witnessed any part of the two attacks and only four called as witnesses in the trial."[38] In his memoir of the case, he summarized their interviews with the rest of the nearby Kew Gardens residents: "The other neighbors added little useful information. Their lack of action on the night of March 13, 1964 was variously explained. Some were just plain indifferent. Others were afraid, confused, or disbelieving. Yet others had no excuse at all." He delineated the differences among the people who lived nearby: "The majority of neighbors were elderly, many in their late sixties and seventies. We attributed their passivity to fear. Some retreated from their original statements to the police, omitting details they believed would cause them to be called as witnesses during the trial." Other people insisted they had called police but could not prove it. Finally the prosecutors spoke with Robert Mozer, then Sophie Farrar,

both of whom had done what they could to help Genovese. Three others—
Andrée Picq, Samuel Koshkin, and Irene Frost—were able to establish the
sequence of events.[39]

Skoller and Cacciatore also asked Victor Horan, Genovese's co-worker,
to testify, as well as Kitty's uncle Vito Genovese, who as a member of her
immediate family had identified her body as required by law, even though
Mary Ann Zielonko already had done so at the hospital. And they called
Mary Ann Zielonko. Skoller wrote: "Although Frank and I knew Mary
Ann and Kitty had been lovers, we never disclosed the nature of their relationship and neither had any detective. Lesbian relationships weren't
generally accepted in those days, and we didn't want theirs to jeopardize
the outcome of the trial." Zielonko was on the stand for a very short time;
she spoke almost inaudibly as she identified Kitty's wallet, which detectives recovered near Moseley's place of employment.[40] None of Genovese's
brothers, nor her sister or parents, attended the trial.

Moseley's family appeared to testify in his defense; his attorneys called
his mother and father, his ex-wife, Pauline, and his second wife, Elizabeth. Moseley also testified on his own behalf. In Skoller's words, "Dressed
in a sport jacket, slacks, shirt, and tie, he maintained the stoic stance he
had adopted from the beginning, never betraying any emotion." Moseley
"testified to his unstable childhood—the constant bickering between his
parents, his mother leaving the family a number of times, and his living
with Alphonse, even after he learned that Alphonse was not his biological father. His testimony was clearly intended to convey such an abnor-
mal childhood and upbringing that it had to result in a severe psychosis."
And in fact the defense team introduced psychiatric reports revealing that
Moseley suffered from schizophrenia.[41]

The Kew Gardens neighbors, the general public, and members of the
media who packed the courtroom also learned for the first time of the series of violent assaults against women that had taken place throughout the
borough in early 1964. Over six weeks, it was learned, Moseley had terrorized at least five women, black and white, killing two of them. Those who
survived testified in court about their horrific experiences. A neighbor of
Anna Mae Johnson spoke on Johnson's behalf. One by one, the rest confronted their assailant, Winston Moseley, the man on trial for the rape and
murder of Kitty Genovese, and described his attacks on them. Their painful testimonies revealed a misogynistic crime spree in Queens.

Alta Morell told a hushed courtroom how, waiting for a bus, she was threatened with a screwdriver on January 31 in South Ozone Park, pulled into a nearby empty lot, and sexually assaulted. She said that her attacker, Winston Moseley, fled with her pocketbook and wristwatch. Just two weeks later, on February 15, and in another part of the borough, Joan Larrinaga was at home sleeping with her baby in her second-floor bedroom. All of a sudden she awoke to find an intruder flashing his knife at them. She begged Moseley not to harm her or her child and offered him money. To her immense relief, he left with her cash and TV set.

Two weeks after the attack on Larrinaga, early in the morning of February 29 in Ozone Park, Anna Mae Johnson was returning home after driving her husband to work. Just as he would do the night he killed Kitty Genovese, Moseley followed her as she drove and then assaulted her on the sidewalk in front of her home. He dragged her into her house and not only robbed her but also shot her repeatedly. When she was dead, he sexually molested her body. Her neighbor testified that he then placed a scarf around Johnson's genitals, lit the scarf, and set her and her house on fire so as to leave no trace of his crime. The next day, on March 1, Virginia Lynn testified that Moseley had climbed into her car in Jackson Heights when she was parked in front of her house during the daytime, waiting for her husband. Lynn said that he put the nose of a rifle against her stomach and demanded her purse; she was able to get out through the opposite door and ran screaming down the block until a motorist eventually stopped to assist her.[42] It would not be until after his deadly assaults on Kitty Genovese in Kew Gardens that Moseley's vendetta against Queens women finally would end.

After a three-day trial, and deliberating for only six hours, the jurors returned their verdict of guilty as charged.[43] On June 15, after hearing from the women Moseley had assaulted, the jury prescribed the death penalty. The *Times* reported that cheers erupted from the spectators in the courtroom. His attorneys filed a mandatory appeal. In August, the paper reported that his execution had been postponed, again insisting, "37 witnesses did nothing." And when Moseley's death sentence was reduced to life imprisonment in 1967, the *Times* article at that time once again reminded readers of the story the paper had created: "The murder of the 28-year-old Miss Genovese near her home on March 13, 1964, drew widespread attention after it became known that 38 of her neighbors had seen or heard the assault but did nothing to summon help." By this time, not surprisingly, many of the Kew Gardens residents who had been implicated in the crime just by virtue of living in the vicinity had left their homes and their community and moved away. Although the intense public attention that had focused on the area faded somewhat, the stigma of apathy that was attached to Kew Gardens ensured that the neighborhood and its residents would never be the same again.[44]

# 5

# THE CITY RESPONDS

Coming at the start of a rapid rise in violent crimes in New York City, the killing of Kitty Genovese served as both a symptom of the disintegration of communities as well as a catalyst for change and activism. The particularities of where the crime took place continued to prove essential to the story's shock value, more so than other details. One year after the first front-page story on the Kew Gardens killing stoked fears among New Yorkers that they could not trust their neighbors, it was clear that the *Times'* version of the crime would be enshrined as the official one. In March 1965 the paper reported that Martin Gansberg had been honored by his colleagues in the Newspaper Reporters Association of New York City for his account "of the public's apathy in the fatal stabbing of a Queens woman." By that time it was not even necessary for the story to include Genovese's name; the mere inclusion of the words "apathy" and "Queens woman" said it all.[1]

Gansberg had returned to Kew Gardens earlier in 1965 to again interview some of the witnesses. In a *Times* feature under the lurid headline "Murder Street a Year Later: Would Residents Aid Kitty Genovese?" he repeated his assertion that people had "opened their windows and looked out at the street" but did nothing to help. In doing so he minimized some of the important facts of the case that he had first reported a year earlier. For example, despite the photograph of Robert Mozer sitting in the local barber's chair which accompanied the article, Gansberg did not mention Mozer's intervention, which interrupted Moseley's first assault on Genovese. Instead he wrote, "The people did not act a year ago, and they are not certain what they would do now." He continued: "The witnesses say if it happened again, they would call the police. Their neighbors are doubtful." Gansberg also did not acknowledge his essential role in creating the *Times* story and instead emphasized the international infamy of the unresponsive neighbors: "A newspaper article put the residents into the public eye. In Istanbul and Moscow, in San Francisco and Miami, in Berlin and elsewhere people read about the 38." He noted the "defensive" responses given by many in the Kew Gardens community. "It can happen any place," they said. "Why pick on us?" Gansberg quoted one of the neighbors, Andrée Picq, who said that she had done what she could but the horror of the situation had immobilized her: "I tried last time; I really tried. But I was gasping for breath and was unable to talk into the telephone."[2]

Gansberg also devoted two paragraphs of his first-year anniversary follow-up story to Karl Ross, "whose apartment was at the head of the stairs at 82–62 Austin Street where Miss Genovese's body was found in the small vestibule." Ross had been friends with Genovese and Zielonko, and Gansberg reported that Genovese called out to him after Moseley first attacked her: "Karl, I'm stabbed . . . Help me." Gansberg described Ross disparagingly as "a husky 5-foot-9-inch trimmer of poodles, whose present address is unknown." In addition to Ross, Gansberg noted that a number of the people who had lived near Genovese at the time of the crime had moved away, including Mary Ann Zielonko. Their serene neighborhood was now a bleak site of sorrow and loss.[3]

On October 13, 1965, another *New York Times* story by Martin Gansberg again took readers back to the scene of the crime. This time it was to witness a political event. Standing alone on a platform on Austin Street, the Republican-Liberal Party candidate for New York City mayor, Congressman John V. Lindsay, used the setting to implore listeners to help him stem the increasing rates not only of crime but also of apathy. Paraphrasing A. M. Rosenthal, he said of Genovese's death, "The tragedy demonstrated

**Figure 11.** Candidate John Lindsay campaigns at the Genovese murder scene on Austin Street in Kew Gardens, Queens, 1965. Photo courtesy of the *New York Times*. Used with permission.

that indifference to one's neighbors was a conditioned reflex of life in New York City," and added, "It's a disease spread by political machines which thrive on public indifference and public apathy and have made you believe nothing can be done about it." He then linked the "disease" of political indifference with the inaction of Genovese's neighbors: "What the Kitty Genovese story tells us is that as long as we permit the political machines to perpetuate the myth that the job of governing New York is hopeless, then apathy and indifference will increase." In doing so he relied on the version of the crime the *Times* had created and continued to promote.[4]

The five-column story on page thirty-five included a large photo of Lindsay speaking to the Kew Gardens crowd. Spotlights illuminated the second-story windows of the apartment where Genovese and Zielonko had lived, as if it were an empty stage set. The place provided an eerie visual reminder of the moment when New Yorkers' belief in community had been badly shaken. Gansberg identified some of those who had been on the scene in March 1964:

> In the crowd of 300 persons that pushed forward to hear Mr. Lindsay were several persons who had been among the 38 witnesses to the slaying of Miss

Genovese on that cold night 19 months ago. They heard her screams for help soon after 3 A.M. as the killer pursued her up the dimly lighted street and stabbed her repeatedly.

Last night they stood in a brisk autumnal breeze and listened as Mr. Lindsay urged them "to join ranks shoulder to shoulder to smash crime in this town." Apathy, he said firmly, doesn't have to be a condition of New York life.

Gansberg used the article to remind *Times* readers of the neighborhood's culpability. He noted that, as Lindsay spoke, "lights shone through the windows of the two apartment houses that overlook the Long Island Rail Road parking lot, where Miss Genovese parked her red Fiat the night of the murder. The lights were on that night also as some witnesses watched parts of the attack by the slayer." He emphasized Lindsay's dramatic assertion—"What the Kitty Genovese story tells us is that something has gone out of the heart and soul of New York City"—as the candidate addressed the people in the apartments nearby, listening from open windows: "That something is hope, morale, spirit, pride, people-to-people responsibility." Lindsay then called on his audience, and all New Yorkers, "to rally to the defense of their neighbors when crime strikes" and promised that his would be an accessible, round-the-clock administration that would help restore a sense of safety and sanity. "We will light this street, all our streets, all our parks, everywhere in this town," he insisted. "We will not rest until decency on the streets and in politics prevails again."[5]

Lindsay's astute use of the Kew Gardens murder scene aided his successful campaign and helped define many of the city's efforts at reform during his mayoralty from 1964 to 1972. Borrowing from Rosenthal's dictum that a renewal of individual responsibility was the best response to Genovese's senseless death, Lindsay insisted that the disfiguring disease of indifference would be cured "only if every citizen was willing to be his brother's keeper."[6] But unlike Rosenthal, he effectively blended appeals for individual involvement with calls for collective action.

In his article Gansberg described the muted reaction of those who had come out to hear the candidate: "The crowd, made up mostly of adults, listened quietly through most of Mr. Lindsay's speech. They interrupted him with applause only once, when he told them that he intended to make certain that 'the double padlock on the front door will no longer be the symbol of New York City.'" He then underlined the lingering aftershocks of Genovese's death. "No one in the crowd wanted to talk about the 'incident,'" he wrote. Gansberg, the reporter whose byline had appeared on the shocking front-page *Times* story that condemned Kew Gardens, and who had spoken previously to many of the people in the crowd, could not get them to talk to him. "Those who had been listed as witnesses by the police ignored questions about their reaction to Mr. Lindsay's remarks," he wrote. "A woman commented: 'Not that again. Why should he be talking about that?'" Their reluctance to speak to Gansberg or any other reporter is understandable. The women and men of Kew Gardens had been vilified for their purported lack of reaction to the assaults, first by the *Times* and then by print and television commentators throughout the city and the nation. They were not about to offer themselves up for public scrutiny once more.[7]

Despite the reluctance of the neighbors to comment, the staging of Lindsay's speech provides a potent example of some of the political uses of the story of Genovese's rape and murder. Her death took place at the start of an unprecedented rise in the crime rate in New York City and helped to spread a new vision of a frightening city, its neighborhoods in chaos.[8] But in addition to electing Lindsay, an energetic young reform-minded mayor, the Genovese crime inspired local and national debates about mid-1960s urban realities. The tensions between individual versus group involvement and accountability surfaced repeatedly as organizers and officials alike searched for possible solutions to the perceived problem of apathy. Ironically, the search for concrete solutions was generated by a commitment to action that stood in sharp contrast to the "sickness" of indifference that the *Times* and, soon, all media would associate with the Genovese case.

## Dial 911

The growing awareness of the need to streamline the city's complex system of reporting emergencies received a jolt in 1964 after the Genovese crime made headlines. Efforts by law enforcement and political leaders to better coordinate New Yorkers' ability to do so were jump-started almost immediately. As one of the few Kew Gardens neighbors who actually glimpsed Moseley's first attack on Genovese when he was a teenager living across

Austin Street in the Mowbray apartment building, Michael Hoffman remembered the difficulty of calling the police in 1964: "In those days, there was no 9-1-1. We had to dial the operator and wait for the eventual connection to the police operator. It took several minutes to get connected to the police and my father told them what we had seen and heard, and that she did walk away but appeared dazed. At that point we couldn't see or hear anything else and we all went back to sleep."[9]

The idea of one centralized emergency number was not a new one: thirty years earlier, in 1934, a London police superintendent had introduced the 999 emergency phone number, and by 1937 it was being used throughout England for calls to police, fire, and ambulance service. In 1957 the city of Sydney implemented 999 services, which expanded to include all of Australia the following year; New Zealand established its 999 system in 1958 as well. Winnipeg, Manitoba, was reportedly the first North American city to use 999, starting in 1959. In the United States, the National Association of Fire Chiefs suggested that a single phone number be developed to report fires in 1957; by 1961 the California Highway Patrol had created a seven-digit number for traffic emergencies.

New York Police Commissioner Michael J. Murphy undoubtedly was aware of many if not all of these efforts when he spoke at an NYPD award ceremony early in April 1964. Murphy assured New Yorkers that he was working to find solutions to the "many complaints about delays in getting responses to calls" made to the police, blaming such delays on the patchwork of telephone numbers in New York's five boroughs. Murphy promised, "The Police Department is seeking to set up a single police telephone number for all five boroughs to speed emergency calls from the public." At the same time, he emphasized that New Yorkers had a duty to "get involved" in reporting crimes.[10]

A few days later, Martin Gansberg followed up on Murphy's suggestion about a single police telephone number for the city. In a long piece in the *Times* that appealed to New Yorkers' pride, Gansberg surveyed eleven "representative" cities, all of which had recently established centralized systems "so that directions to the police in the field can be given out simply and swiftly." The residents of the cities surveyed—which ranged from Boston, Philadelphia, Atlanta, and Miami to Louisville, Cleveland, Chicago, Cincinnati, Salt Lake City, San Francisco, and Seattle—reported general satisfaction. Gansberg noted: "This is in sharp contrast with the situation in New York. Here civic organizations, minority groups and individuals have complained frequently about shortcomings." Headlined "Other City Police Heed Calls Fast," the article noted that the key variable for all of the cities surveyed was that they "use one telephone number for emergency calls to the police. Most of them act while an officer is still taking the call." He quoted Police Commissioner Murphy's claim that New York's current system was too unwieldy and prone to error: "A New Yorker who needs the help of the police can dial the operator or call the department number in his borough. But the borough numbers sometimes pose a problem. For example, the telephone for Staten Island is SAint George 7-1200. Yet the Police Department Official Roster, issued last Jan. 3, gives the exchange as ST. George." He emphasized that Murphy had assigned Captain William Kanz of NYPD's communications bureau to work out a new and better system with the New York Telephone Company.[11]

When *Times* editor A. M. Rosenthal later expanded his writings on the Genovese murder into a book that emphasized the apathy of the thirty-eight "good people" who were her neighbors, he incorporated Gansberg's article about telephone emergency numbers. "It seemed to us that the Genovese story had become entwined with the story of public reaction to the police and the story of police operations," he wrote.[12] The implementation of more efficient communications with the police through a unitary emergency telephone number was part of a broader effort to ease growing tensions over race and crime throughout the city. Rosenthal's steadfast defense of law enforcement personnel in the Genovese case was in stark contrast to the increasing numbers of complaints of police misconduct, especially in largely nonwhite communities in New York. At the same time, people throughout the nation were watching horrific scenes, broadcast nightly into their living rooms, of police violence against civil rights demonstrators. Over the next few weeks, the explosions of racial anger and frustration in Harlem and Bedford-Stuyvesant triggered by the killing of a black teenager, James Powell, by a white off-duty New York police lieutenant, Thomas Gilligan, fueled long-standing charges of excessive use of force by police within and beyond these two areas of the city.

In early July 1964, the image of President Lyndon B. Johnson signing the historic federal Civil Rights Act surrounded by legislators and civil rights leaders made front-page news in New York as it did throughout the nation. Three weeks later, however, some of the same leaders who had celebrated its passage condemned police violence in New York during the Harlem and Bedford-Stuyvesant riots which followed the protests over Powell's death and made explicit comparisons to the brutality faced by civil rights workers in the South. The *New York Amsterdam News* reported the words of the Mid-Queens Citizens Committee for Civil Rights, which declared on July 25, 1964: "We are convinced that James Powell was a victim of cold blooded murder and demand that police lieutenant Thomas Gilligan be immediately suspended pending a full hearing before a full board on which responsible leaders of the civil rights movement and the Negro community are seated. Lt. Gilligan's wanton slaying makes New York no different from Philadelphia, Miss."[13] Congressman Adam Clayton Powell agreed and denounced the police for firing "warning shots" with live ammunition during the riots. The *Times* quoted Powell, who reminded its readers that he was "Harlem's only elected official," as saying: "What has happened in Harlem is without precedent in the history of any police department in any city, including the Deep South. New York City ought to hang its head in shame." Powell and other leaders renewed their calls for more police protection, more black officers, and an independent civilian review board to assess complaints against the police.[14]

In October, one week before New Yorkers would go to the polls to vote in the heated presidential election between the incumbent president and his challenger, Senator Barry Goldwater, who had not only voted against the Civil Rights Bill but also made anticrime rhetoric a central part of his campaign, Mayor Robert Wagner announced that "a new single emergency telephone number would soon be available for calls from anywhere in the city to get police and ambulance help." The special telephone number was part of an effort to "reduce crime at its roots" by developing a comprehensive plan to deal with the growing problem of narcotics addiction in the city. Both initiatives were discussed by the mayor in the context of his administration's commitment to President Johnson's antipoverty program despite the city's worsening economic condition, exemplified by the loss of 84,000 manufacturing jobs between 1959 and 1963.

The following month, with Johnson elected in a landslide, the promise of forthcoming federal aid to combat poverty and crime in the city seemed solid. As legal scholar Jonathan Simon has written, "Crime was an urgent problem, but specifically in the way it was undermining the Great Society on two of its most crucial anchors," which were the urban working class and the civil rights movement. New York and other cities were determined to address concerns about crime, and maintain the liberal coalition in urban areas, by creating more effective local measures that would be supported by federal dollars.[15]

One of these local measures was designed to improve residents' access to law enforcement. Just after Election Day, on November 10 Mayor Wagner proudly announced the new citywide police telephone number for emergencies: 440-1234. According to the front-page article in the *Times*, "when a person dials the new number from a telephone in any of the five boroughs, the call activates new switching equipment at the telephone company's central offices. The equipment, through a series of relays, automatically routes the call directly to the police communications bureau in the borough involved." Wagner himself premiered the system by placing two calls to the Manhattan communications bureau from the porch of Gracie Mansion, the mayor's official residence. Public reaction came quickly and included the predictable complaints from New Yorkers. One prescient letter writer warned that "it would be difficult to dial such a complicated number when a person is being terrorized or is under pressure in other emergency situations in a dark apartment, telephone booth or the like. A more practical approach would have been to use a three or four digit repetitive telephone number such as 111, 999 or the like."[16]

At the federal level, as Johnson moved quickly to address concerns about urban decline, he convened a special President's Commission on Law Enforcement and Administration of Justice. In 1967 the commission offered its many recommendations. Among them was one that called for the establishment of a nationwide telephone emergency reporting number. Johnson also began to allocate increasing amounts of federal monies in direct and indirect assistance to local and state law enforcement, much of it dedicated to improving police operations and introducing new technologies. New York's efforts to manage its burgeoning emergency communications systems soon received a big boost from the federal government.[17]

In January 1968 the *Times* reported on plans "to establish a national emergency telephone number—911—with which police, fire and ambulance services could be summoned from any telephone in the United States." The article quoted Lee Loevinger of the Federal Communications Commission, who promised that the new emergency number eventually would be "better known than 007," the code name of the fictional inter-national spy James Bond. Six months later the paper followed up with a report noting that "New Yorkers making emergency calls to the Police Department will have to dial only three digits—911—to get help." The new number, announced by recently elected mayor John Lindsay, was "part of a broad Police Department effort to reduce the time it takes the public to call the police and for the police to dispatch patrolmen to help the public." Again signaling the city's leading role in efforts to enhance police services, the article noted that New York was the first major American city to implement the 911 system: "According to the telephone company, only one town in Indiana and one in Alabama now have such service."[18]

In a bizarre coda to the history of 911 as a response to increasing racial violence and urban upheavals in the United States in the 1960s, Alabama's Public Service Commission director at the time, who was present at police headquarters for what was reportedly the nation's first 911 call in Febru-ary 1968, was none other than the notorious segregationist Eugene "Bull" Connor. As Birmingham's police chief during pitched battles over school desegregation, Connor had aided and abetted some of the most violent assaults on civil rights advocates in the nation's history as he unleashed police dogs and fire hoses on black children in front of news cameras and photographers from local, national, and international media outlets.[19]

Five months later, on July 2, 1968, in New York, Lindsay, the politician who would be remembered for his attempts to cool rather than inflame racial animus, triumphantly dedicated a new $1.3 million police commu-nications center at 240 Centre Street. "This is, perhaps, the most important event of my administration as Mayor," he declared. "No longer will a citi-zen in distress risk injury to life or property because of an archaic com-munications system." According to the *Times*, which also included three photographs of Lindsay with police personnel at the center as well as a copy of an emergency call record, "The system was officially dedicated when Mr. Lindsay walked to a telephone in the new communications cen-ter and dialed the new emergency number." But the mayor had almost as much difficulty using the new system as he had dealing with city coun-cilors. The *Times* reported, "After several tries, officials told him he was dialing on an inside line, a button was pushed, and his call went through." The article then quoted the mayor's first call: "Do you have a squad car available? Well, you might send one down to lock up the City Council."[20]

Eighteen months later, with the council members still at large, the *Times* reported that 911 was a big hit with city residents—perhaps too much so. A follow-up article noted that, with a 17 percent increase in use in one year's time, "the rapid growth in 911 calls was the major reason Mr. Lindsay called in the recent election campaign for hiring of 4,000 more policemen." Nevertheless, some New Yorkers were not yet clear about what kind of help 911 had been established to provide. According to the commander of the Police Communications Division, Deputy Inspector Anthony Bouza, the new number "has destroyed the knowledge barrier—everyone knows 911—and it has destroyed what might be called the inhibition barrier. People call 911 on the slightest pretext." Bouza reported that callers were clogging the new system with nonemergency complaints, "such as the lack of heat or questions about parking regulations." He noted that there had even been a request for instructions on how to get a divorce.[21]

It is unlikely (though not impossible) that such a question was answered by the officers staffing the new 911 system. But since the easy-to-remember three-digit emergency phone number was unveiled—first locally, then nationally—millions of other requests for help have been handled. The availability of quick access to assistance in emergency situations fundamentally altered expectations of community, of safety and security. Beyond the 911 system, however, New Yorkers also sought answers to the questions raised by the story of the Kew Gardens neighbors and their purported indifference (at worst) or panic (at least) when faced with a frightening and potentially violent situation. Why and how do we appropriately intervene when someone nearby is in danger?

## Bystander Syndrome

In 1966 the *Times* reported on distressing new research by two New York psychologists. The headline "One Witness Better Than 38 in a Crisis, Study Here Shows" heralded a report of a two-year National Science Foundation–supported study of the behavior of witnesses to an emergency. Summarizing the findings of Bibb Latané of Columbia University and John Darley of New York University, the article again repeated the fallacies from the original *Times* front-page story: "The victim of an attack has a better chance of being helped if there is only one witness, rather than

several, according to a study being made here as a result of the Kitty Genovese murder," it began. "Kitty Genovese was slain in the early hours of
March 13, 1964, while, the police learned later, 38 persons looked on from
their apartments—and did nothing. The study, being made by two college professors, has shown that an individual will go to the aid of a victim
if he thinks he is the only one who can help, but that the real or imagined
presence of other onlookers inhibits or restrains him lest he make a fool of
himself."[22]

On December 29, 1968, the paper noted the success of the work un-
dertaken by the Latané-Darley team, again repeating the thirty-eight
witnesses myth: "Two psychologists from Ohio State and Princeton Universities today received a $1,000 award for research on the apathy that
allowed 38 persons to watch passively as Kitty Genovese was murdered
in Queens in 1964." The article reported that, after a three-year study,
researchers had found that "the likelihood of any individual acting as a
'good Samaritan' goes down as the number of witnesses to an emergency
goes up." It went on to note what the authors of the study referred to as
their "depressing findings": that people in crowds "readily 'pass the buck'
convincing themselves that someone else will take care of the emergency."
They had tested college students in situations said to replicate some of the
conditions of the Genovese crime. "The subjects were asked to converse
from separate rooms over an intercom system. Like the witnesses to Miss
Genovese's murder in their isolated apartment windows, they could not
see each other's reactions. One of the group simulated a seizure and called
for help. Of the subjects who thought they were alone with the victim,
85 percent reported the emergency to the experimenter. When two bystanders were present, the percentage dropped to 62 percent. Subjects
placed in groups of five bystanders reacted only 31 per cent of the time."
Other experiments conducted by the team produced similar results.[23]

Writing in *American Scientist* in 1969, Latané and Darley stated that
although the Genovese story had become "the journalistic sensation of the
decade," they did not think that the epithets hurled at the Kew Gardens
neighbors were accurate. "'Apathy' cried the newspapers. 'Indifference,'
said the columnists and commentators. 'Moral callousness,' 'dehumaniza-
tion,' 'loss of concern for our fellow man,' added preachers, professors, and
other sermonizers." The authors did not accept that it was apathy that had
prevented the neighbors from responding. "Actually it was like crowd

behavior in many other emergency situations," they asserted. "Emergencies differ in many ways from other types of situations in which people need help, and these differences may be important. The very nature of an emergency implies certain psychological consequences."[24]

Latané and Darley not only won awards for their research but also changed the field of psychology. The development of their theory of the "Genovese syndrome" or "bystander syndrome," still studied in introductory psychology classes today, led to a new subfield of social psychology and fueled debates about "Good Samaritan" laws. Yet it was based on the blockbuster March 1964 *New York Times* story, with all of its inaccuracies intact and unchallenged. At one point they even presented new ones: "The 38 witnesses to Kitty Genovese's murder did not merely look at the scene once and then ignore it. Instead they continued to stare out their windows at what was going on. Caught, fascinated, distressed, unwilling to act but unable to turn away, their behavior was neither helpful nor heroic; but it was not indifferent or apathetic either."[25] The image of the Kew Gardens neighbors "staring out their windows" without taking action became part of the story of urban apathy despite their insistence that apathy was not a factor.

In addition to the groundbreaking work done by Latané, Darley, and their team of researchers, in 1967 Harry Kaufmann of Hunter College surveyed the impact of moral judgment on bystander behavior. Kaufmann's team, noted Harold Takooshian, a professor of psychology at Fordham University, "found that simply labeling a behavior like 'bystander inaction' as 'illegal' caused people to judge it as more 'immoral.' " Kaufmann's assessment, according to Takooshian, was that "our law clearly sets the tone for what we view as proper behavior." In the early 1980s, Takooshian's own research with colleagues at Fordham found that "the secret of street crime" was nonintervention; that is, "criminals expect witnesses not to intervene." Furthermore, he and his research partners discovered that citizens in urban settings often do not notice crimes taking place around them.[26]

The first social psychologist to assess publicly the Genovese crime's potential impact on the field was Stanley Milgram. Known for his obedience experiments in the early 1960s, in June 1964 he published an article on the incident with Paul Hollander in *The Nation* that began: "It is noteworthy, first, that anger is directed, not toward the crime, nor the criminal, but toward those who failed to halt the criminal's actions. . . . The event is significant, also, for the way it is being exploited." Indeed, "the crime against Miss Genovese no longer exists in and of itself. It is rapidly being assimilated to the uses and ideologies of the day." Milgram and Hollander responded to those who had launched "a general attack on the city . . . as callous, cruel, indifferent to the needs of the people, and wholly inferior to the small town in the quality of its personal relationships" by arguing for the imposition of responsibility for the crime on the man who committed it rather than on Genovese's neighbors or on New York City in general. Perhaps most directly related to the myth of apathy, however, was their observation that the "respectable, law-abiding citizens of Kew Gardens" had thoroughly incorporated the well-known admonition not to take the law into their own hands. They pointed out that the very nature of being law-abiding required that they not take action on their own. The psychologists concluded by reaffirming that helping those in distress, while "a matter of common decency," may not always be observed in practice. They zeroed in on exactly the issue that Rosenthal emphasized in both his May 1964 *New York Times* Sunday magazine essay and his book for McGraw-Hill that year: the perceived need for a strengthening of "person-to-person responsibility." But Milgram and Hollander asked a different question: "What evidence is there in the American community that collective interests have priority over personal advantage?"[27]

The behavior of the bystanders—"unwilling to act but unable to turn away" in Latané and Darley's construction—was in itself fascinating to many observers. One of the first artists to memorialize the neighbors rather than the victim was the folksinger Phil Ochs. Like the participants in the studies, he put himself in the role of one of the witnesses, whether at the Genovese murder site or anywhere "a woman's being grabbed," and sardonically offered rationalizations for inaction in his song lyrics:

> Oh look outside the window, there's a woman being grabbed
> They've dragged her to the bushes and now she's being stabbed
> Maybe we should call the cops and try to stop the pain
> But Monopoly is so much fun, I'd hate to blow the game
> And I'm sure it wouldn't interest anybody
> Outside of a small circle of friends.[28]

Set to an ostentatiously upbeat honky-tonk piano tune, the song—which destroys the barrier between "us" and "them"—raced to the top of the record charts in 1967, the year it was released. It not only provided Ochs with the opportunity to vent his outrage at the reported witnesses but also gave him extensive mainstream radio play, bringing critical acclaim to his paean to passivity. Like the explanation reportedly given by one of the Kew Gardens neighbors—"I didn't want to get involved"—Ochs's refrain of indifference "outside of a small circle of friends" entered the popular lexicon.

The theories of social psychologists also intersected with those of other social scientists, such as the existential psychologist Rollo May. In his book *Love and Will*, published in 1969, just five years after Genovese's death, May analyzed the structure of human existence and specifically studied people's behavior in crisis situations, concluding, "When inward life dries up, when feeling decreases and apathy increases, when one cannot affect or even genuinely touch another person, violence flares up as a daimonic necessity for contact, a mad drive forcing touch in the most direct way possible." The science-fiction writer Harlan Ellison invoked May's words at the end of a dark short story, "The Whimper of Whipped Dogs," first published in 1973.[29] The story tells of the death of a young New York woman in full view of her neighbors, one of whom then herself becomes the victim of a violent intruder. It is significant that Ellison quoted May, who is known for his work defining optimal human existence—a life that is self-actualized, creative, courageous, and free. In Ellison's story, however, it is the city that becomes the perpetrator of violence. Like those who constructed the story of Kitty Genovese and her uncaring neighbors, Ellison blamed the urban setting—specifically New York City—on the increasing apathy supposedly being shown by Americans.

## Community Organizing and the Urban Village

As early as 1949, the black press noted the significance of collective action in New York neighborhoods. "Block Associations Ease Brooklyn Tension" was the headline in the April 2 *Atlanta Daily World* of an article reprinted in local papers. Quoting Thomas Nevins, the principal of a borough junior high school, the report noted that "when colored people began to move into the area there was a great deal of resistance on the part of the old residents but the formation of block associations and community councils have served to break this down." Nevins asserted that he and the other leaders of the block association "made it their duty to 'badger' policemen and the sanitation department into doing an effective job in the area."[30]

On March 14, 1964, the day after news about Genovese's murder first surfaced, a nearly identical report to the one printed in 1949 was published in the *New York Amsterdam News* about a community group in Harlem. "The West 141st Street Block Association this week appealed to residents of the neighborhood for support of its anti-slum, anti-crime program soon to be launched," read the article. "The block association which embraces 140th to 143rd Streets, Lenox and Seventh avenues, was formed about eight months ago after conditions in the area became increasingly deplorable." The residents were pushing for cleanups that addressed not only housing violations but also gambling on the neighborhood's streets. They also wanted "more police protection."[31]

The Genovese crime fueled an increase in community organizing throughout the city, building on long-standing efforts such as tenants' councils and block associations. After learning about the incident, residents of many New York neighborhoods added crime watch programs to the mission statements of existing groups or organized new anticrime patrols to engage in surveillance of strangers and/or to police suspect activities themselves. One of the first block associations was launched on Manhattan's Upper West Side almost immediately after the Kew Gardens murder. Forty years later a *New York Times* article celebrated the group's continuing existence: "Many block associations are formed in response to a problem on their doorstep, like crime or noise, and then fold once the problem has been resolved. But the West 83rd Street Association was formed in reaction to misfortune elsewhere—the 1964 murder of Kitty Genovese, whose screams for help went largely unheeded on a dark street in Kew Gardens, Queens." After hearing news of the crime, a small group of people created a three-block chain of volunteer lookouts from Riverside Drive to Amsterdam Avenue and in 1966 formed their association. "The same core of neighbors who attended block meetings decades ago still attend," reported the *Times*, "but many of them say that the newer and younger residents take less interest in the neighborhood's welfare as the community grows ever more affluent."[32]

Some of the goals and strategies of the neighborhood groups were very similar to those of radical organizations that were not usually included in discussions of tenants' councils or block associations. But activist groups such as the Black Panther Party and the Young Lords also worked within their constituent communities in the 1960s and 1970s, pushing for and in some cases providing basic services where the city's efforts had been woefully inadequate or nonexistent. Their anticrime organizing focused instead on exposing and protesting police brutality. Responding to community needs while challenging official intransigence and violence, they rejected the "partnership solutions to urban violence that were popular with policymakers in the 1960s, such as community policing and War on Poverty development initiatives," as Christina Hanhardt has written, noting that "the call for 'safe streets' has been a rallying cry expressed by both social minorities and property owners in the eras of postwar urban decline and neoliberal development in the United States." The increase in collective action in the 1960s and beyond can be viewed as a response to the perception that official forms of social control were lacking or deficient, as they were in the nineteenth and early twentieth centuries.[33]

As other scholars have noted, some block associations function as "self-help groups" for residents. Members take on assignments that range from removal of garbage to beautification projects; they plan social activities as well as mount crime watch efforts. It is within block or neighborhood associations that tensions between individual responsibility and collective action can come to the fore. Questions such as community formation, protection of members, and rejection of those deemed outsiders bring into bold relief the characteristics that bind a group together as well as the fissures that divide it. For example, researchers have distinguished between groups organized for the prevention of property crimes and personal assaults, assumed to be committed largely by outsiders, and neighborhood groups formed to care for their community and its residents. The lines between these two kinds of groups can and do blur, however, especially when neighborhoods experience rapid changes in the color and socioeconomic status of residents. As one team of researchers wrote, block associations "have been found to increase both the neighboring behavior of residents . . . and their psychological sense of community." Their size and their focus on specific local problems "often make changes at the block level more noticeable to residents, which can result in greater participation and empowerment."[34] In the late 1960s, many community groups evolved into or were organized primarily as guardians of law and order on the local level.

When Martin Gansberg returned to Kew Gardens in 1974 and again surveyed its residents about whether "the same silence could happen now—a decade later," he acknowledged that the people who lived in the neighborhood continued to resist the "apathetic" label that he and other media people had applied to them. He noted that police from the local precinct now praised the neighborhood's engagement. "We have a very active police auxiliary and block watch groups now," police officers told him, as well as a Kew Gardens Improvement Association working to make the area "safer and cleaner." Ten years after the crime that would negatively define their community, the residents of the neighborhood were portrayed as "astute, good people" because of their involvement with local law enforcement. One officer noted that the Kew Gardens police auxiliary was one of the largest in the city and that residents had contributed thousands of hours of their time. The officer also emphasized the positive impact of a more visible police presence in the community due to the reassignment of foot patrols. Gansberg admitted that, unlike other parts of the city, "Kew Gardens has not been a high-crime area and the rate of crime has dropped even more since Miss Genovese was slain," but he emphasized that fear "pervades" the neighborhood. He again mentioned Andrée Picq, still living on Austin Street: "Miss Picq, who testified at the trial of the killer, Winston Moseley (now serving a life term in prison) said she had bought a whistle soon after the incident."[35]

The movement to organize for protection of neighborhoods throughout New York and the nation was quickly brought under the purview of law enforcement. In 1972 the National Sheriffs' Association formally took on the job of managing the burgeoning number of local and national neighborhood watch groups, thus directing the scope and politics of such organizations. But new forms of collective action continued to emerge. Among them were the Guardian Angels. The story of what had happened in Kew Gardens motivated Curtis Sliwa to found the high-profile crime patrol group in 1979. Sliwa remembered: "This Genovese murder on Austin Street shook things up. Everyone got into a funk. Suddenly New York was branded MYOB—Mind Your Own Business. Kitty's murder at first caused an amazing setback for the people of New York City. . . . But for me, the Genovese tragedy taught a different and opposite lesson, to return to the values of my parents and grandparents, when we took responsibility for our own neighborhood." Sliwa and the Guardian Angels have been controversial participants in the city's complicated relationship with citizen patrols of public spaces.[36] According to their website, the essence of the Guardian Angels remains their safety patrols and the involvement of inner-city youth—black, Latino, white, Asian, mixed race—in policing New York hot spots. "By making young people part of the solution rather than casting them as part of the problem," it reads, "The Guardian Angels empowers youth to take pride in their communities and contribute to the safety of their neighborhoods."[37]

Over the years, however, Sliwa has evolved into a local celebrity and radio personality with a very public private life; sometimes the group he helped start has involved itself in questionable campaigns. In their first few years they admitted that they had staged interventions to gain publicity. Some observers have noted further that their in-your-face approach did not guarantee positive results, to the point where "groups such as the Guardian Angels have polarized many as to the effectiveness of community policing." Responses from "established agencies of control" have ranged from "tacit acceptance to outright rejection and suppression." The prerequisite for acceptance from law enforcement seemed to be a willingness to accede to police guidelines. As one observer wrote, "Neighborhood groups have arisen, again to mixed reactions depending on their acceptance of differing police policies in different political communities."[38]

The impulse to protect one's home and neighborhood is not new. Generations of Americans have taken personal responsibility for their families and communities and formed block associations and neighborhood groups of all kinds throughout New York City and the nation. Some are examples of effective community organizing while others have targeted presumed "outsiders," with disastrous results, for nothing more than being the wrong color or age, or wearing the wrong clothes. Starting in the late 1960s, after the explosion of publicity surrounding the Genovese crime, residents continued to organize, defying the myth of urban apathy. They created neighborhood groups in the 1970s in every borough of New York, including one in Kew Gardens.[39]

Echoing the theme of community involvement in the late 1970s was none other than the man responsible for Genovese's death. In April 1977 New Yorkers for the first time heard directly from Winston Moseley. The *New York Times* printed an opinion piece that he authored, headlined "Now I'm a Man Who Wants to Be an Asset." Writing from Attica State

Prison, Moseley referred to the Genovese crime as one "I genuinely regret," adding, "I've been imprisoned many years now and I've wished so many times that I could bring Kitty Genovese back to life, back to her family and friends." He noted, rather dispassionately, that "the crime was tragic, but it did serve society, urging it as it did to come to the aid of its members in distress or danger." He had been through "a trial of fire and death," he wrote, referring to the lessons of the 1971 Attica rebellion. "Misunderstanding, suspicion, animosity, hostility, and virulent hate lashed out and killed viciously and indiscriminately. I saw all that and was sickened. I vowed then and there that I was going to get on the right track and make amends for my own wrongdoing. I learned that human life has great value. In the future I would act responsibly." Moseley also praised the benefits of education as well as activism. He had taken college courses; met two women, a teacher and a nun, who had supported his efforts to change; and earned a bachelor's degree in sociology. "Transformation, a new outlook, caused me to get involved," he wrote.[40]

Then in 1979 journalist Bob Herbert profiled Moseley, a man whose celebrated "transformation" now included blaming his victim. In an article headlined "Kitty Witnesses Still Refuse to 'Get Involved,'" Herbert wrote about an ABC-TV special featuring Moseley which had just aired as a segment of the program *20/20*. In the nationally televised piece, moderated by Sylvia Chase and produced by Aram Boyajian, Moseley was interviewed extensively. Poised and soft-spoken, for the first time he claimed that Genovese had directed a racial slur at him a few days before he assaulted her. Although the incident had never before been mentioned, Moseley claimed that revenge was part of his motivation for the killing. Herbert noted that "Kitty, who was 28, was white and Moseley is black." He reported that Moseley remembered "the act" of killing but not the details of the crime. Herbert also incorporated the theme of witnesses transfixed and immobilized by the crime into his account of the television special, noting: "Samuel and Marjorie Koshkin, who watched the attack for 20 minutes, now live in St. Petersburg, Fla. They refused to answer questions asked by the program's staff. Koshkin said he did not want to 'get involved.'" Herbert ended his article with a quote from Moseley: "Whether I get out on the street or not, or stay in prison, I am going to continue to try to do positive and constructive things to try and make up for those crimes—that crime—that I committed." Moseley made his first application for parole in

1984. He claimed at the hearing that the notoriety of the case made him a victim as well. His request for parole was denied.[41]

Writing in the *New York Times* in 1981, Joel Greenberg asked the question that the Genovese crime had been generating for nearly two decades: "Why do some people turn away from others in trouble?" Remarking, "The incident still stands as a twisted monument to some dark corner of the human character," Greenberg then repeated the story of Kitty Genovese and the thirty-eight witnesses as the *Times* had promoted it. But in his article Greenberg shifted from the trope of apathy to its opposite. "The slaying of Miss Genovese triggered not only a flurry of press reports and investigations," he wrote, "but also, according to some psychologists, a whole new wave of research into altruism." He interviewed researchers at Stanford University who claimed that their research showed that "happy people give so much more," especially to people of equal or higher social status. "When one feels good about oneself, the enhanced sense of competence creates an aura of comradeship with other successful people, according to the psychologists." At the other extreme, not surprisingly, "when the conditions of life become tough, people are unable to give to others." Greenberg quoted one of the researchers as suggesting that perhaps this was part of the explanation for the behavior of the "crowd" in the Genovese case. "This is not the full story" of New York, the researcher said, "but if you live in a society where you're constantly being ground down, then it is unreasonable to expect that you will be kind to others."[42]

Other researchers believed that altruism is based on self-gratification and that completely unselfish behavior is rare if not nonexistent. "There is nothing we are born with that causes us to help without regard for our own welfare," said Arizona State University psychologist Robert Cialdini. Still others claimed that unselfish altruism does occur—in children. "More than 10 years ago," wrote Greenberg, "Dr. [David] Rosenhan [of the National Institute of Mental Health] found that long-term altruism was deeply influenced by parental models. In studying civil rights leaders, he found that people involved in the movement only temporarily displayed a short-term altruism partly motivated by guilt. . . . [M]ore important was that the parents of those who remained to become leaders had exemplified for their children such qualities as perseverance and courage." The article ended with a warning: "In American culture . . . we're fostering the attitude that being empathic or altruistic is too dangerous."[43]

Responses to the Genovese crime fundamentally affected social practices and policies, from the establishment of the first unitary emergency response system to the prioritization of community crime control efforts. Long-standing attempts to improve communication with law enforcement and to build on decades of community organizing throughout New York City received a boost from the publicity surrounding the narrative of uninvolved neighbors. In the social sciences, the Genovese crime fueled investigations by psychologists of individual as well as group behaviors and led to debates about some of the possible causes of inaction as well as action. The psychological theories that resulted found their way into popular culture.

All of these changes underscore the social and political power of the story constructed in 1964 by the *New York Times* yet complicate its main point, that of urban apathy. Organizing by New Yorkers on behalf of a number of social movements—particularly those concerned with challenging injustices based on gender, race, and sexuality—continued throughout the 1980s and 1990s, undermining the idea of civic indifference.

6

# SURVIVING NEW CITY STREETS

Rather than fading with time, the story of Kitty Genovese and the thirty-eight witnesses maintained its utility as a symbol of urban apathy during the 1980s and 1990s, an era of intensifying social change, upheaval, and organizing in New York and throughout the nation. The publicity the crime continued to generate helped to enlarge the agenda of activists, beginning in the mid-1970s with a newly reinvigorated women's movement. The silences in the story promoted by the *Times* inspired feminists to make explicit the prevalence of sexual assaults against women. They also exploded the notion of "lovers' quarrels" as an acceptable reason for nonintervention in intimate partner violence. Furthermore, the myth of urban apathy was turned on its head when activists fighting against the devastating new disease called AIDS took to the streets and courtrooms to expose as criminal the extreme indifference of government to the health and welfare of those affected. The myth also inspired acts of bigotry and vigilantism in an atmosphere of increasing racial animosity as the number and severity of violent crimes in the city skyrocketed alongside expanding ranks of police and rising rates of incarceration.

## Islands of Privilege

New York City was changing fundamentally in the last decades of the twentieth century. Neoliberal policies played out on local, national, and global levels, creating "islands of privilege," as geographer David Harvey has written, "in the midst of large areas of decay."[1] A new and insidious version of the Gilded Age promoted benefits for the city's elites at great cost to the majority of its residents. In terms of both economics and politics, especially with regard to mobilizations for social justice, neoliberalism shaped the present and future of the city and its people. "Its lived effects have been creating a world marked not just by growing income inequality, but also by increasing precariousness for a wide range of people," observed scholars Elizabeth Bernstein and Janet R. Jakobsen in 2012.[2]

The demographic shifts were significant. The city lost just over 10 percent of its total population in the decade from 1970 to 1980, and it was mainly working-class and middle-class people who were being pushed out. According to a report of the city's neighborhoods completed in 2001 by a team of researchers from New York University: "Housing disinvestment and abandonment were rampant, devastating entire communities and leaving in their wake 'bombed-out' neighborhoods where no one but the most disadvantaged dared to go. Housing was destroyed; property tax revenue was lost." Yet, New York being New York, the dire straits of those people left jobless and homeless also created opportunities for others, especially those with considerable resources. But the opportunities were not spread evenly throughout the city. As Harvey emphasized, "Manhattan was secured to the detriment of other boroughs."[3]

Such contradictions are vividly displayed in a January 1979 *New York Times Magazine* story titled "The New Elite and an Urban Renaissance," which celebrated "the rich moving in and the poor moving out" of the city—that is, at 96th Street and below. At one point the long feature proclaimed: "The young gentry gladly endure the urban indignities their parents ran away from. This new breed of professionals is willing to put up with smaller apartments, dirty streets and crime in order to live in chic neighborhoods." Full of photographs of the hot spots and trendy services available in Manhattan, the piece informed *Times* readers that, "hard as it is to believe, New York and other cities in the American Northeast are beginning to enjoy a revival as they undergo a gradual process known by the curious name of 'gentrification'—a term coined by the displaced English poor and subsequently adopted by urban experts to describe the movements of social classes in and around London." The article's author, Blake Fleetwood, provided a brief history lesson for the paper's readers, focusing on the city in the years since World War II. "New York City has lost some two million residents," he acknowledged. "This drop has been largely offset by the substantial immigration of blacks and Puerto Ricans. Unfortunately, these newcomers arrived when the city's manufacturing base, historically the greatest source of employment for new migrants with limited skills, was in serious decline. . . . This massive influx of poor people unable to find work strained city services to the breaking point," while "at the same time, Federal and local governments were encouraging in almost every way possible the flight to the suburbs of the middle and upper-middle classes." He also mentioned the impact during the 1970s of what he called "black flight," the departure of 25,000 African American residents per year, as well as the loss of 69,000 Puerto Ricans, both of which had had a "devastating effect on many neighborhoods in New York," particularly in parts of Brooklyn and the Bronx.[4]

Yet in 1979, only "four years after the doomsayers delivered their eulogies during the worst moments of the fiscal crisis," New York City was coming back from the brink. "Its budgetary problems are still enormous," he admitted, "but the city's spirit has rallied and the business climate has taken a definite turn for the better. . . . Tourism is now New York's second-largest job producer (the garment industry is still the biggest)." Fleetwood pinpointed the city's nascent revival as starting in 1976, with its hosting of the Democratic National Convention and Bicentennial celebrations. Then in 1978 "private enterprise committed nearly a billion dollars to construction in midtown Manhattan. These projects include the A.T.& T., I.B.M., and Fisher Brothers buildings and the renovation of the Chrysler Building, as well as speculative new office towers and high-rise apartments." He also noted some negative aspects of gentrification: "Ironically, the ethnic diversity that is drawing the gentry back to the city, the cultural heterogeneity that has always been the source of so much of New York's character and energy, may become lost in a forest of homogenized highrises and rows of renovated brownstones." But he ended the piece by assuring his privileged readers that the city was indeed theirs for the taking: "The survival and recovery of New York City depends on an educated, integrated urban elite." He then quoted "urban expert" Charles Abrams: "Cities inhabited (chiefly) by the poor are poor cities. And poor cities are poor for the poor as well as the rich."[5]

No mention was made of the activism of community groups that had worked to halt the decline of the city's neighborhoods during the exodus of jobs, people, and capital.[6] The baby-boomer "young professionals" to whom the city was being entrusted were described as single men and women or DINK (Double-Income No Kids) couples. The many attractive young white women pictured in the photos accompanying the *Times* article served mainly as advertisements for the city as a place to enjoy shopping, dining, and "living it up in the wee hours at a midtown discothèque," as one photo's caption put it. What was perhaps understandably ignored was the growing number of cautionary tales for young women about the dangers of a night on the town, especially if one indulged too carelessly in encounters with strangers. In 1975 Judith Rossner had depicted vividly the hidden horrors awaiting sexually adventurous women in her best-selling novel *Looking for Mr. Goodbar*, based on the 1973 murder of a young schoolteacher, Roseann Quinn, in Manhattan. A hit film adaptation debuted in 1977. Both the novel and the film preached the evils of casual heterosexual sex—for women—with barely concealed homophobic undercurrents. It seemed that, by 1973, the affluent metropolitan "Career Girls" of a decade earlier had morphed into wanton lonely "Bachelor Girls," but with the same tragic results.[7]

## Rape Is a Feminist Issue

The *Goodbar* narrative appeared at a time when young women were becoming increasingly vocal about the realities of sexual violence in their lives. As historian Estelle Freedman has written, it took the revival of feminism in the 1960s to move the issue of rape "from silence to public exposure and political activism." One example of this shift was the redefinition of the

Genovese crime as not only a murder but also a rape. Although the details of Moseley's attacks on Kitty Genovese as she lay dying were described in painful exactitude in court documents, the story of the case as promoted by the *New York Times* focused solely on the reported thirty-eight witnesses' failure to come to her aid. In most media accounts that followed immediately in its wake, Moseley's sexual assault was not mentioned. Freedman noted that the rapid pace of change in the 1970s "suggests that the spark of feminist politics ignited a backlog of fear and resentment among American women, many of whom had felt both physically at risk and politically disempowered by the threat of rape."[8]

New York writer and feminist Susan Brownmiller helped light the spark. She resurrected the Genovese story in her book *Against Our Will: Men, Women, and Rape*, published in 1975. Working with New York Radical Feminists, who began discussions of rape in consciousness-raising groups in the fall of 1970, Brownmiller came to an awareness of it as an extremely significant issue. As scholar Maria Bevacqua noted, "before 1970, there had been no feminist analysis of the reality of sexual assault in women's lives." Brownmiller, like many other women who had taken part in movements for racial justice in the 1960s, was well aware of the horrible history of lynching and other forms of vigilante violence against black men throughout the United States that were justified on the basis of accusations of rape by white women. Learning about the personal stories of her friends caused Brownmiller to reassess some of her attitudes about women's experiences with sexual violence. She wrote, "When a group of my women friends discussed rape one evening in the fall of 1970, I fairly shrieked in dismay. . . . I learned that evening, and on many other evenings and long afternoons, that victims of rape could be women I knew—women who, when their turn came to speak, quietly articulated their own experiences." In her book she zeroed in on two high-profile rapists, one white—Albert DeSalvo (the Boston Strangler)—and one black: Winston Moseley. In writing about Moseley, Brownmiller relied on the *Times'* version of the story, including the thirty-eight witnesses. She focused on Moseley's courtroom testimony as well as the descriptions he gave police of violent sexual assaults and murders he committed against several other women in addition to Genovese. "It comes as a surprise to most people that the murder of Kitty Genovese . . . ended in her rape as she lay dying. Winston Moseley, Genovese's 29-year-old killer, later made an extraordinary confession.

'I just set out to find any girl that was unattended and I was going to kill her,' he calmly announced in court."[9]

Brownmiller cited DeSalvo and Moseley as "fairly typical, if unusually dramatic, examples of the men who commit rape-murder." She wrote, "Although 85 percent of all police-blotter rapists go on to commit additional criminal acts that range over the entire spectrum of antisocial behavior, few advance to become rape-murderers. But the few who do cannot be ignored—because it seems probable that the 'support' they received during their raping careers, I mean either their success at eluding capture or the minimal and nontherapeutic prison sentences they served, allowed their escalating violence to proceed unchecked." She also noted: "Moseley was sentenced to life imprisonment for the murder of Kitty Genovese, but there is an addendum to his story. In 1968 he escaped from a prison hospital, captured a woman and held her hostage for hours while sexually assaulting her, and then captured a couple at gunpoint. He beat up the husband and raped the wife before he was reapprehended." What Brownmiller did not mention was that the first woman Moseley assaulted after his escape, Zella Moore, was a black woman.[10]

Moseley had escaped from custody after serving one year of a life sentence at Attica Correctional Facility in upstate New York. While hiding out at a vacant furnished house in the northeastern part of Buffalo, Moseley called the New York State Employment Service to request a maid, hoping that she would arrive by car and he could steal the vehicle. Zella Moore was sent to the house but arrived without a car. Moseley held her captive for eight hours, sexually assaulted her, and threatened to kill her three children if she reported the attacks or told anyone where he was. He finally released her. Despite the horror of what she had endured and the threats he made, Moore contacted the people who owned the house. The next morning, when the owners arrived, Moseley was still there. He attacked them, raped the wife, and then took their car, intending to drive back to New York City. Instead, he ended up in northwestern Buffalo, where he gained entry to the apartment of Mary Kay Patmos, who was at home with her five-month-old baby. When a friend stopped by to visit Patmos, Moseley demanded that she get him a car or he would kill Patmos and her child. The friend called her husband, who contacted the FBI. After nearly an hour's conversation with Moseley, Agent Neil Welch persuaded him to turn over his gun and surrender.

Incredibly, a few days later Zella Moore was charged with aiding a felon because she had failed to inform the police of Moseley's whereabouts. The black community of Buffalo erupted in outrage, and the charge so angered Barbara Sims, the only black lawyer in the Erie County district attorney's office, that she refused to prosecute the case. She was dismissed for insubordination. Sims told the press, "If this had been a white woman raped, do you think they would have brought her into court and charged her with a crime?" The charges against Moore were dropped shortly thereafter.[11]

The disparate treatment of the two black women raped by Moseley in 1964 and 1968 is striking when compared to the extensive coverage of the story of Kitty Genovese and the thirty-eight witnesses. The prosecutor in the Moseley trial, Charles Skoller, noted that the file in the Queens district attorney's office on Anna Mae Johnson's 1964 murder just two weeks before Genovese's was "thin, just a few pages describing the circumstances under which her dead body was found." Furthermore, in reporting Moseley's crimes against women, both black and white, most commentators did not analyze his use of rape as a weapon. One of the few who did was New York Police Department Chief of Detectives Albert Seedman. In a 1974 memoir he emphasized Moseley's sexual assaults and linked the Johnson and Genovese crimes. The heinous details of Johnson's death, which Moseley repeated two weeks later in his attacks on Genovese, largely have been forgotten.[12]

The silences surrounding the outrageous official treatment of Zella Moore and the murder and sexual assault against Anna Mae Johnson underscore criticisms raised by the activist-scholar Angela Davis in 1981 to the work of Brownmiller and others. "During the early stages of the contemporary anti-rape movement," Davis asserted, "few feminist theorists seriously analyzed the special circumstances surrounding the Black woman as rape victim." Addressing the lack of attention to racial realities, she wrote, "The historical knot binding Black women—systematically abused and violated by white men—to Black men—maimed and murdered because of the racist manipulation of the rape charge—has just begun to be acknowledged to any significant extent. Whenever Black women have challenged rape, they usually and simultaneously expose the use of the frame-up rape charge as a deadly racist weapon against their men." She recounted the too often ignored history of organizing by black clubwomen in the late nineteenth and early twentieth centuries, explaining, "Their eighty-year-old

tradition of organized struggle against rape reflects the extensive and exaggerated ways Black women have suffered the threat of sexual violence."
She emphasized the intersection of racism and sexism and insisted that
the feminist anti-rape movement do so as well. "Racism has always drawn
strength from its ability to encourage sexual coercion. While Black women
and their sisters of color have been the main targets of these racist-inspired
attacks, white women have suffered as well. For once white men were persuaded that they could commit sexual assaults against Black women with
impunity, their conduct toward women of their own race could not have
remained unmarred."[13]

Information about sexual assault remained minimal in the media even
with the emergence of a widespread feminist offensive that focused on
violence against women, including what began to be known as domestic
violence. A fatal example of the latter made headlines in December 1974,
in the same Kew Gardens apartment building where many of the reported
Genovese witnesses lived. The *New York Times* featured the story on page
one under the headline "A Model's Dying Screams Are Ignored at the
Site of Kitty Genovese's Murder." The story read, "The latest victim, Sandra Zahler of 82–67 Austin Street, was apparently slain about 3:20 A.M.
Wednesday, when a woman in the next-door apartment on the fifth floor
said she heard screams and the sounds of a fierce struggle." Other neighbors acknowledged that they knew Zahler had been physically attacked
and threatened by a former boyfriend in the past. The reporter quoted one
of them as saying. "The whole thing smacks very much of Kitty Genovese
because nobody called the police." One of the neighbors insisted that she
had contacted police ten years earlier when she'd heard Genovese scream,
but the police had not responded. The article noted, "While most of those
who witnessed the murder of Miss Genovese have moved away from Kew
Gardens, some still remain in the neighborhood and a few still live in the
building where Miss Zahler died."[14]

Reminiscent of the coverage of the "Career Girls" murdered in Manhattan in 1963, much more information about Sandra Zahler was provided
by the *Times* than had been included in stories about Kitty Genovese: "The
model was described as blonde, 5 feet 10 inches tall, and slender." In a
follow-up story in the *Times* on December 28, the significance of the site
and the number of witnesses was again emphasized: "The murder occurred on the same middle-class street where Catherine (Kitty) Genovese

was stalked by a killer and knifed to death early one morning 10 years ago while 38 persons disregarded her cries for help." The article ended with a capsule summary of the rapidly escalating crime rate in the area: "According to a survey of crime trends by The New York Times, the 102nd Precinct, which includes Kew Gardens, experienced from 1968 to 1973 a 118.9 per cent increase in four categories of felonies—homicide, rape, robbery and burglary. Of the 13 other police precincts in the borough, three had a higher percentage increase in the six-year period."[15] The skyrocketing rate of violence against all New Yorkers, and the huge increase in reported rapes, helped to keep the story of Kitty Genovese and the thirty-eight witnesses circulating among the public.

So did feminist organizing. As Estelle Freedman noted, "Grassroots women's groups devoted to stopping rape sprang up across the country, from Washington D.C. to Seattle."[16] In two such instances, activists publicly remembered Kitty Genovese. Two years after *Against Our Will* was published, feminist activists Nikki Craft and Ruth Reinhart in Dallas compiled and distributed a twenty-page newspaper on International Women's Day, March 8, 1977. Their newspaper contained the names and other statistics of men indicted for sex-related offenses from 1960 to 1976 as well as articles and personal testimonies from rape victims. Working their way through sixteen years' worth of criminal files, they named their project after Genovese. According to their account of their efforts, "The Kitty Genovese Women's Project distributed 22,000 copies of their paper, and the response was immediate and positive." They also worked with a local radio station to broadcast their list of accused rapists during its International Women's Day programming. They reported that the station was "flooded with calls from Dallas women." Following the broadcast, a group of wealthy women, calling themselves the Friends of Kitty Genovese, began raising money to run the list in the *Dallas Sunday News*. According to Project activists, "the normally conservative Dallas media, which several years ago laughed at the women's liberation movement, gave the event prime-time and front-page coverage." Genovese herself was mentioned briefly, as the victim of a horrific and deadly assault that had rarely been correctly identified as involving rape as well as murder. [17]

That same year, feminist activists at Michigan State University in East Lansing who had organized the Kitty Genovese Memorial Anti-Rape Collective distributed a fifty-seven-page self-defense pamphlet titled *Disarm*

# DISARM THE RAPIST!

**Figure 12.** Cover art from *Disarm the Rapist!* published by the Kitty Genovese Memorial Anti-Rape Collective, Michigan State University, 1977. Image courtesy of Archives, Michigan State University. Drawing by Marty Waters. Used with permission.

*the Rapist!* In an introduction they related the Genovese story in detail and reiterated the *Times'* tale of indifferent neighbors to emphasize that Genovese "was alone through her ordeal." They also used the story, and Genovese's name, to launch programs to "help prevent the victimization of women." These included education about "the nature and incidence of rape and other sexual assaults against women" and efforts to "destroy the many myths that are perpetrated about rape, rapists, and victims." With annotated maps of high-incidence locations and statistics they had collected, they publicized "danger areas on and around campus" and encouraged women to take practical safety precautions in public as well as in private. They also instructed women in aggressive self-defense techniques and established an anonymous rape hotline for their community. Like the women in Dallas, they trusted that publicity would alarm people into taking action. "Rape is not just a story to tell: it is a terrible reality right here within the MSU community," they asserted. "Olin Health Center unofficially reports the treatment of one rape case per day, while DPS records show over 250 sexual offense crimes (including rape, attempted rape, exhibitionism, peeping toms, etc.) reported last year."[18]

As feminist psychologist Frances Cherry wrote in the early 1980s: "In 1964 we lived in a world that did not recognize by name the widespread abuse of women. The increasing momentum of the women's movement to confront violence in the 1970s allowed for a different framework for my understanding of the murder of Kitty Genovese." She noted her own evolution: "As a graduate student in the early 1970s, in the heyday of bystander intervention research and at the pre-dawning of my own feminist consciousness, I can't claim to have seen anything other than [Bibb] Latané and [John] Darley's point of view." It was while researching the social psychology of rape, she said, that she found information "that shifted the context for the event and altered my framework for thinking about the meaning of Kitty Genovese's death."[19]

By the early 1980s, new sexual horror stories—such as the March 1983 "Big Dan's" barroom gang rape of a young Portuguese woman in New Bedford, Massachusetts, while several male onlookers cheered—raised the specter not just of bystander apathy in the face of brutal public assault but of its active encouragement by witnesses. Twenty years after the Genovese case, media commentators quickly linked the stories. The scholar Helen Benedict wrote, "Virtually overnight, columns and letters appeared all over the country likening the Big Dan's rape to the killing of Kitty Genovese . . . and chiding the accused men, society in general, and individual citizens for allowing such a brutal crime to occur." Benedict emphasized that, unlike the Genovese crime, the Big Dan's case came at a time when the women's movement had made rape a central issue: "The case was taken up by feminists and a huge candlelight march was held in New Bedford protesting violence against women a week after the rape.... The press covered the march at length and the country was reminded that this was no longer 1964, the year of Genovese's death."[20]

The circumstances of the two crimes were radically different. Rather than the brutal rape of an acquaintance by a group of young men in a public place, in the case of Genovese, Moseley had stabbed and later raped his victim in solitude after chasing her down a dimly lit street late at night. He ran away after a neighbor yelled at him and then returned to attack her again inside the small two-story building where she lay bleeding. Only a few witnesses saw the first attack, and the actions of one of them scared Moseley off; another called police but had not comprehended the severity of the assault. There was but one final witness, a friend of Genovese's, who likely saw the second, fatal attack at the bottom of the stairs leading to his apartment. Nevertheless, for different reasons, in both cases the location of the crime was significant. The small port city of New Bedford had a large Portuguese community; almost everyone involved in the Big Dan's case was Portuguese or of Portuguese descent. Regardless of the nature of the crime, the community viewed the resultant media coverage "as a slight to their community and an instance of bigotry," Benedict wrote. Many members of the Portuguese community joined a huge protest in support of the defendants after two of the four men charged were found guilty of aggravated rape in March 1984. The young woman victim fled her home and moved away after she received death threats against her and her children.[21]

By contrast, the women and men who lived in the apartment buildings along Austin Street near Lefferts Boulevard in Queens came from a variety of ethnic backgrounds. Many who caught sight of Genovese's attacker did not realize that Moseley was African American, describing him as "white" to police. Thus it seems that the racial aspects of the crime were not readily apparent at the time to most of those who glimpsed it. A. M. Rosenthal and others at the *Times* decided that race was not a significant factor in the story and so did not comment on it in the paper's coverage. As noted previously, the *Times* did not print a photograph of Moseley until his June 1964 trial, although other papers had printed photographs of him when he was arrested in March. None of them specifically commented on the murderer's race or made it a factor in their analyses of why the neighbors did not intervene. Some, however, did use racially coded language—referring to Moseley as an "animal" or a "monster"—especially during the coverage of his trial. Rosenthal noted, "Moseley did not care whether the women he hunted were black or white, except once, when he made the choice out of curiosity." Instead of racism or misogyny, "apathy" was the rationale that Rosenthal offered for the neighbors' purported inaction.[22]

"Like the Genovese case, the New Bedford rape case raised questions about the mores of urban society that made it a perfect vehicle for this sort of teaching," wrote Benedict. "It was the cheering crowd, more than the actual rape, that inspired public horror and lent itself, like the Genovese murder, to gloomy examinations of societal mores." Benedict made explicit the ways in which the story constructed by the *Times* still held sway even twenty years later. Quoting a *Boston Herald* editorial, she noted its alignment of the two victims. The editors wrote: "The woman, whoever she was, must have known how abandoned Kitty Genovese felt years ago, when her cries for help as she was being slain on a New York street went unheeded by apartment house tenants who heard her and did nothing—either out of fear or because they didn't want to get involved. As for the tenants, their counterparts drink in a New Bedford bar." Benedict also noted what she termed "the mea culpa tone" of some newspaper articles. She quoted an opinion piece from the *Boston Globe*: "Still, this grim tale reminds us that failure is always a possibility, and of just how close we are to those who raped and those who watched and cheered."[23] The *Globe* writer's bizarre identification with perpetrators of criminal sexual assault is reminiscent of Rosenthal's identification with the witnesses who, he claimed, did not act to save Kitty Genovese.

For some people, what both cases highlighted was a need for greater legal protections for victims of crimes. In the *Boston Globe* on March 8, 1984, columnist Ellen Goodman linked the Genovese and New Bedford cases in an argument for "duty to help" laws to prevent violent crimes against women. She reminded her readers: "It is just 20 years since Kitty Genovese became one of the few victims of crime we remember by name. . . . The chilling anniversary of her death occurs just as the New Bedford rape case has come to trial." Goodman pointed out that both cases "touched a sensitive public nerve about callousness as well as crime." Although she repeated the errors of the *New York Times'* version of the Genovese crime and failed to mention that Genovese had been raped as well as murdered, Goodman did note that the bystanders were not "as uncaring as we may have believed at first." She briefly discussed the studies that had been done on witnesses' behavioral responses to emergencies and mentioned Fordham professor Harold Takooshian's observation that public opinion on whether bystanders should be compelled to act had shifted upward in the wake of the New Bedford rape case. "Any 'duty-to-help' law is largely symbolic," she acknowledged. "There is no sure way to compel one person to help another. But widespread adoption of the law would show public support for the ethical instincts to help, the belief that people have responsibility to each other. It would be, finally, a statement that was missing the night of Kitty Genovese's death: We want to get involved."[24]

## Lovers' Quarrels

In 1984 *New York Times* writer Maureen Dowd reported the comments of psychology professor R. Lance Shotland of Pennsylvania State University about studies he had completed of people who witnessed violence between two people who appeared to know each other. "Bystanders who see a man and a woman fighting," he said, "are likely to assume that they know each other, and research shows that bystanders behave very differently if they assume a quarreling man and woman are related rather than strangers." Shotland summarized the differences: "Bystanders who witnessed a violent staged fight between a man and a woman and heard the woman shout 'Get away from me, I don't know you' helped 65 percent of the time. In comparison, those bystanders who heard the woman scream, 'Get away from me, I don't know why I ever married you,' helped only 19 percent of the time.'" Shotland's study helped draw attention to an aspect of the Genovese case that had previously gone largely unremarked upon.[25]

Despite more than a decade of education and activism by feminists on the prevalence of violence against women, a public assault on a woman by a man whom she knew or to whom she was "related" in 1984 still was viewed by many people strictly as a private matter, a situation in which the choice not to interfere was justified. One reader highlighted this aspect of the case in a letter she sent to the *Times* in response to Dowd's March 12 story:

> What immobilized the witnesses was their conviction that the violent man was within his rights because the woman he was brutalizing was his wife or

girlfriend, was his property, was human chattel he was entitled to control by physical abuse. Kitty Genovese was murdered four years before the second wave of the feminist movement claimed violence against women as a political issue central to the civil, legal and sexual inequality of women. Your coverage indicates that the real lesson of her killing, a lesson pointed to by feminists, is still unlearned: people will continue to be indifferent to violence against women as long as the ownership and control of women is viewed as the birthright of men.[26]

Speaking in 2013, Esta Soler remembered the early days of the grass-roots feminist movement to stop violence against women and children. Now the founder of Futures Without Violence, formerly the Family Violence Prevention Fund, in the 1980s she and other feminists organized meetings in their living rooms and met victims of violence in hospitals. "They would come into the emergency room with what police would call 'a lovers' quarrel,'" she told an audience, "and I would see a woman who was beaten, I would see a broken nose and a fractured wrist and swollen eyes. And as activists, we would take our Polaroid camera, we would take her picture, we would wait ninety seconds, and we would give her the photograph. And she would then have the evidence she needed to go to court. We were making what was invisible visible." She continued: "We created this extraordinary underground network of amazing women who opened shelters, and if they didn't open a shelter, they opened their home so that women and children could be safe. . . . We had bake sales, we had car washes, and we did everything we could to fundraise, and then at one point we said, you know, it's time that we went to the federal government and asked them to pay for these extraordinary services that are saving people's lives."[27] In 1984, activists also successfully pressured Congress to pass the Family Violence Prevention and Services Act, the first federal legislation to fund shelters, and ten years later the Violence Against Women Act was authorized.

The feminist media scholar Carrie Rentschler has noted in her work on the origins of the contemporary victims' rights movement that the popular story of Kitty Genovese "represented the old way of reporting on crime, which left the victim out of the story." Furthermore, in the 1980s crime victims "were created not by crime alone but also, more significantly, by their encounters with the criminal justice system."[28] In the 1980s and 1990s, however, many feminists, especially women of color, continued to be critical of advocates and policies that proffered victimhood as a construct and prescribed a one-size-fits-all response to violence between intimate partners, within families and communities, and from society. Some, such as writer and activist bell hooks, challenged the notion of victimhood itself as "disempowering and disabling" and insisted instead on self-empowerment and determination.[29]

## A New Disease's Deadly Odyssey

The necessity for self-empowerment as well as community mobilizations to confront official indifference toward a deadly new disease would become a hallmark of early 1980s activism. At the 1984 Fordham University conference organized by Harold Takooshian to commemorate Genovese's death, the keynote speaker, U.S. Surgeon General C. Everett Koop, likened "interpersonal violence" to an infectious disease. At the time, scientists were just discovering that a virus was likely the cause of the spiraling number of sudden deaths from what was being called Auto-Immune Deficiency Syndrome (AIDS). Koop, however, placed his remarks in a historical rather than a contemporary context. "Violence has become fixed into the agendas of surgeons general," he observed, "for the same reasons that smallpox, malaria, and tuberculosis were the big issues for my predecessors. Those infectious diseases threatened to profoundly disrupt American society then. Violence makes the same threat against our country today." At the Fordham conference, he did not mention the many questions and controversies that were erupting over how to manage the growing AIDS epidemic at local, national, and international levels.[30]

The twentieth anniversary of the Genovese crime coincided with rising panic over the disease, first noted three years earlier in a report issued by the Centers for Disease Control and mentioned in a brief *New York Times* article by Lawrence K. Altman on July 3, 1981. Headlined "Rare Cancer Seen in 41 Homosexuals," Altman's piece identified the new disease as "Gay-Related Immune Deficiency" (GRID), thus inextricably linking what would soon become known as AIDS to gay men. Although the *Times* did not follow up quickly with additional reporting on the disease at the time, it was not alone in its lack of response to the alarming CDC findings.

Journalist Larry Gross noted the "deafening silence" not only from the mainstream press but also from gay publications, including the national gay rights magazine *The Advocate*. Gross wrote of the need for gay and lesbian activists to take stock of the dizzying rate of infection, especially in communities in New York and San Francisco. "Although one of its editors died of AIDS-related cancer in 1981," he noted, "the *Advocate*'s first reference to the disease, in July of that year, quoted a CDC physician about pneumocystis."[31] According to historian Martin Duberman, however, anti-gay forces clearly saw its impact. "By the end of 1981," he wrote, "the reports were no longer a handful and it had become abundantly clear that a devastating new illness was upon us. The *New York Times* didn't think the news worthy of a feature article—although it put a story about the outbreak of a viral illness among the much-beloved Lippizaner horses on the front page. But Jerry Falwell immediately saw the significance of AIDS—and its usefulness in whipping up antigay hysteria. . . . It was a new decade indeed."[32]

The lack of positive coverage of gay people and issues in mainstream media such as the *New York Times* in the 1960s had begun to shift in the following decade, away from reports extolling causal theories about and therapeutic cures for the mental and emotional "sickness" of same-sex desire promoted by New York psychiatrists such as Irving Bieber and Charles Socarides. By the early 1970s, the increasing visibility of gay writers and activists, as well as the studies produced and statements issued by progressive psychologists and psychiatrists, helped weaken the long-perceived link between homosexuality and pathology which had often been promoted in the paper. When the American Psychiatric Association (APA) voted unanimously in 1973 to remove homosexuality from its list of mental illnesses, even the *Times* highlighted the historic shift. Rarely was it noted, however, that these radical changes—at the *Times* and in society—were happening only after decades of courageous and consistent activism. Starting in the 1950s, small groups of gay men, lesbians, bisexuals, transgender people, and their allies organized themselves, first as members of the homophile (love of same) movement and then, increasingly, as gay rights activists, and began to challenge the nearly unanimous belief—enshrined in science and promoted by the news media—that same-sex sexuality was pathological. As New York lesbian organizer Barbara Gittings stated, however, "A stroke of the pen doesn't change attitudes." Bieber and Socarides were among the most vocal opponents of the APA's action declassifying homosexuality as a mental illness and worked to have the policy change overturned. "Mindful of the need for continuing education," Gittings remembered three decades later, "the APA gave the National Gay Task Force exhibit space at several later conventions." In 1976 she was among the activists at the APA convention in Miami who reframed the "sickness" paradigm in the exhibit they presented, titled "Homophobia: Time for Cure."[33]

The sickness of homophobia, however, far from being cured by the early 1980s, was inflamed by fears of the rapid spread of the new and deadly disease. Once again, those who engaged in same-sex sexuality were rendered pariahs. Confusion and misinformation about the sources of infection circulated wildly in rumors, false reports, and scare pieces. Groups that had organized to provide medical information and health services to gay men, such as Gay Men's Health Crisis in New York, founded in 1981, were overwhelmed with demands. As Duberman noted, "What did become clear early on was that the country in general, and the federal government in particular, was simultaneously bent on ignoring or condemning GRID and those who had it."[34]

Soon it was obvious that it was not just sexually active gay men who were at risk. In 1982, Duberman wrote, "the CDC announced three cases of PCP [Pneumocystis carinii pneumonia] among hemophiliacs and thirty-four cases of Kaposi's sarcoma [a rare cancer traditionally associated with elderly men of Mediterranean origin] among Haitians living in the United States. The CDC offered no commentary to accompany the figures, but obviously the 'gay disease' had now been found in several other populations and wasn't strictly confined to gay people. . . . AIDS had also been found in Denmark in 1981, but that was all but unmentioned, as Haiti—in a clear case of racism—was highlighted." In 1983 the *New York Times* Sunday magazine featured a lengthy piece by science writer Robin Marantz Henig on AIDS. In reporting on findings by doctors that the disease likely was sexually transmitted, and echoing the call for immediate changes in sexual behavior, she invoked the image of bystanders that had become associated with the Genovese case to describe those in danger of becoming infected. This time, however, some of the bystanders were perceived as "innocent," helpless victims, while others, by implication, were not. "The groups most recently found to be at risk for AIDS present a particularly poignant problem," she wrote. "Innocent bystanders caught in the path of a new disease, they can make no behavioral decisions to minimize their risk: Hemophiliacs cannot stop taking blood-clotting medication; surgery patients cannot stop getting transfusions; women cannot control the drug habits of their mates; babies cannot choose their mothers." The status of innocent bystander as opposed to those deemed deviant and self-destructive would underscore the government's lack of response. "During the first year and a half of the AIDS crisis, Washington did little—other than indulge in repetitive, homophobic speeches from congressmen like Jesse Helms and William Dannemeyer in which they applauded the Lord's righteous punishment of homosexual immorality and recommended a large-scale quarantine program," Duberman emphasized. "On the state and city levels the records varied somewhat. New York had more than one-third of all AIDS cases in 1982 but reacted more lethargically in the early years than San Francisco or Los Angeles during the same period." It was this devastating reality that would inspire the passionate activism of groups such as the AIDS Coalition to Unleash Power (ACTUP), started in New York in 1987.[35]

The impact of the disease, and the organizing both for and against the growing numbers of people affected by it, reached into communities throughout the city as well as around the world and sometimes created strange political bedfellows. In one such example, the historian Jennifer Brier has written about the fears that accompanied the rapid spread of the disease and the school-based activism that resulted in Queens in 1985. "At a moment when officials presented inconsistent information to the public, and the meaning of AIDS was in flux, parents in Queens became more and more confused and angry," she observed. "Parental concern about proximity to people with AIDS was also fueled by a concurrent public discussion of gay bathhouses and their role in the AIDS epidemic. . . . The *New York Times* regularly ran stories about schools and the gay bathhouses on the same page." Such juxtapositions fueled debates over the relative safety of public spaces. It was in this context that parents in two Queens school districts began to organize against allowing any students with AIDS or what was then called ARC (AIDS-Related Complex) to attend school. Their ultimately unsuccessful efforts to "Save Our Kids, Keep AIDS Out" united white and black parents across racial lines despite the painful history of battles over school desegregation in the borough less than twenty years earlier. Now schoolchildren were in danger of being treated as pariahs regardless of race, ushering in activism that punished rather than aided those in distress.[36]

Brier emphasized that, "As poor African Americans and Africans began to be associated with AIDS, many middle-class African Americans sought to distance themselves from the epidemic, particularly in terms of discussion of drug use. Accepting a model that identity (in this case not being white gay men) shielded people from AIDS even as AIDS activists argued that behavior put individuals at risk, these parents, much like most white Americans, were able to distance themselves from AIDS." The parents' distrust of official assurances of safety were firmly rooted in past experiences with the scientific establishment. "Although for different reasons, African Americans and whites both had reasons to be suspicious of scientists working on behalf of the government," Brier wrote, citing such 1970s disclosures as the U.S. Public Health Service's deadly forty-year Tuskegee Syphilis Study as well as the revelations of gross environmental and health hazards at upstate New York's Love Canal. However, Brier emphasized, "while parents consistently rejected government actions on AIDS as insufficient, they sought remedies within the legal system, and in so doing looked to the state for information and solutions." Queens parents sued the city as school was starting in September 1985, but during the course of their unsuccessful litigation many of their worst fears ebbed when they heard testimony from the city's scientists and doctors, some of whom were themselves parents, providing concrete information about how best to protect all children against infection. What these and other efforts to fight AIDS in the mid-1980s have in common is a determination on the part of many people to reject the pathology of passivity in favor of taking action, both individually and collectively. [37]

## Victims or Vigilantes

The widespread acceptance of what by the mid-1980s was commonly referred to as "bystander syndrome" produced both real-life and fantasy responses to the condition. One of the most significant new vehicles for transmitting the story of Kitty Genovese and the ills of contemporary society was *Watchmen* (1986–87), the best-selling twelve-issue comic book series created by writer Alan Moore, artist Dave Gibbons, and colorist John

Higgins. Not only did *Watchmen* further exaggerate the Genovese story, but also, through the power of its images, it ensured that the story would continue to influence young women and men more than two decades after the crime occurred. True to its era, as one critic has noted, *Watchmen* emphasized urban decay.[38] The by now infamous apathy of Genovese's neighbors is noted by the main character in the series, Rorschach, as one of his motivations for becoming a vigilante:

> Kitty Genovese. I'm sure that was the woman's name.
>     Raped. Tortured. Killed. Here. In New York. Outside her own apartment building. Almost forty neighbors heard screams. Nobody did anything. Nobody called cops.
>     Some of them even watched. Do you understand?
>     Some of them even watched.

This narrative, coupled with the potent images, indelibly imprinted on a new generation the idea of amoral urban high-rise dwellers being entertained by the violent circus in the streets below. In one issue of the comic book, nine panels graphically represent Rorschach's reaction to the news of the murder. They portray an apartment house full of people—supposedly Genovese's neighbors—standing on balconies or in hallways, looking down from their open windows. The witnesses stand in enough light for the reader to see them clearly, suggesting that the witnesses could also clearly see the attacks. They, not the victim, are highlighted, much as Rosenthal had done in his promotion of the story.[39]

Moore and Gibbons uncritically repeated the trope of neighborly indifference and urban apathy, focusing on the headline in the newspaper they show Rorschach reading: "Woman Killed While Neighbors Look On" streams across the front page in big bold letters. Where they added their own bizarre touch was in creating a storyline that involves "the woman"—and they use the name Kitty Genovese—having ordered a dress in a special high-tech fabric from Rorschach's employer. She rejected it because it was, in her words, "ugly." Rorschach remembers this—and remembers her name—when he reads the news. He then fashions a mask out of the fabric to hide his face as he morphs into the antithesis of Genovese's neighbors—a one-man force of righteousness, an urban vigilante. "I knew what people were, then," he says, "behind all the evasions, all the self-deception.

**Figure 13.** Rorschach in *Watchmen* remembering Kitty Genovese's neighbors. Artwork copyright DC Comics. Used with permission.

Ashamed for humanity, I went home. I took the remains of her unwanted dress . . . and I made a face that I could bear to look at in the mirror." Rorschach's decision to go rogue makes more sense to us, the readers of *Watchmen*, than the inaction of Genovese's neighbors. He feels compelled to act when he hears what happened, instead of letting the responsibility fall on someone else's shoulders. He even takes Genovese's rejected dress and uses it to literally look at the world through her experience. He describes the fabric as "black and white. Changing shape . . . but not mixing. No gray." It is clear that he has a very cut-and-dried view of justice.[40]

To Rorschach, the people who failed to step in and help are no better than the actual murderer. In the *Watchmen* version of reality, people—in the guise of masked vigilantes—don't sit back and watch what is going on around them. They attempt to fight back. The success or failure of the fight doesn't matter; what matters is that they tried. The panels showing Rorschach and the bystanders are powerful examples of how Moore and Gibbons incorporated supposedly real information into the entertaining genre of comic books. The Genovese murder is presented as an atrocious blot on human nature. Where the fantasy world of *Watchmen* steps up and takes responsibility, the real world—in the person of the supposed thirty-eight witnesses—does nothing. According to this logic, our real world seems no better then the corrupt and war-torn one of *Watchmen*.

It is a chilling conclusion, especially given the real-life example of "subway vigilante" Bernhard Goetz, who grew up in Kew Gardens. Goetz personified the "fight back" mentality portrayed in *Watchmen*. In December 1984 he opened fire on four young black men on a city subway train after one of them demanded money from him, paralyzing one of them for life. His violent outburst polarized people throughout New York and beyond. "Angry Citizens in Many Cities Supporting Goetz" was the headline of the *New York Times* story on January 7, 1985. The article began, "The shooting took place on a New York City subway, but what Bernard Hugo Goetz did on Dec. 22 after he was harassed by four teen-agers has become something greater than a local phenomenon." The reporter noted that the case had "hit a real raw nerve" and seemed to resonate especially with radio and television talk show audiences throughout the country. "Although the case has inspired a national discussion about crime and the rights of people to protect themselves," she continued, "nowhere has the talk and emotion been more profound than in New York." Even the city's mayor,

Ed Koch, while condemning Goetz for taking the law into his own hands, commented on a news show that he understood the fear and frustration felt by city dwellers: "The rights of society have been impinged upon, and what they're saying is they're fed up. I'm fed up, too."[41]

By 1989, however, when asked by Douglas Martin of the *Times* for his comments on urban apathy on the twenty-fifth anniversary of Genovese's murder, the mayor replied: "Today the likelihood of a crowd averting its eyes and not going to the defense of someone in trouble is much less likely.... Today what we have to worry about is vigilantism. It is the other extreme." Martin had returned to Kew Gardens to ask residents whether they thought New York was "a community or a jungle." He reported: "There were surely no answers in the long halls of the apartment building across the street from where Kitty died. It was here most of the 38 witnesses were said to live. Some residents who lived here then have become too old to talk, some afraid to come to the door, some forever angry." He quoted one unnamed woman as saying: "I really don't want to discuss that case. It has bothered me for a long time." She insisted that she had called the police, even though there is no record of such a call.[42]

In May of that same year, Sam Roberts wrote in the *Times* about crimes that "vividly crystallize abstract but passionate assumptions, demonstrating the depths to which society has sunk and resonating in the minds of everyman or everywoman as potential victims." Roberts noted the Genovese crime as one of these signal events: "It brought home—home to the middle-class community of Kew Gardens, Queens—the depths of urban anomie and rekindled a primal fear that the big city is a place in which you are likely to be abandoned in your hour of need." Roberts also recounted the 1986 case of Michael Griffith, "a black man chased to his death on a Howard Beach highway by a gang of white youths," and noted that the attacks on Griffith and two other black men in a nearly all-white Queens neighborhood, one of whom survived being beaten with a bat, had become "a benchmark of racial animosity in New York's simmering melting pot where, other than in clashes with police, when white kills black it's news." He ended his review of crimes that raise "fundamental questions about moral and legal codes" with the infamous 1989 Central Park case in which five black youths were convicted of raping a white female jogger despite the lack of evidence linking them to the crime. "The rape tested New Yorkers' resolve to reclaim their parks and other public spaces and prompted debate—in black and white communities—of the causes of teen-age crime. Also, it fed the resentment of many blacks who believe that had the victim been nonwhite or poor the case would not have provoked such an outcry."[43]

Roberts's inclusion of the charges made by members of the black community regarding the victim's race and class status in the widely publicized Central Park rape case underscored the significance of a continuing issue: that of disparate media coverage of victims of heinous crimes. As Rosenthal had written twenty-five years earlier: "If Miss Genovese had been killed on Park Avenue an assistant would have called the story to my attention, I would have assigned a top man, and quite possibly we would have had a front-page story the next morning. If she had been a white woman killed in Harlem, the tension of the integration story would have provided her with a larger obituary. If she had been a Negro killed in Harlem she would have received a paragraph or two."[44]

## New Yorkers Are Questioning Life in Their City

By 1990, one *Times* writer asserted, "New York City is looking in the mirror these days and does not like what it is seeing." William Glaberson's article, headlined "Chilled by Violence, New Yorkers Are Questioning Life in Their City," captured the prevailing mood of an intense war-weariness among many residents. "In what suggests a citywide morale crisis, New Yorkers are talking about New York to each other, to reporters and to just about anyone who will listen. They talk about murders and muggings, homelessness and drugs. They wonder whether new perceptions and new realities about the difficulties of New York life will leave a permanent mark." Glaberson acknowledged that the problems were not New York's alone: "Some of the city's politicians and other boosters worked overtime last week to remind people that New York was well down on the list of dangerous American cities, ranking ninth last year, for example, well below Washington, Detroit, New Orleans, Dallas and Baltimore. But if there are some stubborn misperceptions that have always plagued the city's image, there are some sobering realities as well. After a decline in crime rates in the early part of the 1980's, statistics show a sharp increase in the last several years in such violent crimes as murder and robbery, with current rates climbing even higher. Last year there were 1,905 murders, more than ever before in the city's history, according to Police Department statistics."[45]

With crime rising again in the early 1990s, it was voters in Queens who provided a political margin that in 1993 would elect former federal prosecutor Rudolph Giuliani as mayor of New York. He won the borough with just over 100,000 votes in an election in which his margin of victory throughout the city was approximately half that number of votes. "Very much an outer-borough ethnic himself," Steven Malanga wrote in 2004, "Giuliani captivated Queens voters with his agenda of tough-on-crime policing, budget and tax restraint, and welfare reform." For some, Giuliani symbolized a city desperate for safety and stability; for others, his ascendancy marked a low point in the conservative law-and-order attitudes that had been promoted nationally for decades.[46]

For the architect of the Genovese story, the thirtieth anniversary of the crime was a time of despair. In his "On My Mind" column of March 15, 1994, A. M. Rosenthal asserted, "In our city and country, there is more violence, more apathy toward it, not less." He noted that in the thirty years since Genovese's death, " 'apathy' is not really news anymore. Every week, sometimes often in one week, somebody gets murdered before witnesses in our city—an execution on a drug corner, or death in a drive-by splatter of bullets. When I see the scene in my mind, I know that there must have been lots of witnesses—in the streets, or watching from windows. But the thought that they walked away or pulled their heads in does not startle me anymore. I take it for granted. If I were still an editor I would probably not bother to send reporters to search out witnesses, it seems so commonplace now, silent witnesses."[47]

Less than five years later, things had changed. In December 1998 a headline in the *Times* proclaimed, "Homicides Decline below 1964 Level in New York City." The article began, "The number of killings reported so far this year in New York City has fallen to 606, putting the city on a pace to end the year with fewer homicides than it had in 1964, when The Beatles played 'The Ed Sullivan Show,' the Verrazano-Narrows Bridge opened and a woman named Kitty Genovese was killed in Queens." It noted multiple reasons for the record decline—"experts point to the stronger economy, a drop in the number of people in their late teens and early 20's, the waning of the crack epidemic, and an increase in the number of people behind bars"—while simultaneously reiterating the official version of the Genovese story: "But while the city is on a pace to log even fewer homicides this year than it did in 1964, when 636 people were reported killed—among them Kitty Genovese, who was stabbed to death as 38 neighbors heard her screams and did nothing—little else about the nature of crime in the city and the criminal justice system remains the same."[48]

The article pointed out that the size of the police department had increased (from about 25,900 to nearly 40,000), as had the number of arrests, which had "skyrocketed" from 93,627 in 1964 to 396,237 in 1998, "largely a result of the Police Department's crackdown on 'quality of life' crimes." This was a reference to what was often referred to as "broken-windows" policies, from the title of a 1982 *Atlantic* article written by James Q. Wilson and George Kelling. As historian Marilynn Johnson explained: "According to their theory, police could reduce crime by adopting a tough enforcement stance that includes minor 'quality of life' offenses such as public drinking and urination, panhandling, street peddling, truancy, turnstile jumping, squeegee washing, etc. Arresting such violators prevents them from committing more serious offenses, allows police to apprehend those with illegal weapons, drugs, or outstanding warrants, and sends a message that the streets are under control."[49]

Despite the findings of a 1994 investigation into police practices initiated by David Dinkins, New York's first African American mayor, which exposed not only widespread corruption but also extreme brutality, his newly elected successor, Mayor Guiliani, ignored recommendations to appoint an independent police monitor and instead implemented his "zero tolerance" policies. By the end of the decade, law enforcement personnel were crediting those policies with drastically reducing New York's crime rate. These policies provided many more opportunities for stopping, frisking, and arresting large numbers of people, overwhelmingly in nonwhite neighborhoods. As Johnson noted, for many New Yorkers, especially white residents living in rapidly gentrifying neighborhoods, "quality of life policing was a welcome policy that seemed to revive and reclaim a decaying urban core."[50]

In 1989, community activists of all races who had organized for years to stop police violence against New Yorkers thought they had found a reliable ally in David Dinkins. According to Johnson, "Dinkins' strong stance on civil rights—including support for an independent CCRB (Civilian

Complaint Review Board)—helped him win the votes of blacks, Latinos, and white liberals." Dinkins focused instead on community policing strategies and then was quickly overwhelmed by the epidemic of crack cocaine and crime that swept the city, to which he responded by adding considerably to the ranks of the city's police department during his one term in office. The videotaped beating of motorist Rodney King by some members of the Los Angeles Police Department, who were then acquitted in 1992 of the charges against them, fueled anger there and elsewhere, including New York. Thousands of New Yorkers held largely peaceful demonstrations and vigils, although some violence was reported in Jamaica, a neighborhood of Queens, and in Harlem. The mobilizations overall revealed the growing power of community organizing to challenge police violence.[51] But the enforcement of "zero tolerance" under the Giuliani administration meant increased brutality, harassment, and racial and sexual profiling in many New York communities. "Activists in the city's African American, Latino, Asian American, gay, and homeless communities insisted that police used quality of life policing to target and abuse the city's poor, nonwhite, and socially stigmatized residents," Johnson argued. "For these citizens, city streets had become *less* safe, and the quality of life had deteriorated."[52]

The controversial practices associated with this style of policing often are contrasted with community policing efforts, in which officers are assigned specific neighborhoods to patrol, investing time and energy into gaining the trust of the people in the community. As reported in the 1998 *Times* article, however, decreasing crime rates were used by some police officials to justify moving away from the more labor-intensive strategies of community policing in favor of computerized crime statistics and neighborhood-based antidrug sweeps. The article quoted Police Commissioner Howard Safir: "I'm not going to be bullied by community activists who say, 'We want feel-good cops.'" Rather, he insisted, "the bottom line is crime reduction."[53] The "bottom line" of New York's dropping crime rate also included a huge increase in the incarceration rate. The article noted that the numbers of people in the state's prisons had mushroomed from 19,439 in 1964 to more than 69,000 in 1998. Sociologist Andrew Karmen noted: "In those days there was a greater emphasis on rehabilitation, alternatives to incarceration, and getting to the root causes of crime. Today there's more emphasis on punishment and incarceration. But it's an open question whether or not the criminal justice system deserves the credit for the drop in crime."[54] Increasingly, it is clear that it does not.

A decade later, legal scholar Jonathan Simon returned to the impact of community displacement in establishing the connections he had studied among housing, homicide, and mass incarceration since the 1950s. Simon specifically linked the Kitty Genovese crime with "broken windows" policing strategies. He wrote that the transformation of many city dwellers from renters to home owners in the 1950s had brought about the desertion of the cities for the suburbs and a shift in support for crime control methods that protected property values. "The post-WWII trend of suburbanization helped to lay the foundation for mass incarceration," he asserted. "Mass incarceration is, in fact, a racial strategy." He reported that in 1999, "just under one percent of working-age white males were in prison (itself a historic high) but 7.5 percent of working-age black males were." Simon then reprinted the infamous March 1964 *New York Times* story about Genovese's death and the thirty-eight Kew Gardens witnesses and noted its impact particularly on the field of psychology. He also acknowledged critiques of the story: "As a piece of popularized social science with a highly problematic empirical base, Kitty Genovese's case and the bystander effect might be compared to the highly influential 'broken windows' theory about the effects of increasing enforcement of minor public-order laws, except that instead of influencing mayors and police chiefs, the Genovese case was a 'broken windows' theory for middle-class families, one that constituted a powerful advertisement for moving out of urban apartment buildings and into suburban cul-de-sacs." He argued that the politics of racial separation and the politics of crime were "integral to each other" and framed by the politics of place.[55]

"Place" always was a significant factor in the shock value of the story of Kitty Genovese and the thirty-eight witnesses. The Kew Gardens neighborhood, with its semi-suburban location and small-scale community orientation, led many to perceive it as a friendly enclave in the midst of a sometimes cold, often dangerous, decaying megalopolis. The reported failure of its residents to "do the right thing" is what kept the story alive despite growing questions about its validity. These questions, which threatened the very premise on which the myth of urban apathy was constructed, had been discussed privately for two decades. By the early years of the twenty-first century, the myth was increasingly being challenged publicly.

# 7

# CHALLENGING THE STORY
# OF URBAN APATHY

The women and men who lived near Kitty Genovese in 1964 became the subject of the story of her death two weeks after the crime was committed and remained in the spotlight—or, to put it more appropriately, on the hot seat—for fifty years. They came in for far more attention, analysis, and criticism than anyone else involved in the case, including the murderer, Winston Moseley. Although some of Genovese's neighbors challenged the portrayal of their community immediately after the murder, and repeated their objections every time they were given the chance for years afterward, it had little impact on the public's acceptance of the myth of urban apathy. The tale of thirty-eight uninvolved witnesses endured for decades despite the fact that the number was never verified and only a handful of Genovese's Kew Gardens neighbors were called to testify at Moseley's trial.

In 1965 some two hundred more murders were reported in New York than in 1964, further fueling residents' fears about their vulnerability. It was becoming increasingly difficult for New Yorkers to feel safe. People were leaving the city in record numbers. But one of those who remained on Austin Street, and who would defend his neighbors and his community every time he was given the chance, was Frank Facciola. He repeatedly resisted the characterizations of Kew Gardens appearing in the media and was among a handful of residents who pushed back against the opprobrium directed at the women and men who had lived near Genovese. For the most part, however, their voices were lost in the thunderous denunciations of apathy and indifference emanating from the media, law enforcement, scholars, and artists.[1]

But anniversaries of the Genovese crime provided occasions for many reporters to return to Kew Gardens and talk with some of the people who had remained in the neighborhood as well as the many newcomers who had later made it their home. A hint of Kew Gardens residents' consistent rebuttals to the story the *Times* had created appeared in a ten-year anniversary story, again written by Martin Gansberg, in 1974. While not rejecting the urban apathy myth, Gansberg admitted that some people continued to challenge their neighborhood's bad name: "At the time of the slaying, some oldtime residents objected to the fact that newspapers, radio and television had paid so much attention to the neighborhood. They recalled similar incidents elsewhere and related favorable events in Kew Gardens that they felt should have been reported in the press. There are some now who feel [the murder] should not be looked into again. Newer residents, reminded of the Genovese slaying, were optimistic about neighborhood help."[2]

Gansberg's small gesture of recognition that the people of Kew Gardens continued to defend themselves against misrepresentation was significant. Beginning in the 1980s, a growing number of writers and researchers would complicate and, in some cases, challenge the official *New York Times* version of the story of Kitty Genovese and the thirty-eight witnesses. As crime rates rose in the city, some articles revealed the difficulty of appropriately responding to frightening or dangerous events. A 1982 *Times* article, headlined "Heroism in Modern Times," sympathetically examined what the author called "the heroism of ordinary people suddenly trapped in situations of great menace." In an example of routine reinforcement of the *Times'* narrative, however, one psychologist the reporter interviewed declared: "In some cases, 'heroic' would mean having the simple courage to make a phone call to the police. . . . That certainly would have helped in the case of Kitty Genovese."[3]

## Neighborhood Wound That Refuses to Heal

For those Kew Gardens neighbors who themselves felt stigmatized simply for living near the scene of a horrible crime, the twentieth anniversary of Genovese's death in 1984 was a time for profound sorrow and yet another round of recriminations about their alleged inaction—recriminations that many of them continued to resist. Local dailies sent reporters to talk to the Kew Gardens neighbors early in March. "Nathan Levine saw the cameras and the notepads and he knew what was coming, wrote Kenneth Gross of *Newsday*. "'You're going to stir it up again, aren't you?' he said bitterly. 'You people keep coming around and bringing it up again.'" Interviewed for the March 11, 1984, issue, Levine, who owned a store on Lefferts Boulevard near the site of the murder, insisted, "I don't accept this business about not getting involved." As Gross put it, "Levine has spent the greater part of his adult life defending his community against the media knives." Levine was not alone in rejecting the media's negative portrayal of his neighborhood. Gross also interviewed another local business owner, Bobby Tobin. "You want the truth?" Tobin asked him. "The truth is it didn't happen. There weren't 38 people who heard that. No way."[4]

He also heard from longtime Kew Gardens defender Anthony Corrado, the owner of the upholstery store on Austin Street who had helped Genovese and Zielonko when they were moving into their apartment in 1963. Corrado insisted yet again: "It was noisy [that night]. Very noisy street. The bar, you know? People didn't know what was happening. They though it was just noisy customers from the bar. I know one guy wanted to come down, but his wife said it was just noisy customers from the bar." Another neighbor whose apartment faced Austin Street and who was asleep when the first attack took place insisted that "people came out to help. . . .[T]hey came out when, unfortunately, it was too late. And I happen to know someone called the police. I believe that there were two calls. Of course the police deny it. But there were calls."[5]

Gross went on to describe some of the changes that had taken place in the neighborhood in the two decades since Genovese was killed: "The art theater on Lefferts Boulevard has been replaced by an X-rated movie theater. And the turnover in rentals has increased. There is a decidedly Asian influence crowding out the old German shops. But the neighborhood looks roughly the same. The buildings are well maintained. The residents look prosperous." But, he added, "the topic festers just under the surface—a wound that refuses to heal." He quoted another longtime neighbor, "one of the German-American residents," who said of the story about the neighborhood's lack of involvement: "What happened that night has become a myth. It is what we have read about. We don't know what is true and what is myth. This story doesn't exist."[6]

Writing in the *Daily News* on March 11, 1984, reporters John Melia and Don Singleton asked, "Did the case of Kitty Genovese and her reportedly hard-hearted neighbors shame all Americans to the point where we would be more likely to play good Samaritan should the occasion arise?" They too reported on the responses of the current Kew Gardens residents. "It's a shame you news people have to bring this up all the time," said an older woman "who did not want her name published." Despite seeking anonymity, she insisted: "Nobody in [this neighborhood] is apathetic. I know it isn't true that 37 people heard her screams and failed to call the police. I was here, and we are not like that." They also reported the opposing comments of another resident who was not at home the night of the killing. " 'This neighborhood is a disgrace,' said Margaret Walrath, who was working at a radio station at the time Kitty was slain. 'I believe that people heard but didn't want to help. I don't think they'd help today either.' " Melia and Singleton then made an important point about the story's construction and the significance of its continued circulation in the media: "The fact is that the issues raised by the Kitty Genovese case are so basic that it would be unrealistic to expect them to have been changed by a single event, however out of proportion it may have been blown." They then concluded: "The killing of Kitty Genovese was a tragedy. But maybe that tragedy was more private and less public than has been suggested by some police officials and some reporters—and it should be noted that both groups had something to gain from the way they told the tale."[7]

## A Fundamental Issue of the Human Condition

Many of the challenges to the official version of the Genovese story reflected growing tensions between calls for individual responsibility in an increasingly hostile urban environment, as Rosenthal promoted in his book *Thirty-Eight Witnesses,* and the significance of collective action in creating social change. As *New York Times* writer Maureen Dowd noted in 1984, the story "crystallized what people were only beginning to feel about urban life in America: the anonymity, the lack of human contact, the feeling of not being able to control one's environment." Dowd quoted psychologist Stanley Milgram: "The case touched on a fundamental issue of the human condition, our primordial nightmare. . . . If we need help, will those around us stand around and let us be destroyed or will they come to our aid? Are those other creatures out there to help us sustain our life and values or are we individual flecks of dust just floating around in a vacuum?" Hewing largely to the *Times'* official version, Dowd emphasized the ongoing impact of the crime. "It's held the imagination because [in] looking at those 38 people, we were really looking at ourselves," she wrote, quoting Fordham law professor Peter J. O'Connor. "We might not have done anything either. That's the ugly side of human nature."[8]

Dowd noted the studies and writings done in the two decades since Genovese's death—"over 1,000 articles and books attempting to explain the behavior of bystanders in crises"—and summarized some of the findings and recommendations for changes in the law, starting with a shift in focus from criminal to victim. The Genovese murder "mobilized people's thinking around the need for society to respond to the victimization of people," she wrote, quoting psychology professor Morton Bard. Dowd noted the proliferation of neighborhood watch groups and safety patrols, installation of the 911 emergency telephone number, as well as increases in victims' rights advocacy. "Lobbying groups have sprung up to protect the rights of the victim," she observed, "and crime-stoppers units with payment for anonymous tips are common in big city police departments." She also emphasized the *New York Times'* role in shaping the Genovese story, noting that a *Times* reporter, "retracing the investigation with detectives, said witnesses offered several reasons for their inaction." She then quoted Harold Takooshian, who provided a more nuanced and detailed explanation of the reactions of the neighbors in Kew Gardens: "We realize now that the reasons were more complex. . . . Some might have wanted to get involved but didn't know what to do."[9]

Another March 1984 *New York Times* piece gave Kew Gardens residents an opportunity to speak for themselves. Although its provocative headline, "The Night That 38 Stood By as a Life Was Lost," once again misrepresented the responses to the crime, the unsigned article provided examples of how the case still haunted the people who lived in the neighborhood. For example, "It flashes through Margaret Swinchoski's mind each time she walks past the Kew Gardens, Queens, train station: This was where Kitty Genovese met her killer." A newcomer to the area, Swinchoski was aware of its infamy before she moved to New York. "Even in the small town in Vermont where Miss Swinchoski grew up, Catherine Genovese's case became a shocking symbol of apathy. Now Miss Swinchoski lives in the same quiet, middle-class neighborhood where Miss Genovese was slain 20 years ago as she tried to make her way from her car, parked in the train station lot, to her apartment on Austin Street." The article highlighted the constant fear that the young woman felt. "I walk here during the day but not at night," said Swinchoski, "because of what happened then and because of what might happen now."[10]

The article reiterated much of the original *Times* story but corrected a significant error, pointing out that Moseley had made two attacks on Genovese rather than the three initially reported. Yet the article also repeated the urban legend that "witnesses watched from behind their curtains—one couple pulled up chairs to the window and turned out the light to see better." The writer then turned to some of the people who had lived through the trauma of the murder and allowed them, finally, to defend themselves. One of the more outspoken was Bernard Titowsky, owner of the Austin Book Shop, who remembered seeing blood near the entrance to his store the morning after Genovese's death. "Time and rain washed most of it away," he told the reporter. Like Facciola, he insisted that the Kew Gardens residents had been unfairly portrayed. "No one wants to give the people that lived here any credit,' he said. "They just want to use it as a sociology lesson."

The last word was given to one neighbor who had in fact gone to Genovese's aid the night she was killed. The article concluded by quoting an unnamed eighty-three-year-old woman who lived nearby. "She was awakened at 3:30 A.M. that night when a friend called to say he had seen the attack but was intoxicated and did not want to deal with the police." Contrary to the stereotype of the indifferent bystanders, the woman immediately took action. "She put on a coat over her nightgown and went down the street to find a door ajar and Miss Genovese crumpled behind it." The horror of finding her neighbor bleeding on the floor had not lessened in twenty years. The neighbor remembered, "She was dying . . . making noises like, 'Uh, uh, uh,' like she couldn't breathe." She alerted another neighbor, she said, who called the police. The article ended with a plea for understanding and a hope that people would forget the story that had been told about the neighborhood. "We weren't apathetic," the woman said. "There are good people here. There's so much else bad in the world. Poor Kitty."[11]

## Stigma Remains from Genovese Case

Regardless of the rare inclusion of their voices in a handful of news accounts twenty years after the murder, the people of Kew Gardens continued to be described as morally deficient in their response to the Genovese killing—lacking in awareness, compassion, and courage. Nevertheless, a few intrepid writers uncovered additional information, and, following their instincts that the official version of the story as promoted by the *Times* "just didn't add up," they attempted to rehabilitate the reputation of the Kew Gardens community.

One veteran Queens reporter did not mince words as he examined the construction of the Genovese story. "Did the people of Kew Gardens get a bad rap when Kitty Genovese was killed?" wondered reporter John Melia in 1984. Melia had returned to the neighborhood on the twentieth anniversary of Kitty Genovese's death, and he succinctly summarized what had happened there in the weeks and months after the crime. "One week after the murder," he wrote, "a newspaper report stated that 39 [*sic*] of her neighbors watched as Genovese was attacked three times by Moseley and ignored her dying pleas for help. Other papers scrambled to find these cold-hearted people who merely batted an eyelash and then returned to bed as blood was spilled up and down their street. The uproar was deafening, politicians castigated the people of Kew Gardens for their apathy, the police couldn't believe how little these people cared, the public was disgusted."[12]

Melia took the news media to task for their vilification of Kew Gardens. An experienced reporter for the *New York Daily News* who had spent years working in Queens, he retraced the crime scene and looked carefully at the location, noting the physical features of the landscape, then wrote a short but powerful piece in March of that year. It again placed Genovese's neighbors at the center of the story, but with a significant difference. Melia noted that in the twenty years since the crime, "newspapers, including this one, have dredged up the death of Kitty Genovese on a periodic basis to take the pulse of Kew Gardens and see if the patient is recovering." Unlike most other commentators, however, Melia cast the community as victim rather than perpetrator. "Maybe the trail was cold after two decades," he wrote, "but the people we interviewed—people who lived on Austin St. at the time—were almost unanimous in feeling that whatever they said about that night would be distorted by the press." He quoted neighbors who had lived near or known Genovese, women and men who disputed their collective portrayal as apathetic onlookers. "We are not bad," Melia reported one neighbor saying emphatically. He then shared the "rumblings" among reporters who had covered the immediate aftermath of the murder and Moseley's trial and who also had doubts about the story's veracity: "We heard a story of one reporter, sent out by his editor to find these witnesses, who came back literally begging that the story not run because there was nothing there. He told his editor that the witnesses did not exist in the numbers claimed. But it was too late, the people of Austin St. in Kew Gardens had been stamped with the indelible mark of Cain—the story ran, full of appropriate outrage and horror."[13]

Melia also detailed his own doubts about the number of actual eyewitnesses. In addition to recounting some of the errors made in the *Times'* front-page story of Moseley's attacks on Genovese, he reminded his readers of the specifics of an urban, rather than suburban, environment: "In reconstructing the crime, you have to remember that it was 3:30 on a winter morning, a time when most people are in bed asleep and windows are closed, a time when people are not easily roused. Most of all, you should take into account that this is a street in a large city. Admittedly, it is a relatively quiet city street, day or night, but a city street nevertheless, with all the attendant noise."[14] He concluded that on a cold winter morning well before dawn, few people who were awakened by Genovese's calls for help would have understood what they were hearing. In analyzing police reports of the neighbors' responses, he found that most of the neighbors who lived in the apartment buildings nearby and were interviewed by detectives immediately afterward said that they heard something but saw nothing.

Melia's thoughts were featured prominently as part of a twentieth-anniversary feature on the crime in the *Daily News*. His story was reproduced on a website built by one Kew Gardens resident, attorney and local historian Joseph De May. De May moved to Kew Gardens in November 1974, ten years after the Genovese crime. He started law school at St. John's University the following January. Although he knew of the case and had a general understanding of what had happened, he did not know the details. He had chosen the Kew Gardens neighborhood for its accessibility—close to the LIRR, buses, and subways—and affordability. His large one-bedroom apartment—$155 a month was the rent, he remembered recently—was one block from Lefferts Boulevard and local shops. He was happy living in Kew Gardens and settled into the neighborhood, remaining there after he graduated and began to practice maritime law. At one point he found an old photograph of a building that once had stood where his apartment now was and he began to learn more about Kew Gardens; in the process he discovered an affinity for local history.

When he began his research into the neighborhood, De May's efforts inevitably led him to the early morning hours of March 13, 1964. As he started reading news accounts of the crime, the description of the murder in the front-page *New York Times* article caught his interest. Over the next few years, after reviewing court documents as well as news articles on the case, De May created a detailed set of links to information about the Kitty Genovese story on a website he established in 1990. Under the headline "What You Think You Know about the Case Might Not Be True," De May provided excerpted copies of Moseley's confession to Queens police and other official documents to raise questions about what actually happened the morning of Genovese's murder. Perhaps most important, he enabled website visitors to leave comments. One reader, Michael Hoffman, a retired New York Police Department officer who had moved to Florida, wrote to De May to say that not only did he remember the murder, which occurred when he was a teenager, but also he had seen enough of Moseley's first assault on Genovese to yell to his father to call the police. Hoffman's memories of that morning provided evidence to support De May's growing belief that at least some people in the neighborhood had contacted the local precinct. He also reproduced the testimony given during Moseley's trial by Robert Mozer, who testified in court that he had successfully interrupted Moseley's attack after hearing a woman's cry for help. Although Moseley ran off, he returned shortly thereafter. While Mozer's actions are mentioned very briefly in the *Times*' front-page story and in Rosenthal's book, they are not described as the significant intervention that they were. In fact, they are not commented on at all.[15]

In interviews, De May always insists that he is not an apologist for Kew Gardens. He has emphasized the individual responses of different residents

**Figure 14.** Joseph De May (left) and Harold Takooshian (right) at the entranceway to Kitty Genovese's apartment in Kew Gardens on the forty-fifth anniversary of the crime. Photo taken by Marcia M. Gallo, March 2009.

of Kew Gardens and refuted the idea that they functioned as a cohesive group. "Usually the bystander syndrome theory says that when you have a group of people, everyone is looking to someone else to take action," he told an interviewer. "But in this particular case, you didn't have a group of people. You had individuals." He does not excuse the neighbors who failed to act. "You know," he said, "I think there were probably a number of people who knew that there was something more than just . . . a lovers' quarrel at stake, and they may not have taken any action. You can justly criticize them for that." But De May noted the exaggerations of some media accounts: "My point is that we didn't have what the *Herald Tribune*, I think, described at the time as being a scene reminiscent of the Roman Colosseum with the Romans watching the Christians being slaughtered while they cheered them on. It's that scenario that didn't happen, not that the witnesses were . . . blameless."[16]

Despite the questions raised by De May and others, best-selling books such as *The Tipping Point* by Malcolm Gladwell, published in 2000, kept the essential details of the *Times* story before the public, now updated with all the rhetorical embroidery that had been added in the preceding decades. It was not until the fortieth anniversary of the crime that challenges to the story secured major media attention. The shocking assertion that there may not have been thirty-eight witnesses to the crime first surfaced in the very pages of the paper that had constructed the cautionary tale in the first place, the *New York Times*. It was accompanied by another surprise: the disclosure that the victim had been involved in a lesbian love affair at the time of her death.

## Kitty—40 Years Later

Writer Jim Rasenberger agreed to prepare a feature on the Genovese case for the *Times* to publish in 2004. "When I began researching in November 2003 the article that appeared in the New York Times on February 8," he related, "I started with two questions. The first was factual: what exactly occurred in those early morning hours of March 13th, 1964? The second question was more philosophical: what did the events of that night mean? In other words, what lessons or morals could we draw from the death of Kitty Genovese?" He pointed out that "within days of the front-page, March 27th *New York Times* article on the 38 witnesses, everyone in New York was speculating on how this could have happened."[17]

Rasenberger ran down some of the more ridiculous reasons offered for the reported failure to act four decades earlier—television hypnosis, "male insufficiency"—and noted that the search for answers continued. But his focus was on the errors of representation made by the original front-page *Times* story. "This was in fact how the story was originally reported on March 27th," he wrote. "I quote: 'For more than half an hour, 38 respectable, law-abiding citizens in Queens watched a killer stab a woman in three separate attacks in Kew Gardens.'" Rasenberger added, "No wonder there was such contempt for the people of Kew Gardens for months after the murder." But "like all myths," he acknowledged, "it is not quite true. . . . It turns out the great majority were not *eye* witnesses, but *ear* witnesses, and what they heard was likely fragmentary and confusing, through closed windows on a chilly night."[18]

In fact, after consulting the available sources, augmented by his own research, Rasenberger came to believe that the story of thirty-eight witnesses had been exaggerated. The article he then wrote was prominently displayed in the *Times*; it filled the top half of the first page of the city section and continued inside for a full page. "Kitty—40 Years Later" remains one of the most thoughtful of the thousands of essays and articles published about the Kew Gardens murder. It not only expanded public awareness of the humanity of the people who had been Kitty Genovese's neighbors but also provided important information about the victim herself—namely, that Genovese had been a "vivacious, generous" person, very close to her family, and that the "roommate" she shared her Austin Street apartment with, Mary Ann Zielonko, had been her lover. It also began to break the stranglehold that the "thirty-eight witnesses" myth had had on the Genovese story for forty years. In 1964, an accurate depiction of Genovese and the female lover who mourned her likely would have shifted the focus of media attention to her sexuality and torpedoed the *Times'* emphasis on urban apathy. Despite Albert Seedman's revelations of Genovese's lesbian relationship in 1974, the impact of Jim Rasenberger's story thirty years later was immediate. Finally, the world knew more about the woman behind the name associated with "bystander syndrome."

One month later, at a 2004 fortieth-anniversary commemorative forum at Fordham University, Rasenberger joined eight other invited panelists— as well as a surprise guest A. M. Rosenthal, who sat in the audience— to discuss the continuing relevance of the case. "Four decades later, the

Genovese murder conjured enough emotion and curiosity to fill Room 109 of McMahon Hall on March 9 for a public forum titled 'Remembering Catherine 'Kitty' Genovese 40 Years Later,'" the university newspaper reported. At the forum, Rasenberger asserted again that the *Times'* story of thirty-eight witnesses was exaggerated; the timing and locations of the assaults on Genovese made it impossible for the neighbors interviewed by police to have seen both of the attacks. In fact, it seems most likely that only one, Karl Ross, actually witnessed the final, fatal attack. This does not excuse the passivity of the handful of neighbors who did see Moseley attack Genovese or hear her screams for help. Nevertheless, as Rasenberger concluded, "whether or not we choose to overlook the inaction of these 38, they were hardly monsters for us to judge with moral superiority. In that situation, would we have behaved differently? According to psychology researchers, maybe not."[19]

But the most shocking testimony at the commemoration came from Rosenthal himself. Retired from the *Times* but still writing a weekly column for the *Daily News*, he was invited by Harold Takooshian, the organizer of the event, to come to the podium at the front of the room from his seat in the audience after the nine panelists had concluded their brief presentations. First thanking literary agent Andrew Blauner, who had seen to it that Rosenthal's book on the Kitty Genovese case was republished in 1999 by the University of California Press, Police Commissioner Murphy (in absentia), for pointing him toward the case, and panelist Charles Skoller, to whom he nodded, for prosecuting "the monster" who killed Genovese, Rosenthal began his comments by insisting, as he looked at Rasenberger, "Yes, thirty-eight!" He then went on to disavow his own story.[20]

Rosenthal stated emphatically that he had "never said, nor did anybody at the *New York Times* say, that there were thirty-eight people peering out of a window. . . . [W]e took the intelligence of the reader to understand that." This shocking admission went unremarked upon at the forum, possibly because Rosenthal provided a deeply personal and moving account of his oldest sister's sudden death from pneumonia decades earlier, a death he referred to as a "murder." "Bess was returning home two nights before New Year's through a path in Van Cortlandt Park when a man, a pervert, exposed himself. She ran, and she ran, and she ran," he recounted, his anger obvious. His sister arrived home in a drenching sweat on the cold winter night. Within two days, she was dead. "I still miss our darling

Bess," he said, "and feel Bess was murdered by this criminal who took her life away, no less than the monster who killed Kitty Genovese." He explicitly linked the loss of his beloved older sister to the death of Kitty Genovese. "What does that have to do with Catherine Genovese? She was Catherine Genovese," he insisted.[21]

Rosenthal's sorrow, more than fifty years after his sister's death, was palpable. Connecting the loss of his sister to his experiences abroad, he offered a deeply personal assessment of the experience of apathy:

> While I was a foreign correspondent in Poland, Nepal, India, Pakistan, and Bangladesh, I remember walking past dead and dying bodies in the streets of Calcutta. What did I do to help? Nothing. It was too bad, and I carried all these things with me. Sometimes, I would carry an apple to give to a beggar. And I ask myself, was there any difference between those thirty-eight witnesses and me? Does God count how many people we pass by? I don't know. But I do know I will never walk past a corpse again, thanks to the valuable lesson I learned from these two noble women—my dear sister Bess and Kitty Genovese.[22]

Despite Rosenthal's powerful personal revelations forty years later, the fact remains that the story of Kitty Genovese had become a worldwide sensation because of the *Times'* explicit and repeated assertions that more than three dozen people had watched her die and done nothing. Rosenthal not only made the number the central point of the story but also titled his book on the crime *Thirty-Eight Witnesses*. When he took the podium at Fordham in 2004, however, he minimized the number and its significance. The creator of the myth of urban apathy debunked the very premise on which it was founded.[23]

The official version of the story lived on despite such potent challenges to it, which continued to mount during the first decade of the twenty-first century. The many questions about the veracity of the tale of thirty-eight witnesses reached popular as well as scholarly audiences. For example, toward the end of the decade a pair of best-sellers helped to expose the exaggerations and omissions of the original story. By then, with crime rates dropping and the numbers of city dwellers increasing, their challenge to the story's emphasis on urban apathy was well received by many people who were seeking new twists on old truisms.

## Unbelievable Stories about Apathy and Altruism

When economist Steven Levitt and writer Stephen Dubner published a follow-up to their first successful book, *Freakonomics*, they took on even more "mind-blowing topics," in the words of one reviewer. For the millions of readers who devoured their 2009 book *SuperFreakonomics*, Levitt and Dubner's assessment of the Kitty Genovese story provided an antidote to the conclusion that "human beings are the most brutally selfish animals to ever roam the earth."[24] After recounting the basic details of the story as constructed by the *New York Times* and reprinting excerpts from the infamous first paragraph of the March 1964 news item, Levitt and Dubner noted that the impact of the article was "immediate and explosive," adding that it had inspired more research than had been done on the Holocaust. They asked, "Does our apathy really run so deep?" Briefly placing the story of the crime in its historical context, they discussed the spike, then drop, in crime rates in the United States since the Genovese killing. Initially, they noted, "the story wasn't big news, especially in the *Times*. It was just another murder, way out in Queens, not the kind of thing the paper of record gave much space." Citing information posted by De May, they detailed the significant facts of the case, such as the early morning hour, the dimly lit street on which Moseley first accosted Genovese, and the location of the second and fatal attack out of view of almost all nearby residents.[25]

Levitt and Dubner's particular contribution to the growing number of challenges to the official story was their focus on the then teenaged Kew Gardens neighbor Michael Hoffman. He had sworn in 2003 in an affidavit that he had heard Genovese's screams, glimpsed Moseley's attack, and yelled for his father, who called the local precinct. Hoffman believed that the police response was slow because what his father reported was not a murder in progress but rather a possible domestic disturbance that appeared to have ended. "The attacker had fled and the victim had walked off, if shakily, under her own power," said Hoffman. With a low-priority call like that, "the cops don't put down the donuts as fast as if it were to come across as a homicide call." While quoting Hoffman, Levitt and Dubner acknowledged that Hoffman, himself a former New York City police officer, and De May "both have an incentive to exonerate their neighborhood from the black eye the Genovese murder gave it."[26]

Yet they also highlighted another important factor that undercut the notion of the supposed apathy of the area's residents—the fact that Moseley's capture in another Queens neighborhood had been due to quick action by residents there—and questioned why this information was rarely included in the story of Kitty Genovese and the thirty-eight witnesses. They concluded on a note of irony: "A man who became infamous because he murdered a woman whose neighbors failed to intervene was ultimately captured because of . . . a neighbor's intervention." By including their challenges to the official version of the story in their best-selling book, Levitt and Dubner added to the increasing public skepticism about the condemnations of the Kew Gardens neighbors in particular and bystander behavior in general.[27]

### The Construction of a Parable

One instance of skepticism Levitt and Dubner cited was a team of psychologists who, in 2007, didn't just air their misgivings about the role of the bystanders in the Genovese case; they labeled the story a parable. British psychologists Rachel Manning, at the University of the West of England in Bristol and Mark Levine and Alan Collins, both at Lancaster University, published an article in the journal *American Psychologist* in which they examined the impact of the official version of the Genovese story on the field of social psychology. In their article, titled "The Kitty Genovese Murder and the Social Psychology of Helping: The Parable of the 38 Witnesses," they argued, "The events of that night in New York in 1964 paved the way for the development of one of the most robust phenomena in social psychology—[Bibb] Latané and [John] Darley's (1970) 'bystander effect' (the finding that individuals are more likely to help when alone than when in the company of others)." After examining extracts of Winston Moseley's trial transcripts and other legal documents associated with the rape and murder of Kitty Genovese, Manning and her team concluded, "The story of the 38 witnesses is not supported by the available evidence."[28]

Their concerns focused on the impact the story had had on social science research, especially bystander intervention research. The team asserted, "We suggest that the story of the 38 witnesses, and its message that groups have a negative effect on helping, has meant that psychologists have been slow to look for the ways in which the power of groups can be harnessed to promote intervention." Manning, Levine, and Collins clarified at the beginning of their paper that they did not intend to upend the pioneering work done by their colleagues. Rather, they wanted to "draw a clear distinction between the story itself" and the decades of research into helping behavior that it had generated. They praised the work of Latané and Darley on the bystander effect, regardless of the inaccuracies in the official version of the story. "It does not matter to the bystander effect that the story of the 38 witnesses may be misconceived," they insisted. "What does matter for the present purposes is the perseverance of the story of the 38 witnesses and the way it has populated and dominated the imagination of those who think about helping behavior in emergencies."[29]

They noted the pervasiveness of the *Times'* version of the events of March 13, 1964, in the ten most commonly used undergraduate psychology textbooks. "The Kitty Genovese story appears in all of them," they found. "In seven books it is accorded its own text box, subsection or picture. In two, the story is used both as an exemplar of helping behavior and as a guide to best practice in research methods. . . . All textbooks give the impression that Kitty Genovese was killed on the street where the murder could be seen by others." Furthermore, "almost all texts suggest that the 38 witnesses watched from their windows as the murder unfolded before them. . . . All claim that nobody intervened, or called the police, until after Kitty Genovese was dead."[30]

Manning and her colleagues detailed the questions that had been raised for nearly a decade about the veracity of the story and concluded, "Thus the three key features of the Kitty Genovese story that appear in social psychology textbooks (that there were 38 witnesses, that the witnesses watched from their windows for the duration of the attack, and that the witnesses did not intervene) are not supported by the available evidence." The psychologists drew on and quoted from many of the published challenges to the official story. They noted that, despite the availability of other versions of the events, social psychology textbooks continued to publicize the account constructed by the *Times*. "It is interesting to speculate why that might be," they stated as they turned to the role of mythmaking as a "byproduct of pedagogy," arguing that it is particularly problematic in psychology. They also challenged the presentation of the Kew Gardens residents as "a group" and proposed that instead they could more accurately be understood a collection of individuals. "This figure of the group as the source of collective inaction," they wrote, must be taken in its historical context. In the story of Kitty Genovese, it is the group's passivity that is dangerous. "By challenging the story of the 38 witnesses," they concluded, "we begin to uncover alternative formulations of the potential of the group in the context of helping behavior."[31]

Not surprisingly, their piece caused controversy in social science circles, and the authors were criticized by other psychologists who had conducted studies of various aspects of bystander inaction. Harold Takooshian, for example, discounted their conclusions that "an iconic event in the history of helping research—the story of the 38 witnesses who remained inactive during the murder of Kitty Genovese—is not supported by the available evidence." It was not, however, the intention of Manning and her team to disparage the findings of social scientists over the years. As they wrote, "By focusing on real life behavior in emergencies—but varying the number of people believed to be present—Latané and Darley were able to argue something which was counterintuitive (for the historical moment), that the presence of others inhibits helping."[32]

Although they contributed to the growing literature that raised important questions complicating the parable of the thirty-eight witnesses, they did not dispel it. As Susan Whitbourne wrote in *Psychology Today* in 2010, "Many introductory psychology classes still use this case to illustrate the bystander effect." She repeated some of the corrections to the official story that by this time were well known: "Some neighbors did try to help but many simply didn't hear or see the crime and there literally was nothing they could have done to save her life. The facts of the story aside, the bulk of research evidence has mounted over the years to substantiate the bystander effect principle. Study after study continues to prove that the larger the crowd, the less likely anyone is to offer help."[33]

Challenges to the story's implications for our understanding of human behavior continue to mount. In 2011 *New York* magazine reported a study co-authored by Brown University psychology professor Joachim Krueger. The team found that being in a group decreases helping behavior except in those situations in which there is a clear and discernable threat. "It's counterintuitive," Krueger was quoted as saying. "As the costs of a behavior become higher, you should be less likely to help." Even more heartening, Krueger said, the study revealed that when the costs of intervention are immediate, physical, and dangerous, "the bystander effect goes away." The article concluded, "Here it's worth noting that the *New York Times* coverage instrumental in enshrining Genovese's murder in legend was less than completely accurate: There may have been just three eyewitnesses to the attack; most neighbors only heard portions of it; it's possible none saw the final assault and murder." The author pointed out that Krueger's findings seemed to indicate that "had there really been thirty-eight people who watched Genovese get attacked, they would have been more likely to come to her aid, not less so."[34]

John Melia had first pointed out many of these inaccuracies more than twenty-five years earlier in his writings in the *Daily News*. They would reappear two years later, this time in the pages of the newspaper that was responsible for the construction of the story. As challenges to the official *New York Times* version increased throughout the first decade of the twenty-first century, one of the most significant came on January 30, 2013, from the Gray Lady herself.

## Timeless Book May Require Some Timely Fact Checking

In a prominent essay in the Books section of the *New York Times*, headlined "Timeless Book May Require Some Timely Fact Checking," Leslie Kaufman began by quoting the well-known phrase "Journalism is meant to be the first draft of history." She continued: "Newspaper articles fit that mold nicely, fading into the archives. But books are not so neat." She noted that the increasing digitization of books provided greater opportunities for the rerelease of older works, "and in some cases the common interpretation of their subject matter has evolved or changed significantly." For Kaufman, a case in point was the recent reissue by Melville House of A. M. Rosenthal's *Thirty-Eight Witnesses: The Kitty Genovese Case*. Noting the book's age and its original publication date only a few months after the murder, she wrote: "It was a gruesome story that made perfect tabloid fodder, but soon it became much more. Mr. Rosenthal, a Pulitzer Prize–winning reporter who would go on to become the executive editor of The New York Times, was then a new and ambitious metropolitan editor for the paper who happened to be having lunch with the police commissioner 10 days after the crime." Kaufman detailed Rosenthal's development of the theme of "community callousness" and the rapidity with which he produced his book, as well as the groundswell of interest it generated. "In the years since, however, as court records have been examined and witnesses reinterviewed, some facts of both the coverage and the book have been challenged on many fronts, including the element at the center of the indictment: 38 silent witnesses. Yet none of the weighty counter-evidence was acknowledged when Mr. Rosenthal's book was reissued in digital form by Melville—raising questions of what, if any, obligation a publisher has to account for updated versions of events featured in nonfiction titles."[35]

Although "for the most part," she wrote, "people in the industry agree that there is not a high burden on a publisher to update books based on new evidence about old events, or even to acknowledge that new facts or interpretations exist," she did note one publisher's decision to add material about the sexual abuse scandal at Pennsylvania State University discovered in 2011 to a book about former football coach Joe Paterno. Interestingly, though she did not mention it, Rosenthal's thirty-eight witnesses theme was invoked in at least one Philadelphia newspaper in reference to the silence of those at Penn State who knew or suspected that sexual molestation was being committed but did not intervene.[36]

Kaufman provided a list of sources, including Melia's 1984 article in the *Daily News* and Jim Rasenberger's 2004 feature in the *Times*, although neither writer was named. She quoted Assistant District Attorney Charles Skoller as well as the literary agent Andrew Blauner, who was instrumental in ensuring that Rosenthal's *Thirty-Eight Witnesses* remained in print. She concluded by quoting Rosenthal's response to Rasenberger: "In a story that gets a lot of attention, there's always somebody who's saying, 'Well, that's not really what it's supposed to be. . . . There may have been 38, there may have been 39, but the whole picture, as I saw it, was very affecting."[37]

One longtime media observer and critic of the *Times, New York Daily News* writer David J. Krajicek, applauded Kaufman's article. He wrote on his blog on January 31, 2013, "The *New York Times*, to its credit, was willing to take on one of its late iconic editors in a story about the infamous Kitty Genovese murder," further noting that Rosenthal's version of the story "was debunked any number of times." Krajicek then reprinted an article he had published in 2011 under the headline "A Random Murder: The Killing of Kitty Genovese." In it, Krajicek flatly stated: "No one saw Moseley 'stalk and stab' Genovese for 30 minutes. Prosecutors said there were as few as six witnesses, and a handful of others heard the scream, which the *Daily News* called 'just the faintest of cries.' Yes, decisive action by a neighbor might have spared Genovese. But the witnesses were more drowsy and confused than apathetic. One was drunk. The father of the teen said he got short shrift when he called cops. One man said he didn't call because he was certain that neighbors had done so. A single quaking couple did admit they chose not to get involved." Beyond adding his voice to the chorus of knowledgeable critics of the thirty-eight witnesses trope, as Rasenberger had done in 2004, Krajicek also provided information about Genovese's life and her lover Mary Ann Zielonko, details that now are included in most updated accounts of the crime.[38]

## 50 Years Later, New York Murder Still Fascinates

In 2014 a flood of articles appeared to commemorate the fiftieth anniversary of Kitty Genovese's death. Most of them disputed the *Times'* original front-page story on the events of March 13, 1964, and many complicated the meaning of the tragedy. Writing for the Associated Press, Karen Matthews declared that Genovese's cries for help "still echo, a symbol of urban breakdown and city dwellers' seeming callousness toward their neighbors." Headlined "50 Years Later, New York Murder Still Fascinates," her article, reprinted in newspapers around the country and throughout the world, led off with the myth of urban apathy. A police historian, Thomas Reppetto, told her that the case "caught the spirit of the time," adding, "It seemed to symbolize that society no longer cared about other people." Matthews then questioned the myth, writing, "While more recent reporting—some of it by the *Times* itself—found that the number of people who actually saw the murder was greatly exaggerated and that some neighbors did try to help, the Genovese case left its mark on public policy and psychology." After reviewing the basic facts of the story and noting its role in the adoption of the 911 system, the passage of "Good Samaritan" laws to protect people who help those in trouble, and the development of the psychological theory of the "bystander effect," she returned to the issue of urban apathy, observing: "The story seemed to show that New York was an urban hell where no one would lift a finger to help a neighbor. 'It fit some people's anti-New York perspective,' said Philip Zimbardo, a retired professor of psychology at Stanford University." Matthews concluded by quoting James Solomon, a writer and filmmaker who had been very close to the Genovese story and, since the late 1990s, to Genovese's brother Bill, with whom he was working on a documentary, *The Witness*, about Bill Genovese's journey of coming to terms with his sister's death. Solomon hoped to ensure that the rich life of Kitty Genovese would be included in the coverage of this anniversary of her death. "She was a daughter and a sister and a lover and a colleague," Solomon said. "She wasn't just a victim."[39]

Some news reports again featured the people who lived in Kew Gardens. For example, reporting for New York 1 Radio News, Ruschell Boone traveled to the area for his update of the story. He left no doubt that neighbors were still defending themselves against the charges of indifference they had endured for decades. "This neighborhood hasn't changed much in fifty years," said Boone, "and neither has the opinion of the people who continue to dispute stories that Kitty Genovese was brutally stabbed on Austin Street while thirty-eight witnesses, most of them from the Mowbray apartment building, did nothing to help." One neighbor, Aaron Adler, told him, "It's a bum rap, yeah." Adler remembered John Lindsay's campaign appearance on Austin Street and added that he "had heard so much about [the people of] Kew Gardens and their lack of sympathy." Boone also interviewed Bill Corrado, who now owns his father's furniture store, still located on Austin Street. In response to a question about indifference, Corrado countered, "It wasn't that type of neighborhood." His father, Anthony, had been a staunch defender of his community. Bill Corrado remembered that his father had been "quite upset" when friends of his said that they had called, or attempted to call, police to report the crime. Boone concluded his short report on a fatalistic note about the resilience of the myth of urban apathy: "Fifty years later, the truth of the original story still appears to be in doubt. But after so many years, it's likely the name Kitty Genovese will continue to raise the image of New Yorkers who didn't care enough to help."[40]

What was striking about the media coverage fifty years after the crime was that, although the errors in the original story have now become part of its telling, no one contrasted the myth of urban apathy with the reality of mobilizations for social change that New Yorkers were then, and still are, engaged in. The social and political activism that helps define the city and sustain its vitality fundamentally relies on involvement. It was in part because such involvement has been an integral aspect of the city's life that the myth of urban apathy caught New Yorkers' attention in the first place.

Epilogue

# KITTY, FIFTY YEARS LATER

Artists as well as activists have been in the vanguard of the promotion of the Kitty Genovese story since its inception. In large part because of their efforts, it endures regardless of increasing challenges to its basis in fact. Through cultural productions—from Phil Ochs's sardonically upbeat "Outside Of a Small Circle of Friends" to Harlan Ellison's gripping short story "The Whimper of Whipped Dogs," from the four-color graphic portrayals in *Watchmen* to the power of LuLu LoLo's reenactment of Mary Ann Zielonko's personal grief—the story of "the dying girl that no one helped" has been transmitted to new generations for five decades.

In the first years of the twenty-first century, two women artists—one a celebrity, the other less well known—utilized the story of Kitty Genovese in new works. Although one relied on the *Times* version and the other acknowledged the questions raised about its accuracy, both of them remind us of the singular impact this crime has had. Singer-songwriter Emmylou Harris recorded "Lost Unto This World" in 2003. It included a reference to Kitty Genovese and extended the questions worldwide: "I was murdered by the high way / And my cries went up in vain." Harris discussed the song online, reiterating the original *Times* version: "I'd been reading this book about America's relationship to international genocide. And it made me think about the slaughter of women, in particular. There's another thing that's been haunting me for years and that is the Kitty Genovese story. This was a girl who was stalked and stabbed over a half-hour period in 1964 while dozens of people heard her screams and watched and didn't even pick up the phone to call the police. That event horrified me. I always thought I wanted to write about it, but it didn't happen until these pieces came together, and I thought about female genocide."[1]

In 2012, on the blog Writing Without Paper, poet Maureen Doallas provided a poignant example of how the story of Kitty Genovese has evolved. Indirectly referring to Mary Ann Zielonko's description of Genovese, Doallas subtly updated the legend. Her closing lines take note of both the controversies and the story's impact: "What's said to have taken / place, what might have / occurred, who saw it all / and acted, or didn't, how / the story made it / to *The New York Times* / and went viral, never was / exactly what anyone claimed / the night of March 13, / when Kitty smiled— / *she had a great smile*— / for the very last time." Doallas wrote about the impact the news of the crime had had on her as a young girl. "Not yet 12 at the time, I well remember the news stories and still get a chill reading about it."[2]

Like Doallas, I find that my reactions to the Kitty Genovese story have not faded with the years. Because of the power of the narrative that was constructed in 1964, most of us now know much more about Kitty Genovese, her killer Winston Moseley, her neighbors, and the power of indifference than we did then. But despite our awareness of the errors and exaggerations, the silences and misplaced blame of the official version, the story still matters. It matters because it raises the central question of how we engage with those around us, individually and collectively, when they need our help.

"That monster is in all of us," Bill Genovese said to a hushed audience in a large meeting room on the third floor of Fordham University's Manhattan campus on a cold, bright Saturday in March 2014. The handsome sixty-something younger brother of Kitty Genovese was seated in his wheelchair behind the table where conference panelists had delivered their remarks about his sister's murder and were now responding to questions and comments. Among the crowd of researchers, writers, filmmakers, students, family, friends, and former neighbors who had gathered for a fiftieth-anniversary commemoration of her death, his comments about her murderer were striking for their thoughtfulness and generosity. Referring to what he described as the physical and psychological deterioration of Winston Moseley in the two months before he spotted Kitty in her red Fiat, Genovese related his experiences as a U.S. marine in Vietnam. "I saw decent people turn into killers, because of the situation they were in," he said. His insights were noteworthy amid some panelists' characterizations of Moseley—at age seventy-nine the longest-serving inmate in a New York penal institution—as an "animal" and a "monster." Bill Genovese emphasized that he did not harbor hate against the man who killed his sister. He reminded those gathered that it is far easier to externalize evil than to acknowledge its existence even in seemingly "normal" people.[3]

This lesson may be the main one that A. M. Rosenthal hoped to teach his readers. The final three sentences of his short book *Thirty-Eight Witnesses: The Kitty Genovese Case* highlight the decisions each person must make when confronted suddenly by someone—a stranger, a neighbor—in need of assistance. "There are, it seems to me, only two logical ways to look at the story of the murder of Catherine Genovese," he wrote in 1964. "One is the way of the neighbor on Austin Street—'Let's forget the whole thing.' The other is to recognize that the bell tolls even on each man's individual island, to recognize that every man fears the witness in himself who whispers to close the window." Rosenthal's depiction of the people who lived in Kew Gardens as uncaring led him to insist that "we" must behave better than "they" did. He marshaled his anger at the Kew Gardens neighbors, as Nicholas Lemann wrote in the *New Yorker* in 2014, in order to "enshrine the apathy narrative."[4]

Rosenthal's construction of the story of indifference rested on the incongruity of the place—a small village-like neighborhood in semi-suburban Queens—and the large number of neighbors—thirty-eight—who watched an attack on an innocent person and did nothing. While the location of the attacks is incontrovertible, the number and nature of the "witnesses" has been in contention for five decades. Almost since the first front-page report was printed in the *Times* on Friday, March 27, 1964—just below the fold and extending for nearly a full page inside the first section, accompanied by large photographs of the neighborhood—people have argued about the

**Figure 15.** The apartment buildings on Austin Street in Kew Gardens, where Kitty Genovese lived and died, as seen from the Long Island Rail Road station. Photo courtesy of the *New York Times*. Used with permission.

number of bystanders or the extent of their knowledge of what had happened. "Since then, everything has pivoted on the 38 witnesses," Bill Genovese told a reporter for the *Daily News* in 2014. "There wouldn't have been a story without that." He added, "I've always wondered about the veracity of the claim."[5]

He is not alone. Two books that claimed to tell the "true story" of the crime appeared among a spate of publications marking the fiftieth anniversary of Kitty Genovese's death. Their authors came to opposite conclusions using essentially the same sources. Both utilized personal interviews as well as police and court documents, but one author, Kevin Cook, supported the assertion, made publicly since the mid-1980s, that the number of actual witnesses to Moseley's two attacks was far smaller than initially reported. Furthermore, Cook took pains to acknowledge the efforts by the Austin Street neighbors who did call the police or go to Kitty Genovese's aid. Catherine Pelonero, by contrast, challenged the "dangerous revisionism" she saw in updated accounts of the case and insisted instead that the original *Times* story was correct. She came to the conclusion that many of

the Kew Gardens neighbors had behaved badly. But as Lemann emphasized in his review of the two books, "The *Times'* version of the Genovese story represents a version of reality that was molded to conform to a
theory."[6] In addition:

> Some of the fascination that racialized, sexualized violence attracts surely
> rubbed off on the story—it became clear from photographs and from other
> outlets that Genovese was white and attractive and that Moseley, a repeat
> rapist, was black—but the gist of the piece lent itself perfectly to Sunday ser-
> mons about a malaise encompassing all of us.
>
> It was a way of processing anxieties about the anonymity of urban life,
> about the breakdown of the restrictive but reassuring social conventions of
> the fifties, and, less directly, about racial unrest, the Kennedy assassination,
> and even the Holocaust, which was only beginning to be widely discussed,
> and which seemed to represent on a grand scale the phenomenon that one
> expert on the Genovese case calls Bad Samaritanism.[7]

Lemann gave credit to Jim Rasenberger, who challenged the hegemony
of the official version of the case in 2004 in the *Times* itself, as well as the
British psychologists Rachel Manning, Mark Levine, and Alan Collins,
whose incisive article in *American Psychology* in 2007 examined how the
group apathy aspect of the story had affected social science research. Lemann did not mention the reporting done by John Melia of the *Daily News*
in 1984, though he did make the all-important point that, in contradiction
to Rosenthal's reputation as an exacting journalist, his "convictions about
the crime were so powerful that he was impervious to the details of what
actually happened."[8]

Lemann's astute assessment of the story helped to close some of the
gaps between the differing accounts of "what actually happened" to Kitty
Genovese on the morning of March 13, 1964. Perhaps most significantly, he
explained some of the motivations behind, as well as the meanings drawn
from, the story's creation. One member of the groundbreaking team of researchers responsible for the development of psychological theories about
bystander behavior did take issue with Lemann's essay. Bibb Latané wrote
to the *New Yorker* to correct the record regarding his team's findings.
"Abe Rosenthal was indeed responsible for creating a myth, as Nicholas
Lemann writes regarding the circumstances surrounding the murder of

Kitty Genovese, but the myth was not, as Lemann suggests, that some three dozen people heard and failed to report screams on a March night fifty years ago," Latané argued. "Instead, it was Rosenthal's insistence that the cause was moral decay, urban alienation, or 'apathy,' which Rosenthal considered a disease, 'a symptom of a terrible reality in the human condition.'" Latané clarified that what he and his colleagues had found was that, "far from being an illness, failure to respond results from social influence, the understanding of which can be used to help individuals act in closer accord with their moral predispositions." He ended his letter by emphasizing that "the myth of apathy was initiated by a headline written after Kitty's murderer had been caught—as a result of a citizen reporting a crime in progress, and the reason the story went viral was that New York and the nation were in the midst of a decade of rising—not falling, social concern."[9]

Further consideration of the myth's impact on social mores—especially regarding sexuality, race, and crime—reveals that sizable gaps remain even in revisionist versions of the story. For example, Lemann's sensitivity regarding neighbor Karl Ross (about whom he wrote, "He was thought to be gay, at a time when gay New Yorkers had a lot to fear, both from attackers on the street and from the police") is rare and commendable. Since 1964 Karl Ross has been the Kew Gardens character everyone loves to hate. It is easy to see why. Ross had been a friend of both Genovese and Zielonko; Kitty called out to him for help when Moseley found her at the bottom of the stairwell leading up to Ross's apartment; and a phone call to police after he glimpsed Moseley assaulting her might have saved Genovese's life. One can only imagine how—or if—Ross has lived with this knowledge and his memories of that early morning nightmare over the years. His inability to overcome his fears, and the deadly impact of his intoxication, cannot have been easy for him to reconcile.[10]

Lemann also reminded readers that "three months before the murder, Rosenthal had assigned a five-thousand-word story that ran on the *Times* front page under the headline 'Growth of Overt Homosexuality In City Provokes Wide Concern.' The fact that Kitty Genovese herself was gay evidently escaped his notice." Yet Lemann's suggestion that Rosenthal somehow did not "notice" that Kitty Genovese was involved in a same-sex relationship lets the legendarily homophobic *Times* editor off the hook. As gay staffers such as Charles Kaiser have documented, Rosenthal's discomfort (at best) with homosexuality was well known at the *Times* during his editorial tenure there. Furthermore, as involved as he was in the story's creation and promotion, it is inconceivable that Rosenthal did not know at least as much about Genovese as the police and prosecutors handling the case did. For him to assert in his writings that "she lived alone" while knowing full well that Genovese shared her apartment and her life with Mary Ann Zielonko can only be explained as an attempt to continue to fit Genovese into an Ideal Victim mold and keep the story's focus on the neighbors' apathy.[11]

Genovese's good friend Angelo Lanzone has said that Rosenthal tried repeatedly to talk with Zielonko after the crime; Zielonko refused his overtures. When she finally did speak to the media in 2004, and the *Times* printed Jim Rasenberger's account of their relationship, it did not escape Rosenthal's notice. In fact, at the 2004 Fordham commemorative conference Rosenthal directly chastised Rasenberger. "I can't believe you outed her—we would not have done that," he said. Rasenberger responded, "Abe, times have changed."[12]

Times have changed with regard to other gender and sexual norms as well. Although the establishment of the 911 emergency response system and the results of psychological research on bystanders are routinely noted in books and articles on the crime's impact, rarely is it acknowledged that the Genovese case changed our understandings of and responses to rape and other forms of misogynistic assaults. Both revisionists and defenders of the official version tend to erase the impact of the Genovese crime on contemporary attitudes toward violence against women, and the responses are still often driven by the race of the victim. The differential media treatment given to Moseley's other victims, especially Anna Mae Johnson, the young African American woman he murdered and raped, persists fifty years after the crimes were committed. This was first brought to my attention in 2011 as I reviewed the official police and court documents in the Genovese case at the Queens County Courthouse in Kew Gardens. A young black female clerk who brought in the Moseley files commented angrily that although there was great interest in Kitty Genovese, no one seemed to care much about his other victim—"the black woman." Her remark startled me then and has only grown in its importance since.

Although he was indicted for both Johnson's and Genovese's murders, Moseley was never prosecuted in the Johnson case despite the heinous details of the crime, which he committed just two weeks before he assaulted Genovese. The case includes serious errors on the part of the Queens medical examiner in misreading gunshot wounds for stab wounds. After Moseley's confession, Johnson's body was exhumed, and a reexamination supported his version of the crime, which both Cook and Pelonero include in detail in their books along with the diagram Moseley drew for police of the murder scene. Yet the district attorney's failure to prosecute him for the Johnson crime is not addressed. Although Moseley has remained imprisoned for decades for his deadly assault on Kitty Genovese, Anna Mae Johnson once again was marginalized. Because Moseley was never formally or legally held accountable for her murder and rape, she and her family never received justice through the court system or in the media.[13]

The initial reports that some of the Kew Gardens neighbors took Moseley's attacks on Genovese as "a lovers' quarrel" and thus did not intervene also failed to elicit public commentary in 1964. It was not until the feminist movement of the 1970s began to redefine sexual assault and intimate partner violence as criminal that such instances of bystander inaction were called into question. This is but one example of how Genovese crime writers have "missed the story," as Peter C. Baker asserted in his fiftieth-anniversary commentary in *The Nation*.[14]

Kitty Genovese's murder and rape inspired a groundswell of organizing in the 1970s and beyond, ranging from anti-rape projects to women's self-defense groups, in direct contradiction to the *Times'* laments about indifference. It helped usher in fundamental shifts in the practices and policies of law enforcement, as well as medical personnel, judges, and politicians, to name and prevent violence against women. In 2014 her death was cited as an influence on the recent reauthorization of the federal Violence Against Women Act, specifically in the provisions that address sexual violence on campus. According to a blog dedicated to "shattering the silence on sexual violence," Genovese's story "became one of the most well-known rape cases in American history and became the quintessential example in advocacy for bystander intervention education. While March 14 [*sic*] has always been associated with a tragic memory, with the enactment of Campus SaVE in 2014, this date will represent both a sad remembrance of the past and a hopeful look towards a safer future." The Campus Sexual Violence Elimination, or Campus SaVE, legislation aims to reform and

**Figure 16.** Sketch of Kitty Genovese by Bill Rose. Image courtesy of Joseph De May. Used with permission.

strengthen sexual assault prevention and response programs at American colleges and universities.[15]

Fundamentally, the dominance of the apathy narrative has meant that urban community organizing campaigns—from the Citywide Committee for Integrated Schools to Occupy Wall Street—are overshadowed in popular memory. Rosenthal's fear of indifference—that "sickness" he warned against so insistently—seems misplaced when we consider the histories of organizing for social justice and the civil rights of people of all colors, races, genders, sexualities, abilities, and ages. Since the mid-1960s, movements to educate about and organize against poverty, crime, mushrooming incarceration rates, police violence, war, immigration restrictions, environmental destruction, and greed have all become crucial parts of the stories we tell of the American people. So too are the efforts of those who resist progressive change and instead mobilize to defend the status quo and the privileges of the select few. But despite fluctuations in the numbers of people involved as well as the strategies and tools used by organizers (Twitter accounts have replaced the Xerox machines of yesterday), we must not discount the realities of activism. Looking back at 1964, a momentous time for individual as well as collective involvement, one wonders: Whose "apathy" was Rosenthal worried about? Was it the white middle- and upper-class *Times* readers who concerned him, many of whom were becoming disaffected with the growing militancy of civil rights activism? Or was his emphasis on individual responsibility a harbinger of the neoliberal policies that soon would define the city, the nation, and the world?

As Nicholas Lemann concluded in his essay, "the real Kitty Genovese syndrome has to do with our susceptibility to narratives that echo our preconceptions and anxieties."[16] In 1964, the story of the deadly assaults on a cold Queens street startled New Yorkers into questioning their notions of safety and security. The many cogent critiques of the story, and the myth of urban apathy that resulted from it, expose the very real fears that the upheavals of the mid-1960s generated among many inhabitants of the nation's largest metropolis. The media's emphasis on the crime as representative of a city in decline revealed both perceptions and realities of a changing New York, but the story struck a chord everywhere. The vulnerability and isolation of contemporary life seemed to be personified by the tale of the young woman who was murdered in public as her neighbors watched and did nothing, regardless of whether or not the story was true.

# NOTES

**Prologue**

1. Martin Gansberg, "37 Who Saw Murder Didn't Call the Police," *New York Times*, March 27, 1964, 1, 38; A. M. Rosenthal, "Study of the Sickness Called Apathy," *New York Times Magazine*, May 3, 1964, SM 24.

2. Jim Rasenberger, "Kitty: 40 Years Later," *New York Times*, February 8, 2004, CY 1, 14.

3. Elaine Tyler May, "Security against Democracy: The Legacy of the Cold War at Home," *Journal of American History* 97, no. 4 (March 2011): 944; Khalil Gibran Muhammad, *The Condemnation of Blackness: Race, Crime, and the Making of Modern Urban America* (Cambridge: Harvard University Press, 2010), 272–73.

4. A. M. Rosenthal, *Thirty-Eight Witnesses* (New York: McGraw-Hill, 1964); reprinted, with a new introduction, as *Thirty-Eight Witnesses: The Kitty Genovese Case* (Berkeley: University of California Press, 1999; New York: Melville House, 2008, 2012). Hereafter cited as Rosenthal, *Thirty-Eight Witnesses*, with the date of the edition in parentheses. Cite here is to the 1999 printing, xxiv–xxv.

5. Martin Gansberg, "37 Who Saw Murder Didn't Call the Police," *New York Times*, March 27, 1964, 1.

6. Memorandum of Law, Respondent's Brief, *People of the State of New York v. Winston Moseley*, Indictment no. 542–64, Queens County Criminal Term, 1964.

7. Ibid.

8. "Queens Barmaid Stabbed, Dies," *New York Daily News*, March 14, 1964, 1; "Woman, 28, Knifed to Death," *Long Island Press*, March 13, 1964, 1; "Queens Woman Is Stabbed to Death in Front of Home," *New York Times*, March 14, 1964, 26.

9. After a few years, Rosenthal's book went out of print, but in 1999 it was updated and reprinted by the University of California Press with a cover that featured Genovese and emphasized the number of purported witnesses to the crime.

10. Rosenthal, *Thirty-Eight Witnesses* (1999), viii.

11. John Melia, interview with author, August 25, 2013 (e-mail and telephone); on the *New York Times'* status as the American "newspaper of record," see Edwin Diamond, *Behind the Times: Inside the New* New York Times (Chicago: University of Chicago Press, 1996), 274, 319; Shannon Martin and Kathleen A. Hansen, "Examining the 'Virtual': Publication as a 'Newspaper of Record,'" *Communication Law and Policy* 1, no. 4 (1996): 574–96; Seth Mnookin, *Hard News: The Scandals at the* New York Times *and Their Meaning for American Media* (New York: Random House, 2004), xii–xiii.

12. Joseph Goulden, *Fit to Print: A. M. Rosenthal and His Times* (Secaucus, N.J.: Lyle Stuart, 1988): 15.

13. Chris Greer, *News Media, Victims, and Crime* (London: Sage, 2007), 21–22.

14. For example, see Keith Soothill and Sylvia Walby, *Sex Crime in the News* (London: Routledge, 1991); Marian Meyers, *News Coverage of Violence against Women: Engendering Blame* (Newbury Park, Calif.: Sage Publications, 1997), and *Mediated Women: Representations in Popular Culture* (New York: Hampton, 1999); Martin Innes, 'Signal Crimes and Signal Disorders: Notes on Deviance as Communicative Action,' *British Journal of Sociology* 55, no. 3 (2004): 335–55.

15. Greer, *News Media, Victims, and Crime,* 22.

16. Gale Miller and James Holstein, eds., *Constructionist Controversies: Issues in Social Problems Theory* (New York: Aldine De Gruyter, 1990).

17. Kathy M. Newman, "Kitty Genovese, American Icon," the Greater Good Science Center, University of California, Berkeley, September 1, 2006. http://greatergood.berkeley.edu/article/item/kitty_genovese_american_icon (accessed January 23, 2013).

18. Rasenberger, "Kitty: 40 Years Later"; Sonia Sotomayor, *My Beloved World* (New York: Alfred A. Knopf, 2013), 111–13; Jeffrey Zaslow, "What We Can Learn from Sully's Journey," *Wall Street Journal*, October 14, 2009, D1; Alan Moore and Dave Gibbons, *Watchmen* (New York: DC Comics, 1986); Michael Schwirtz, "Man in '84 Subway Shooting Faces Marijuana Charges," *New York Times*, November 3, 2013, A28.

19. Rosenthal, *Thirty-Eight Witnesses* (1999), 73.

## 1. Urban Villages in the Big City

1. E. B. White, "Here Is New York," reprinted in *Empire City: New York through the Centuries,* eds. Kenneth T. Jackson and David S. Dunbar (New York: Columbia University Press, 2002), 697.

2. Ibid.

3. Kenneth T. Jackson, introduction to *The Neighborhoods of Queens*, by Claudia Gryvatz Copquin (New Haven: Yale University Press and the Citizens Committee for New York City, 2007), xxii, xxv–xxvii; Mel Watkins, "Rodney Dangerfield, Comic Seeking Respect, Dies at 82," *New York Times*, October 6, 2004, http://www.nytimes.com/2004/10/06/arts/06dangerfield.html (accessed January 13, 2013).

4. Nicole Steinberg, ed., *Forgotten Borough: Writers Come to Terms with Queens* (Albany: State University of New York Press, 2011); "Queens, the Forgotten Borough," n.d., www.nyny.com/neighborhoods/ (accessed July 24, 2013); Jackson, introduction, xxiv, xxvii; Aaron Rutkoff and Nick Abadjian, "Catherine of Braganza: The Fall of a Queen," The Queens Spin, *Queens Tribune,* n.d., http://www.queenstribune.com/anniversary2003/queenscatherin (accessed January 6, 2013).

5. Vincent F. Seyfried and Jon A. Peterson, "Historical Essay: A Thumbnail View," http://www.queensbp.org/content_web/tourism/tourism_history.shtml (accessed July 20, 2013); F. Scott Fitzgerald, *The Great Gatsby* (New York: Charles Scribner's Sons, 1925).

6. Seyfried and Peterson, "Historical Essay: A Thumbnail View."

7. Andrew Wiese, *Places of Their Own: African American Suburbanization in the Twentieth Century* (Chicago: University of Chicago Press, 2004), 149. Sugar Hill was a fashionable residential neighborhood in Harlem.

8. Joanne Reitano, *The Restless City: A Short History of New York from Colonial Times to the Present* (New York: Routledge, 2006), 159–60; Robert A. Caro, *The Power Broker: Robert Moses and the Fall of New York* (New York: Vintage Books, 1975), 773.

9. Eric C. Schneider, *Vampires, Dragons, and Egyptian Kings: Youth Gangs in Postwar New York* (Princeton: Princeton University Press, 1999), 47; Peter Eisenstadt, *Rochdale Village: Robert Moses, 6,000 Families, and New York City's Great Experiment in Integrated Housing* (Ithaca: Cornell University Press, 2010), 81.

10. Joshua B. Freeman, *Working-Class New York: Life and Labor since World War II* (New York: New Press, 2000), 143–44.

11. Michael Jones-Correa, *Between Two Nations: The Political Predicament of Latinos in New York City* (Ithaca: Cornell University Press, 1998), 14.

12. Freeman, *Working-Class New York,* 172–74.

13. Edith J. Cayhill and Thomas Furey, "The Move Is to the Suburbia within the City—Queens," *World Tribune and Sun,* July 11, 1963, quoted in Sylvie Murray, *The Progressive Housewife: Community Activism in Suburban Queens, 1945–1965* (Philadelphia: University of Pennsylvania Press, 2003), chap. 1, n. 10.

14. Freeman, *Working-Class New York,* 172–74.

15. Clarence Taylor, "Conservative and Liberal Opposition to the New York City School-Integration Campaign," in *Civil Rights in New York City: From World War II to the Giuliani Era,* ed. Clarence Taylor (New York: Fordham University Press, 2011), 97.

16. John D'Emilio, *Lost Prophet: The Life and Times of Bayard Rustin* (New York: Free Press, 2003), 338–43, 365–68, 375.

17. Daniel Perlstein, "The Dead End of Despair: Bayard Rustin, the 1968 New York School Crisis, and the Struggle for Racial Justice" in Taylor, *Civil Rights in New York City,* 126; "2nd School Boycott On: Galamison Goes It Alone in Key Test of His Power," *Long Island Press,* March 16, 1964, 1.

18. "8 Queens Schools Target of Pickets," *Long Island Press,* March 16, 1964, 1.

19. "An Open Letter," *Long Island Press,* March 15, 1964, 4.

20. "Parents Off for Albany," *Long Island Press,* March 17, 1964, 9.

21. Taylor, "Conservative and Liberal Opposition to the New York City School-Integration Campaign," 95, 105–8.

22. "Queens Woman Is Stabbed to Death in Front of Home," *New York Times,* March 14, 1964, 26.

23. Claudia Gryvatz Copquin, "Kew Gardens," in *The Neighborhoods of Queens,* 115.

24. Richmond Hills Historical Association, "About Alrick Man," http://www.richmondhill history.org/alrickman.html (accessed January 10, 2013).

25. Copquin, "Kew Gardens," 116.

26. Rosenthal, *Thirty-Eight Witnesses* (1964), 28–29.

27. Ibid. (1999), 7–8.

28. Ibid., xi; Rosenthal, *Thirty-Eight Witnesses* (1964), 17–18.

29. Martin Gansberg, "37 Who Saw Murder Didn't Call the Police," *New York Times,* March 27, 1964, 1, 38.

30. Diana Shaman, "If You're Thinking of Living in Kew Gardens," *New York Times,* March 3, 1985, R8; Jennifer Bleyer, "Café and Society," *New York Times,* January 30, 2005, http://www.nytimes.com/2005/01/30/nyregion/thecity/30blis.html (accessed May 30, 2012).

31. Copquin, "Kew Gardens," 116–17.

32. John Roleke, "Kew Gardens in Queens, New York—Neighborhood Profile," About. com, http://queens.about.com/od/neighborhoods/a/Kew-Gardens-New-York.html (accessed January 7, 2013).

33. Martin Gansberg, "Murder Street a Year Later: Would Residents Aid Kitty Genovese?" *New York Times*, March 12, 1965, 35; Gansberg, "Kew Gardens Slaying: A Look Back," *New York Times*, March 17, 1974, BQLI 1, 15; Steven Malanga, "Why Queens Matters," *City Journal*, Summer 2004, http://www.city-journal.org/html/14_3_why_queens_matters.html (accessed January 31, 2014).

## 2. Hidden in Plain Sight

1. Mary Ann Zielonko, "Remembering Kitty Genovese," SoundPortraits, National Public Radio, March 13, 2004, http://soundportraits.org/on-air/remembering_kitty_genovese/transcript. php (accessed November 12, 2008).

2. Jim Rasenberger, "Kitty, 40 Years Later," *New York Times*, February 8, 2004, CY 1, 14; Edward Weiland, "Kitty Worshipped Life in the City, and Died in Its Lonely Streets," *Long Island Press*, March 14, 1964, 1.

3. Weiland, "Kitty Worshipped Life in the City," 1; Angelo Lanzone, e-mail, July 6, 2010, copy in author's possession. See also Certificate of Marriage Registration, Rocco A. Fazzolare and Catherine S. Genovese, October 22, 1954, City of New York, Office of the City Clerk.

4. James Solomon, comments of William Genovese included in e-mail to author, November 14, 2013.

5. Karen Tongson, *Relocations: Queer Suburban Imaginaries* (New York: New York University Press, 2011), Kindle e-book, loc. 258, 405; Eric C. Schneider, *Vampires, Dragons, and Egyptian Kings: Youth Gangs in Postwar New York* (Princeton: Princeton University Press, 1999), 32–33.

6. Weiland, "Kitty Worshipped Life in the City," 1, 2.

7. Miriam Cohen, *Workshop to Office: Two Generations of Italian Women in New York City, 1900–1950* (Ithaca: Cornell University Press, 1992), 182.

8. Joshua Freeman, *Working-Class New York: Life and Labor since World War II* (New York: New Press, 2000), 167–69.

9. Betty Friedan, *The Feminine Mystique* (New York: W. W. Norton, 1963); Joanne Meyerowitz, "Beyond the Feminine Mystique: A Reassessment of Postwar Mass Culture, 1946–1958," in *Not June Cleaver: Women and Gender in Postwar America, 1945–1960*, ed. Joanne Meyerowitz (Philadelphia: Temple University Press, 1994), 229–62.

10. "Statement by the President on the Establishment of the President's Commission on the Status of Women," December 14, 1961, http://www.jfklibrary.org/Asset-Viewer/Archives/JFK POF-093-004.aspx (accessed November 25, 2013).

11. U.S. Equal Employment Opportunity Commission, Equal Pay Act of 1963 (Pub. L 88-38), http://www.eeoc.gov/laws/statutes/epa.cfm (accessed April 19, 2014).

12. Angelo Lanzone, e-mail, September 10, 2010, copy in author's possession; Angelo Lanzone, interview, December 2, 2010, and January 20, 2011, Las Vegas, transcript in author's possession.

13. Lanzone e-mail and interview.

14. Lanzone e-mail and interview; Mary Ann Zielonko, interview by telephone, July 16, 2009, transcript in author's possession; Jeff Pearlman, "Infamous '64 Murder Lives in Heart of Woman's 'Friend'," Tribune Newspapers. *Newsday*, March 12, 2004. http://articles.chicagotribune.com/2004-03-12/news/0403120260_1_winston-moseley-catherine-kitty-genovese-gay-bar (accessed January 23, 2013). Also found as Pearlman, "Grief Was Private for Public Murder," *Newsday*, March 14, 2004 http://articles.orlandosentinel.com/2004-03-14/news/0403140082_1_ kitty-genovese-talkative-york (accessed June 26, 2010).

15. Pearlman, "Grief Was Private for Public Murder"; Mary Ann Zielonko, "Remembering Kitty Genovese," SoundPortraits, NPR, March 13, 2004, http://soundportraits.org/on-air/remembering_kitty_genovese/transcript.php (accessed November 12, 2008).

16. Zielonko interview; Pearlman, "Grief Was Private for Public Murder"; Liz Goff and Aaron Rutkoff, "Remembering Kitty Genovese," *Queens Tribune,* March 11, 2004, http://www.queenstribune.com/feature/RememberingKittyGenovese.html (accessed February 23, 2011).

17. Claudia Gryvatz Copquin, *The Neighborhoods of Queens* (New Haven: Yale University Press and the Citizens Committee for New York City, 2007), 117; The Big Apple Blog: Crew Gardens (Kew Gardens), June 28, 2008, http://www.barrypopik.com/index.php/new_york_city/entry/crew_gardens_kew_gardens (accessed January 31, 2014).

18. Goff and Rutkoff, "Remembering Kitty Genovese."

19. Ibid.; Lanzone interview; Zielonko interview.

20. Angelo Lanzone, e-mail, July 6, 2010, copy in author's possession; Zielonko interview.

21. Zielonko interview; Rasenberger, "Kitty, 40 Years Later"; LuLu LoLo (Lois Pascale Evans), interview by author, New York, June 21, 2011, transcript in author's possession.

22. Lanzone interview.

23. James Baldwin, "The Male Prison," in *Nobody Knows My Name: More Notes of a Native Son* (New York: Dell, 1962), 157.

24. Robert C. Doty, "Growth of Overt Homosexuality in City Provokes Wide Concern," *New York Times,* December 17, 1963, 1.

25. Daniel Chomsky and Scott Barclay, "The Editor, the Publisher, and His Mother: The Representation of Lesbians and Gays in the *New York Times,*" *Journal of Homosexuality* 60, no. 10 (2013): 1389–1408; Marcia M. Gallo, "The Parable of Kitty Genovese, the *New York Times,* and the Erasure of Lesbianism," *Journal of the History of Sexuality* 23, no. 2 (May 2014): 273–94.

26. Joan Nestle, "Restriction and Reclamation," in *Queers in Space: Communities, Public Places, Sites of Resistance,* ed. Yolanda Retter, Anne-Marie Bouthillette, and Gordon Brent Ingram (San Francisco: Bay Press, 1997), 63. See also Alix Buchsbaum Gender, "Risking Everything for That Touch: Butch-Femme Lesbian Culture in New York City from World War II to Women's Liberation" (Ph.D. diss., Rutgers University, 2014).

27. Ernest Havemann, "Homosexuality: Why?" *Life,* June 26, 1964, 79.

28. "Cross-Currents," *The Ladder* 8, no. 10 (July 1964): 23.

29. For examples of fiction, see Vin Packer [Maryjane Meaker], *Spring Fire* (New York: Gold Medal Books, 1952); Claire Morgan [Patricia Highsmith], *The Price of Salt* (New York: Coward-McCann, 1952); Ann Bannon [Ann Weldy], for Gold Medal Books: *Odd Girl Out* (1957), *I Am a Woman* (1959), *Women in the Shadows* (1959), *Journey to a Woman* (1960), *The Marriage* (1960), *Beebo Brinker* (1962); Valerie Taylor [Velma Nacella Young], for Gold Medal Books: *Whisper Their Love* (1957), *The Girls in 3-B* (1959), *Stranger on Lesbos* (1960), and for Midwood-Tower: *A World without Men* (1963), *Unlike Others* (1963), *Journey to Fulfillment* (1964); Artemis Smith [Annselm Morpurgo], for Beacon Books: *Odd Girl* and *The Third Sex* (both 1959).

30. For examples of nonfiction, see Ann Aldrich [Maryjane Meaker], for Gold Medal Books: *We Walk Alone* (1955), *We Too Must Love* (1958), *Carol in a Thousand Cities* (1960), *We Two Won't Last* (1963); Donald Webster Cory, *The Lesbian in America (New York: Citadel Press, 1964);* Jess Stearn, *The Grapevine* (New York: McFadden Books, 1964).

31. Stearn, *The Grapevine,* 318–19. See also Martin Meeker, *Contacts Desired: Gay and Lesbian Communications and Community* (Chicago: University of Chicago Press, 2006).

32. Zielonko interview; Lanzone interview.

33. Weiland, "Kitty Worshipped Life in the City," 1.

34. Ibid., 2.

35. Zielonko interview.

36. Ibid.; Brent Curtis, "Woman Recalls Partner's Brutal Murder," *Rutland (Vt.) Herald & Times*, March 14, 2004, 1.

37. Curtis, "Woman Recalls Partner's Brutal Murder," 1.

38. Zielonko interview; LuLu LoLo interview.

39. Zielonko interview; Curtis, "Woman Recalls Partner's Brutal Murder," 1.

40. Zielonko interview.

41. LuLu LoLo interview; LuLu LoLo, *38 Witnessed Her Death, I Witnessed Her Love: The Lonely Secret of Mary Ann Zielonko (Kitty Genovese Story)*, http://www.lululolo.com/theater/38witnessed.html (accessed June 22, 2011); Eva Yaa Asantewaa, "Fringe Benefits," *InfiniteBody: Arts, Culture and the Creative Mind*, August 19, 2009, http://infinitebody.blogspot.com/2009/08/fringe-benefits.html (accessed June 22, 2011).

42. Albert A. Seedman and Peter Hellman, *Chief! Classic Cases from the Files of the Chief of Detectives* (New York: Arthur Fields Books, 1974), 123–24.

43. Seedman and Hellman, *Chief!*, 123–24; Julie Lee, letter to the editor, "Misleading and Irrelevant," *New York Magazine*, September 1975, 25.

44. Euan Bear, editorial, "Reclaiming Herstory," *Out in the Mountains*, April 4, 2004, 4.

45. Jim Rasenberger, "Kitty, 40 Years Later," *New York Times*, February 8, 2004, CY sec. 14, 1, 9; see, for example, Diane Anderson-Minshall, "12 Crimes That Changed the LGBT World," *Advocate*, May 7, 2012, www:Advocate.com (accessed May 8, 2012).

46. Bear, "Reclaiming Herstory."

47. Jennifer K. Wood, "In Whose Name? Crime Victim Policy and the Punishing Power of Protection," *NWSA Journal* 17, no. 3 (Fall): 5.

**3. Thirty-Eight Witnesses**

1. "Woman, 28, Knifed to Death," *Long Island Press*, March 13, 1964, 1; "Police Seek Help in Barmaid's Slaying," *Long Island Press*, March 17, 1964, 1.

2. Thomas Noyes and Fred Carpenter, "Suspect Held as Killer of 2 LI Women," *Long Island Press*, March 19, 1964, 1, 2; Wallace S. Sayre and Herbert Kaufman, *Governing New York City: Politics in the Metropolis* (New York: W. W. Norton, 1965), 82–84.

3. Noyes and Carpenter, "Suspect Held as Killer of 2 LI Women"; Hannah Arendt, *Eichmann in Jerusalem: A Report on the Banality of Evil* (New York: Viking Press, 1963); A. M. Rosenthal, *Thirty-Eight Witnesses* (Berkeley: University of California Press, 1999), xiv–xv.

4. Memorandum of Law, *The People of the State of New York v. Winston Moseley*, Supreme Court of the State of New York, Queens County: Criminal Term, Indictment no. 542/64, 7–10; Winston Moseley, "The Years Flew By," memoir dated 1948 and 1949, Aram Boyajian Papers, Columbia University Rare Book and Manuscript Library.

5. David Anderson, "4 Kew Gardens Residents Testify to Seeing Woman Slain on Street," *New York Times*, June 10, 1964, 50.

6. "Queens Man Seized in Death of 2 Women," *New York Times*, March 20, 1964, 21.

7. Thomas Noyes and Fred Carpenter, "Suspect Held as Killer of 2 LI Women," *Long Island Press*, March 19, 1964, 1.

8. "Two Admit Same Slaying, Baffle Cops," *New York Daily News*, March 22, 1964, 1; Rosenthal, *Thirty-Eight Witnesses* (1999), 9.

9. Arthur Gelb, *City Room* (New York: Penguin, 2004), 344.

10. Joseph C. Goulden, *Fit to Print: A. M. Rosenthal and His Times* (Secaucus, N.J.: Lyle Stuart, 1988), 15–17; Edwin Diamond, *Behind the Times: Inside the New York Times* (New York: Villard Books, 1994), Kindle e-book (2013), loc. 3307–3347; Gerald Lanson and Mitchell Stephens, "Abe Rosenthal: The Man and His Times," *Washington Journalism Review* (July–August 1983): 22–28. See also Harrison E. Salisbury, *Without Fear or Favor: The New York Times and Its Times* (New

York: Times Books, 1980); Turner Catledge, *My Life and the* Times (New York: Harper & Row, 1971); Gay Talese, *The Kingdom and the Power* (New York: World Publishing Co., 1969).

11. John Shafer, "The Ugly Genius of A. M. Rosenthal (1922–2006)," *Slate*, May 11, 2006, http://www.slate.com/articles/news_and_politics/press_box/2006/05/am_rosenthal_19222006. html (accessed February 23, 2010); Robert D. McFadden, "A. M. Rosenthal, Editor of The Times, Dies at 84," *New York Times*, May 11, 2006, http://www.nytimes.com/2006/05/11/ny region/11rosenthal.html?pagewanted=all&_r=0 (accessed February 23, 2010).

12. Charles Kaiser, "When the New York Times Came Out of the Closet," NYRblog, *New York Review of Books*, September 25, 2012, adapted from Kaiser's afterword in *On Being Different: What It Means to Be a Homosexual*, by Merle Miller (New York: Penguin Books, 2012), http://www.nybooks.com/blogs/nyrblog/2012/sep/25/when-new-york-times-came-out-closet/ (accessed June 25, 2013); Michelangelo Signorile, "Out at the *New York Times*: Gays, Lesbians, AIDS and Homophobia inside America's Paper of Record," *Huffington Post*, November 28, 2012, http://www.huffingtonpost.com/2012/11/28/new-york-times-gays-lesbians-aids-homophobia_n_2200684. html (accessed June 12, 2013). See also Martin Duberman, *Midlife Queer: Autobiography of a Decade, 1971–1981* (New York: Scribner, 1996), and *Hold Tight Gently: Michael Callen, Essex Hemphill, and the Battlefield of AIDS* (New York: New Press, 2014); James Kinsella, *Covering the Plague: AIDS and the American Media* (New Brunswick: Rutgers University Press, 1989).

13. A. M. Rosenthal, n.d., AMR/4, 12, A. M. Rosenthal Papers, Manuscripts and Archives Division, New York Public Library.

14. Goulden, *Fit to Print*, 26–27, 31.

15. Rosenthal, *Thirty-Eight Witnesses* (1999), 6.

16. Goulden, *Fit to Print*, 38–39; Diamond, *Behind the* Times, loc. 818.

17. Goulden, *Fit to Print*, 43–48; Diamond, *Behind the* Times, loc. 856.

18. Rosenthal, *Thirty-Eight Witnesses* (1999), xii.

19. A. M. Rosenthal, "There Is No News from Auschwitz," *New York Times Magazine*, August 31, 1958, 5.

20. Ibid.; Jack Benjamin, letter to the editor, *New York Times Magazine*, September 14, 1958, 6.

21. McFadden, "A. M. Rosenthal, Editor of The Times, Dies at 84."

22. Rosenthal, *Thirty-Eight Witnesses* (1999), 5.

23. Ibid., xii.

24. Gelb, *City Room*, 340.

25. Ibid., 342–43.

26. Ibid., xii; A. M. Rosenthal, "Please Read This Column!," On My Mind, *New York Times*, November 5, 1999, http://www.nytimes.com/1999/11/05/opinion/on-my-mind-pleasereadthiscol umn (accessed December 24, 2012); McFadden, "A. M. Rosenthal, Editor of The Times, Dies at 84"; Goulden, *Fit to Print*, 92; Lanson and Stephens, "Abe Rosenthal: The Man and His Times," 25; Gelb, *City Room*, 363–65; Robert C. Doty, "Growth of Overt Homosexuality in City Provokes Wide Concern," *New York Times*, December 17, 1963, 1.

27. McFadden, "A. M. Rosenthal, Editor of The Times, Dies at 84"; Gelb, *City Room*. 376.

28. Rosenthal, *Thirty-Eight Witnesses* (1999), xiii, 13; Richard J. H. Johnston, "Mitchell Denies Murdering Girl," *New York Times*, March 5, 1965, 34.

29. Report of District Attorney, Queens County Investigation Bureau, March 20, 1964, Defendant: Winston Moseley, Case no. 542–64, March 23, 1964, Arresting Officer Mitchell Sanz, Detective John Carroll, Assistant District Attorney Phillip J. Chetta, Stenographer J. Bownes. Hereafter cited as Report of District Attorney, Queens County Investigation Bureau, March 20, 1964.

30. Rosenthal, *Thirty-Eight Witnesses* (1999), 9–14.

31. "Suspect Committed in Slaying of Two," *New York Times*, March 26, 1964, 27.

32. Martin Gansberg, "37 Who Saw Murder Didn't Call the Police," *New York Times*, March 27, 1964, 1.

33. Ibid.

34. Ibid., 1, 38; Charles E. Skoller, *Twisted Confessions: The True Story behind the Kitty Genovese and Barbara Kralik Murder Trials* (Austin, Tex.: Bridgeway Books, 2008), 33–35; Rosenthal, *Thirty-Eight Witnesses* (1999), 38.

35. Jim Rasenberger, "Kitty, 40 Years Later," *New York Times,* February 8, 2004, CY, sec. 14, 1, 9; A. M. Rosenthal, comment at "Remembering Catherine 'Kitty' Genovese 40 Years Later: A Public Forum," Fordham University, New York, March 9, 2004, DVD in author's possession; Charles Skoller, comment, "The Kitty Genovese Murder and the Social Psychology of Helping," *Psychology and Crime News,* http://www.crimepsychblog.com (accessed March 11, 2009).

36. Martin Gansberg, "37 Who Saw Murder Didn't Call the Police"; Skoller, *Twisted Confessions,* 33–35; Rosenthal, *Thirty-Eight Witnesses* (1999), 38.

37. Joseph De May, telephone interview by author, March 13, 2009, transcript in author's possession.

38. Charles Mohr, "Apathy Is Puzzle in Queens Killing," *New York Times*, March 28, 1964, 21.

39. Martin Gansberg, "Police to Honor 3 Who Gave Help," *New York Times*, March 31, 1964, 37.

40. Martin Gansberg, "New Way to Call Police Aid Sought," *New York Times*, April 2, 1964, 1.

41. Rosenthal, *Thirty-Eight Witnesses* (1964), 57, 60.

42. Loudon Wainwright, "The Dying Girl That No One Helped," *Life*, April 10, 1964, 21.

43. Ibid.

44. Ibid.

45. Jean-Claude van Itallie, notes for "Woman Murdered," script for *The Murdered Woman*, performed April 17 and 20, 1964, Martinique Theater, New York, Jean-Claude van Itallie and Open Theater Collections, Kent State University Special Collections and Archives, File A45 M8 1964.

46. Sally Banes, *Greenwich Village 1963: Avant-Garde Performance and the Effervescent Body* (Durham: Duke University Press, 1993), 44–45.

47. Mike Boehm, "Theater, Enlightened? That's His Goal," *Los Angeles Times*, October 29, 2004, E30; Gene A. Plunka, *Jean Claude van Itallie and the Off-Broadway Theater* (Newark: University of Delaware Press, 1999), 26; Jean Claude van Itallie, "The Open Theater (1963–1973): Looking Back," *Performing Arts Journal* 7, no. 3 (1983): 31.

48. Thomas Buckley, "Rape Victim's Screams Draw 40, but No One Acts," *New York Times,* May 6, 1964, 38; Kenneth Gross, "Bronx Crowd Deaf to Cries of Beaten Girl," *New York Daily News*, May 5, 1964, 10.

49. John Sibley, "Woman Who Became Involved to Help Police Now Regrets It," *New York Times*, May 11, 1964, 1.

50. Arlene Teichberg, "We Must Care," letter to the editor, *New York Times,* May 16, 1964, SM 22; "Look Closely," *New York Amsterdam News*, July 18, 1964, 20. See also Mohr, "Apathy Is Puzzle," 21; "40 Shun Pleas of Girl in N.Y. after Attack," *Chicago Tribune*, May 6, 1964, 12; "The City: Not Getting Involved," *Time*, May 15, 1964; Jerry Cohen, "Big-City Americans Turn Backs on Distress Calls," *Los Angeles Times*, May 31, 1964, B1; "N.Y. Stabbing Is Re-enacted," *Washington Post*, August 2, 1964, B6; Matt Weinstock, "Other Side of Non-involvement," *Los Angeles Times*, August 9, 1964, 17.

51. Peter Duffy, "100 Years Ago, the Shot That Spurred New York's Gun-Control Law, *New York Times,* January 23, 2011, http://cityroom.blogs.nytimes.com/2011/01/23/100-years-ago-the-shot-that-spurred-new-yorks-gun-control-law/ (accessed January 18, 2013); Richard Mark, "No Weapons for Protection," letter to the editor, *New York Times*, April 1, 1964, 38; John C. Gmelch, "Further Disarming the Citizen," letter to the editor, *New York Times,* April 3, 1964, 32.

52. "Secretary in Queens Stabs Her Attacker; Now Faces Charges," *New York Times*, July 6, 1964, 31; Charles Grutzner, "A Defensive Arm May Be Illegal," *New York Times*, July 7, 1964, 37; Emanuel Perlmutter, "Citizen Weapons Gain Popularity," *New York Times*, July 12, 1964, 38.

53. Weinstock, "Other Side of Non-Involvement," 7. The *Los Angeles Times* featured extensive coverage of the Genovese crime, both in 1964 and in the years following: at least seven stories appeared from May to December 1964 and continued in 1965 and through the next several years. In 1967 one long piece titled "The Kitty Genovese Syndrome" linked apathy to foreign policy, particularly regarding military interventions in Vietnam and the Congo. The coverage in the *Los Angeles Times*, however, generally was more sympathetic to "the witnesses" than was true of other newspapers, including the *New York Times, Washington Post,* and *Chicago Tribune*. In columns written by Paul Coates and Matt Weinstock, in particular, the *Los Angeles Times'* focus was often on the many reasons why bystanders might not involve themselves in dangerous or frightening situations. In addition, in 1965 Coates traveled to Kew Gardens to interview Genovese's neighbors. In his column, datelined "Shame Street, N.Y.," he became one of the first to challenge the myth of urban apathy. Coates wrote: "But it is not entirely true that everybody on this guilty street was afraid to help a dying girl. When I went back there, the other day, I found one woman who doesn't have to share the shame of Austin St. Her name—Greta Schwarz." He then described the efforts Schwarz made to help Genovese after being summoned by Karl Ross. See Paul Coates, "The Crime on Austin Street," *Los Angeles Times*, September 1, 1965, 3.

#### 4. The Metropolitan Brand of Apathy

1. Sarah M. Johnson, "Commitment to Others," letter to the editor, *New York Times,* March 31, 1964, 34.

2. David Singleton, "Apathy to Crime Discussed," letter to the editor, *New York Times,* March 31, 1964, 34.

3. Milton M. Goldman, "Passivity before Crime," letter to the editor, *New York Times,* April 5, 1964, 32.

4. Rosenthal, *Thirty-Eight Witnesses* (1964), 53.

5. A. M. Rosenthal, "Study of the Sickness Called Apathy," *New York Times Magazine,* May 3 1964, SM 24.

6. Ibid.

7. Ibid.

8. Amon Elon, introduction to *Eichmann in Jerusalem: A Report on the Banality of Evil,* by Hannah Arendt (1963; New York: Penguin, 2006), x–xiii.

9. Hans Neisser, letter to the editor, *New York Times,* and response, May 24, 1964, SM 62.

10. Arthur J. Olsen, "Echoes of Nazis Disturb Germans," *New York Times*, February 25, 1963, 3.

11. David Binder, "Blood Shortage Worsening Here," *New York Times*, March 26, 1962, 1; Dr. Graham B. Blaine Jr., "Moral Questions Stir Campuses," *New York Times*, January 16, 1964, 73; Peter Kihss, "Charter Reform: Big Question for City after 25 Years without Change," *New York Times*, October 2, 1961, 26; Joseph C. Ingraham, "Auto Makers Face Critical Six Weeks of '64 Model Year," *New York Times*, September 21, 1963, 26; Clyde H. Farnsworth, "Non-Professionals Quiet," *New York Times*, April 2, 1963, 61.

12. Fred Powledge, "The Student Left: Spurring Reform," *New York Times*, March 15, 1965, 1; Fred Powledge, "N.A.A.C.P. Seeking a Million Voters: Registration Drive Waged throughout the North," *New York Times*, August 23, 1964, 44.

13. For all quotations throughout this discussion, see Rosenthal, "Study of the Sickness Called Apathy," SM 24, 66, 69–70, 72.

14. Joseph De May, telephone interview with author, July 21, 2013; affidavit of Michael Hoffman, www.oldkewgardens.com (accessed February 23, 2010).

15. Report of District Attorney, Queens County Investigation Bureau, March 20, 1964; David Anderson, "4 Kew Gardens Residents Testify to Seeing Woman Slain on Street," *New York Times*,

June 10, 1964, 50; Martin Gansberg, "Murder Street a Year Later: Would Residents Aid Kitty Genovese?" *New York Times*, March 12, 1965, 35, 37.

16. Fred Powledge, "White Liberals Here Extend Fight for Integration," *New York Times*, June 5, 1964, 17; Martin Arnold, "Galamison Bars New Unity Role," *New York Times*, March 31, 1964, 26; introduction, Ellen Lurie Collection, Center for Puerto Rican Studies, Hunter College, City University of New York. In 1993 the Ellen Lurie School P.S. 5, a full-service community school serving children and their families in grades K–5, opened in Washington Heights in partnership with the Children's Aid Society.

17. "The Vietnam Crisis," *New York Times*, February 27, 1964, 30.

18. Rosenthal, *Thirty-Eight Witnesses* (1964), 73.

19. Congress of Racial Equality, "How CORE Views the Fair: Symbol of American Hypocrisy," Elliot Linzer Collection, Civil Rights Movement Archives, Queens College, City University of New York, http://archives.qc.cuny.edu/civilrights/items/show/11 (accessed July 28, 2013). See also Brian Purnell, " 'Drive Awhile for Freedom': Brooklyn CORE's 1964 Stall-In and Public Discourse on Protest Violence," in *Groundwork: Local Black Freedom Movements in America*, ed. Jeanne Theoharis and Komozi Woodard (New York: New York University Press, 2005), 45–76; George Lipsitz, *A Life in the Struggle: Ivory Perry and the Culture of Opposition* (Philadelphia: Temple University Press, 1995); John D'Emilio, *Lost Prophet: The Life and Times of Bayard Rustin* (Chicago: University of Chicago Press, 2004).

20. Lawrence Samuels, *The End of the Innocence: The 1964–1965 World's Fair* (Syracuse: Syracuse University Press, 2007), xvi.

21. After the murders, the Chaney family in Meridian received numerous threats. With assistance from the Goodman and Schwerner families, they moved to New York. In 1966 Goodman's parents, Robert and Carolyn, established an activist foundation to "carry on the spirit and purpose" of their son's life, the Andrew Goodman Foundation; http://www.andrewgoodman.org (accessed February 24, 2014). In 1967 New York's West Side Civil Rights Committee dedicated Freedom Place in honor of Schwerner, Goodman, and Chaney. Ben Chaney established the James Earl Chaney Foundation in 1998 to honor his brother; http://www.freedomsummer.com (accessed February 24, 2014). See Seth Cagin, *We Are Not Afraid: The Story of Goodman, Schwerner, and Chaney and the Civil Rights Campaign for Mississippi* (New York: Macmillan, 1988). See also Hank Klibanoff, "The Lasting Impact of a Civil Rights Icon's Murder," *Smithsonian Magazine*, December 2008, http://www.smithsonianmag.com/history/the-lasting-impact-of-a-civil-rights-icons-murder-92172099/?no-ist= (accessed February 24, 2014).

22. Marilynn S. Johnson, *Street Justice: A History of Police Violence in New York City* (Boston: Beacon Press, 2003), 235.

23. Ibid.

24. Ibid., 236.

25. Malcolm X, "The Ballot or the Bullet," in *Malcolm X Speaks: Selected Speeches and Statements*, ed. George Breitman (New York: Grove Press, 1990), 24–25.

26. Layhmond Robinson, "New York's Racial Unrest: Negroes' Anger Mounting," *New York Times*, August 12, 1963, 1.

27. Martha Biondi, "How New York Changes the Civil Rights Movement," *Afro-Americans in New York Life and History: An Interdisciplinary Journal,* July 1, 2007, reprinted at Fighting for Justice: New York Voices of the Civil Rights Movement, http://www.nyc.gov/html/cchr/justice/downloads/pdf/how_new_york_changes_the_civil_rights_movement.pdf (accessed June 9, 2013).

28. Clarence Taylor, "Conservative and Liberal Opposition to the New York City School-Integration Campaign," in *Civil Rights in New York City: From World War II to the Giuliani Era*, ed. Clarence Taylor (New York: Fordham University Press, 2011), 95; Martha Biondi, *To Stand and Fight: The Struggle for Civil Rights in Postwar New York City* (Cambridge: Harvard University Press, 2003), 286.

29. Brian Purnell, "'Taxation without Sanitation Is Tyranny': Civil Rights Struggles over Garbage Collection in Brooklyn, New York, during the Fall of 1962," in *Civil Rights in New York City,* 53–55.

30. "2,000 in Puerto Rican Rights March," *Long Island Press,* March 2, 1964, 7.

31. "Top Cop Blasts 3 Rights Leaders," *Long Island Press,* March 16, 1964, 1.

32. Malcolm X, "The Ballot or the Bullet," 26.

33. M. S. Handler, "Malcolm X Sees Rise in Violence," *New York Times,* March 13, 1964, 20.

34. Rosenthal, *Thirty-Eight Witnesses* (1964), 8.

35. Ibid., 18, 20–21.

36. Charles E. Skoller, *Twisted Confessions: The True Story behind the Kitty Genovese and Barbara Kralik Murder Trials* (Austin, Tex.: Bridgeway Books, 2008), 35.

37. Ibid., 51–53.

38. Charles Skoller, "The Kitty Genovese Murder and the Social Psychology of Helping," *Psychology and Crime News,* www.crimepsychblog.com (accessed March 11, 2009).

39. Skoller, *Twisted Confessions,* 54–56.

40. Ibid., 65–67.

41. Ibid., 69–72.

42. Memorandum of Law, District Attorney, *People of the State of New York v. Winston Moseley,* Indictment no. 542-64, Queens County Criminal Term, 1964, 12–13.

43. Skoller, *Twisted Confessions,* 76–77.

44. David Anderson, "Moseley Recalls 3 Queens Killings," *New York Times,* June 11, 1964, 30; "Moseley Execution Delayed," *New York Times,* August 11, 1964, 22; Martin Gansberg, "Murder Street a Year Later: Would Residents Aid Kitty Genovese?" *New York Times,* March 12, 1965, 35; Ronald Maiorana, "Genovese Slayer Wins Life Sentence in Appeal," *New York Times,* June 2, 1967, 37.

**5. The City Responds**

1. "Reporters' Group Announces Award," *New York Times,* March 24, 1965, 27.

2. Martin Gansberg, "Murder Street a Year Later: Would Residents Aid Kitty Genovese?" *New York Times,* March 12, 1965, 35, 37.

3. Ibid., 37.

4. Martin Gansberg, "Lindsay, Recalling the Genovese Murder, Deplores Apathy," *New York Times,* October 13, 1965, 35.

5. Ibid.

6. Ibid. Lindsay was quoting Mayor Wagner's comments about citizen involvement made the previous year. See Irving Spiegel, "Neighborly Spirit Asked by Wagner," *New York Times,* May 8, 1964, 42.

7. Martin Gansberg, "Lindsay, Recalling the Genovese Murder, Deplores Apathy," 35.

8. In 2012 the New York City government website announced, "All Time Record Lows for Murders and Shootings." The press release noted: "Comparable murder statistics date back to 1963 when the city recorded 548 homicides. The most murders New York City recorded in a single year was 2,245 murders in 1990—an average of six murders a day. Today, New York City averages closer to one murder a day—even though the city's population has grown by roughly a million people since 1990"; http://www.nyc.gov/html/nypd/html/pr/pr_2012_all_time_records_lows_for_murders_and_shootings.shtml (accessed May 14, 2013).

9. Steven D. Levitt and Stephen J. Dubner, *SuperFreakonomics: Global Cooling, Patriotic Prostitutes, and Why Suicide Bombers Should Buy Life Insurance* (New York: HarperCollins, 2009), 129–30

10. Martin Gansberg, "New Way to Call Police Aid Sought," *New York Times,* April 2, 1964, 1; "Public Is Urged to Report Crimes," *Long Island Press,* April 2, 1964, 1.

11. Martin Gansberg, "Other City Police Heed Calls Fast," *New York Times*, April 4, 1964, 33.

12. Rosenthal, *Thirty-Eight Witnesses* (1964), 57.

13. "Harlem Paper Asks for Board," *New York Times,* July 22, 1964, 19.

14. Ibid.

15. Jonathan Simon, "Governing through Crime Metaphors," in *Brooklyn Law Review* 67 (Summer 2002): 1055–56.

16. Theodore Jones, "A Call to 440-1234 Now Brings Police," *New York Times*, November 11, 1964, 1; Nicholas A. Addams, letter to the editor, *New York Times*, November 17, 1964, 40.

17. "The Evolution and Development of Police Technology," Seaskate, Inc., Washington, D.C., July 1, 1998, prepared for the National Committee on Criminal Justice Technology, National Institute of Justice.

18. David Burnham, "Dial 911 for the Police in City Starting Monday" *New York Times*, June 27, 1968, 35.

19. Gary Allen, "The History of the 911 Emergency Telephone Number," *Dispatch Magazine*, http://www.911dispatch.com/911/history/ (accessed July 18, 2011); Michael R. Curry, David J. Phillips, and Priscilla M. Regan, "Emergency Response Systems and the Creeping Legibility of People and Places," *Information Society* 20, no. 5 (November–December 2004): 357–69.

20. David Burnham, "Police Emergency Center Dedicated by Mayor," *New York Times*, July 2, 1968, 43.

21. "Success of 911 Puts Strain on Police Here," *New York Times*, November 29, 1968, 35.

22. "One Witness Better Than 38 in a Crisis, Study Here Shows," *New York Times*, July 10, 1966, 56.

23. "Study of a Slaying Brings Award to 2," *New York Times*, December 29, 1968, 31; Bibb Latané and John Darley, "Bystander 'Apathy,' " *American Scientist* 57, no. 2 (Summer 1969): 244–68.

24. Latané and Darley, "Bystander 'Apathy,' " 245.

25. Ibid., 266.

26. Harold Takooshian, "Remembering Catherine 'Kitty' Genovese 40 Years Later: A Public Forum," *Journal of Social Distress and the Homeless* 5, no. 1 (January 2005): 68–70.

27. Stanley Milgram and Paul Hollander, "The Murder They Heard," *The Nation*, January 15, 1965, 602–4.

28. Phil Ochs, "Outside Of a Small Circle of Friends," *Pleasures of the Harbor*, CD (A & M Records, 1967).

29. Rollo May, *Love and Will* (New York: W. W. Norton, 1969), quoted in Harlan Ellison, "The Whimper of Whipped Dogs," in *Deathbird Stories* (1975; E-Reads 2009), Loc. 483 of 5200.

30. "Block Associations Ease Brooklyn Tension," *Atlanta Daily World* (via National Negro Press Association), April 2, 1949, 6.

31. "Block Group Plans Own Cleanup," *New York Amsterdam News*, March 14, 1964, 9.

32. Ian Alterman, "From Tragedy a Sense of Community: One Aftermath of the Genovese Murder," letter to the editor, *New York Times*, February 15, 2004, CY 11; Paul Berger, "Here, They Really Do Know Your Name," *New York Times*, June 4, 2006, http://query.nytimes.com/gst/fullpage.html?res=9E01E5DD1731F937A35755C0A9609C8B63&module=Search&mabRewa rd=relbias%3Ar (accessed January 25, 2014).

33. Christina Hanhardt, "Butterflies, Whistles, and Fists: Gay Safe Street Patrols and the New Gay Ghetto, 1976–1981," *Radical History Review*, Queer Futures Issue 2008, no. 100 (Winter 2008): 61–85; Werner J. Einstadter, "Citizen Patrols: Prevention or Control?" *Crime and Social Justice* 21–22 (January 1984): 200–212.

34. Douglas D. Perkins, Paul Florin, Richard C. Rich, Abraham Wandersman, and David M. Chavis, "Participation and the Social and Physical Environment of Residential Blocks: Crime and Community Context," *American Journal of Community Psychology* 18, no. 1 (February 1990): 83–115.

35. Martin Gansberg, "Kew Gardens Slaying: A Look Back," *New York Times*, March 17, 1974, BQLI 1, 15.

36. Curtis Sliwa, remarks at "Remembering Catherine 'Kitty' Genovese 40 Years Later: A Public Forum," Fordham University, New York, March 9, 2004, DVD in author's possession.

37. "Guardian Angels—Keeping It Safe," http://www.guardianangels.org/safety.php (accessed July 1, 2013).

38. Einstadter, "Citizen Patrols: Prevention or Control?" 201; Dareh Gregorian, "Curtis Sliwa, Guardian Angels Founder, Testifies He Can't Pay Ex $13G a Month," *New York Daily News*, December 9, 2013, http://www.nydailynews.com/new-york/curtis-sliwa-pay-13-000-month-article-1.1542705 (accessed March 12, 2014); David Gonzalez, "Sliwa Admits Faking Crimes for Publicity," *New York Times*, November 25, 1992, B1, B2.

39. John Avlon, "Crime Watch Groups Viewed Suspiciously after Trayvon Martin Killing," *The Daily Beast*, March 26, 2012, http://www.thedailybeast.com/articles/2012/03/26/crime-watch-groups-viewed-suspiciously-after-trayvon-martin-killing.html (accessed April 26, 2014).

40. Winston Moseley, "Today I'm a Man Who Wants to Be an Asset," *New York Times*, April 16, 1977, 15.

41. Bob Herbert, "Kitty Witnesses Still Refuse to 'Get Involved,'" *New York Daily News*, October 1979; Greg Smith, "Kitty Killer: I'm Victim Too Says Notoriety Causes Him Hurt," *New York Daily News*, August 5, 1995, http://www.nydailynews.com/archives/news/kitty-killer-victim-notoriety-hurt-article-1.697583 (accessed March 10, 2014); Michael Gannon, "Genovese Murderer Denied Parole Again," *Queens Chronicle*, November 17, 2011, http://www.qchron.com/editions/queenswide/genovese-murderer-denied-parole-again/article_9e1cb892-5637-5713-9c33-db14de0d6b99.html (accessed March 10, 2014).

42. Joel Greenberg, "Why Do Some People Turn Away from Others in Trouble?" *New York Times*, July 14, 1981 http://www.nytimes.com/1981/07/14/science/why-do-some-people-turn-away-from-others-in-tr.html?module=Search&mabReward=relbias%3Ar (accessed March 2, 2014).

43. Ibid.

## 6. Surviving New City Streets

1. David Harvey, "The Neoliberal City," lecture, Dickinson College, February 1, 2007, https://www.youtube.com/watch?v=rfd5kHb-Hc8&feature=em-share_video_user (accessed May 10, 2014). See also David Harvey, *A Brief History of Neoliberalism* (New York: Oxford University Press, 2005); and Jason Hackworth, *The Neoliberal City: Governance, Ideology, and Development in American Urbanism* (Ithaca: Cornell University Press, 2007).

2. Elizabeth Bernstein and Janet R. Jakobsen, introduction, "Gender, Justice, and Neoliberal Transformations," *The Scholar & Feminist Online*, no. 11.1–11.2 (Fall 2012–Spring 2013), http://sfonline.barnard.edu/gender-justice-and-neoliberaltransformations/introduction/ (accessed May 11, 2014).

3. Harvey, "The Neoliberal City"; Glynis Daniels and Michael H. Schill, *State of the City's Housing and Neighborhoods, 2001* (New York: New York University, Center for Real Estate and Public Policy, NYU School of Law, 2001), 1.

4. Blake Fleetwood, "The New Elite and an Urban Renaissance," *New York Times Magazine*, January 14, 1979, 22, 26.

5. Ibid., 22.

6. See, for example, accounts of community organizing to rebuild a devastated South Bronx in the mid- to late 1970s in Alexander von Hoffman, *House by House, Block by Block: The Rebirth of America's Urban Neighborhoods* (New York: Oxford University Press, 2003), 23–32.

7. Ibid., 26, 34. See also Judith Rossner, *Looking for Mr. Goodbar* (New York: Simon & Schuster, 1975). Like the novel from which it was adapted, the 1977 film of the same name, starring Diane Keaton and Richard Gere, and directed by Richard Brooks for Paramount Pictures, tells of the murder of a young white woman who works during the day as a dedicated schoolteacher while

frequenting the bars and discos at night searching for male sex partners. See also Sady Doyle, "Kill Me Maybe: 1975's *Looking for Mr. Goodbar* and the Never-Ending Panic over Young Women and Casual Sex," *Slate Book Review*, June 12, 2012, http://www.slate.com/articles/arts/books/2012/06/girls_and_sex_once_more_looking_for_mr_goodbar_.html (accessed May 11, 2014).

8. Estelle B. Freedman, *Redefining Rape: Sexual Violence in the Era of Suffrage and Segregation* (Cambridge: Harvard University Press, 2013), 276–77.

9. Maria Bevacqua, *Rape on the Public Agenda: Feminism and the Politics of Sexual Assault* (Boston: Northeastern University Press, 2000), 32; Susan Brownmiller, *Against Our Will: Men, Women, and Rape* (New York: Fawcett Columbine, 1975), 8, 198–199.

10. Brownmiller, *Against Our Will*, 206, 200.

11. Martin Gansberg, "Genovese Killer Is Hunted Widely," *New York Times*, March 20, 1968, 35; Maurice Carroll, "Genovese Slayer Yields Gun, Gives Up," *New York Times*, March 22, 1968, 1; "Hostage Held Captive by Moseley Called in Buffalo Inquiry," *New York Times*, April 23, 1968, 30.

12. Albert A. Seedman and Peter Hellman, *Chief! Classic Cases from the Files of the Chief of Detectives* (New York: Arthur Fields Books, 1974), 110.

13. Angela Y. Davis, "Myth of the Black Rapist," in *Women, Race, and Class* (New York: Random House, 1981), 172–201. In her award-winning book *At the Dark End of the Street: Black Women, Rape, and Resistance—A New History of the Civil Rights Movement from Rosa Parks to the Rise of Black Power* (New York: Knopf, 2010), historian Danielle L. McGuire updated the history of black women's activism against sexual violence.

14. Robert D. McFadden, "A Model's Dying Screams Are Ignored at the Site of Kitty Genovese's Murder," *New York Times*, December 27, 1974, 1, 46.

15. Ibid., 46; Selwyn Raab, "Police Seek Ex-Boyfriend of Slain Woman in Queens," *New York Times*, December 28, 1974, 27; Emanuel Perlmutter, "Suspect Gives Up in Queens Slaying," *New York Times*, December 29, 1974, GN 1.

16. Freedman, *Redefining Rape*, 278.

17. Jane Loader, "Exposing the Rapist Next Door," *Seven Days*, April 25, 1977; "Kitty Genovese Memorial Project," newsletter, March 8, 1977, Boston Women's Health Book Collective Records, ser. 10, Arthur and Elizabeth Schlesinger Library on the History of Women in America, Radcliffe Institute for Advanced Study, Harvard University.

18. Kitty Genovese Memorial Anti-Rape Collective, *Disarm the Rapist!* (East Lansing, Mich., 1977), American Radicalism HV6558.K5, Michigan State University Special Collections.

19. Frances Cherry, "Kitty Genovese and Culturally Embedded Theorizing," in *The "Stubborn Particulars" of Social Psychology* (London: Routledge, 1995), 20–21. See my discussion of Latané and Darley in chapter 5.

20. Helen Benedict, *Virgin or Vamp: How the Press Covers Sex Crimes* (New York: Oxford University Press, 1992), 89.

21. Ibid., 92–94, 131–134.

22. Rosenthal, *Thirty-Eight Witnesses* (Berkeley: University of California Press, 1999), xiv–xv.

23. Benedict, *Virgin or Vamp*, 92–93, 94.

24. Ellen Goodman, "Crimes of Uninvolvement," *Boston Globe*, March 8, 1984, 19.

25. Maureen Dowd, "20 Years after the Murder of Kitty Genovese, the Question Remains: Why?" *New York Times*, March 12, 1984, B1, B4.

26. Dorchen Leidholdt, "People Indifferent to Violence Against Women," letter to the editor, *New York Times*, March 20, 1984, 22.

27. Esta Soler, "How We Turned the Tide on Domestic Violence (Hint: The Polaroid Helped)," TED talk, December 2013, transcript in author's files, http://www.ted.com/talks/esta_soler_how_we_turned_the_tide_on_domestic_violence_hint_the_polaroid_helped/transcript (accessed April 4, 2014).

28. Carrie A. Rentschler, *Second Wounds: Victims' Rights and the Media in the U.S.* (Durham: Duke University Press, 2011), 5, 34; Benedict, *Virgin or Vamp,* 98–99.

29. bell hooks, *Killing Rage, Ending Racism* (New York: Henry Holt and Co., 1995), 51, 56.

30. "Apathy Reduced, Conferees Report," *New York Newsday,* March 11, 1984, 30.

31. Larry P. Gross, *Up from Invisibility: Lesbians, Gay Men, and the Media in America* (New York: Columbia University Press, 2002), 95–96.

32. Martin Duberman, *Midlife Queer* (New York: Scribner, 1996), 227.

33. Barbara Gittings, "The Vote That 'Cured' Millions," *Gay and Lesbian Review Worldwide* 14, no. 4 (2007): 17–18; Richard D. Lyons, "Psychiatrists, in a Shift, Declare Homosexuality No Mental Illness," *New York Times,* December 16, 1973, 1. See also Charles Kaiser, "When the *New York Times* Came Out of the Closet," *New York Review of Books,* September 25, 2012, http://www.nybooks.com/blogs/nyrblog/2012/sep/25/ (accessed June 22, 2013); Michelangelo Signorile, "Out at the *New York Times*: Gays, Lesbians, AIDS and Homophobia inside America's Paper of Record," Huffington Post, November 28, 2012, http://www.huffingtonpost.com/2012/11/28/new-york-times-gays-lesbians-aids-homophobia_n_2200684.html (accessed June 12, 2013).

34. Martin Duberman, *Hold Tight Gently: Michael Callen, Essex Hemphill, and the Battlefield of AIDS* (New York: New Press, 2014), 49.

35. Ibid., 55, 60; Robin Marantz Henig, "AIDS: A New Disease's Deadly Odyssey," *New York Times Magazine,* February 6, 1983, http://www.nytimes.com/1983/02/06/magazine/aids-a-new-disease-s-deadly-odyssey.html (accessed March 16, 2014) . For interviews with surviving members of the AIDS Coalition to Unleash Power (ACTUP/New York), see the ACT UP Oral History Project coordinated by Jim Hubbard and Sarah Schulman, http://www.actuporalhistory.org/index1.html (accessed August 25, 2014).

36. Jennifer Brier, " 'Save Our Kids, Keep AIDS Out': Anti-AIDS Activism and the Legacy of Community Control in Queens, New York," *Journal of Social History* 39, no. 4 (Summer 2006): 965–87. See also Jennifer Brier, *Infectious Ideas: U.S. Political Responses to the AIDS Crisis* (Durham: University of North Carolina Press, 2009).

37. Jennifer Brier, " 'Save Our Kids, Keep AIDS Out,' " 974–75.

38. James O'Ehley, "Kitty Genovese and The Watchmen," Sci-Fi Movie Page, http://www.scifimoviepage.com/upcoming/previews/watchment-1.html (accessed February 7, 2013).

39. Alan Moore and Dave Gibbons, *Watchmen* (New York: DC Comics, 1986), chap. 6, 10.

40. Ibid.

41. Esther B. Fein, "Angry Citizens in Many Cities Supporting Goetz," *New York Times,* January 7, 1985, http://www.nytimes.com/1985/01/07/nyregion/angry-citizens-in-many-cities-supporting-goetz.html (accessed January 25, 2014).

42. Douglas Martin. "Kitty Genovese: Would New York Still Turn Away?" *New York Times,* March 11, 1989, http://www.nytimes.com/1989/03/11/nyregion/about-new-york-kitty-genovese-would-new-york-still-turn-away.html (accessed January 25, 2014).

43. Sam Roberts, "When Crimes Become Symbols," *New York Times,* May 7, 1989 http://www.nytimes.com/1989/05/07/weekinreview/the-region-when-crimes-become-symbols.html (accessed February 1, 2014). See also Roberts, "A Racial Attack That, Years Later, Is Still Being Felt," City Room, *New York Times,* December 18, 2011, http://cityroom.blogs.nytimes.com/2011/12/18/a-racial-attack-that-years-later-is-still-being-felt/ (accessed March 14, 2014). The five men convicted in the 1989 Central Park rape case were exonerated in 2002 after DNA evidence was matched to an assailant, Matias Reyes, who had never been considered a suspect but was in jail for other physically violent crimes. In 2003, Antron McCray, Raymond Santana Jr., Kevin Richardson, Yusef Salaam, and Kharey Wise filed a lawsuit against the city of New York for malicious prosecution, emotional distress, and racial discrimination. They sued for $50 million each. For the next ten years, the city fought the lawsuit but in June 2014 agreed to a settlement. See Benjamin Weiser,

"5 Exonerated in Central Park Jogger Case Agree to Settle Suit for $40 Million," *New York Times*, June 19, 2014 http://www.nytimes.com/2014/06/20/nyregion/5-exonerated-in-central-park-jog ger-case-are-to-settle-suit-for-40-million.html (accessed September 1, 2014).

44. Rosenthal, *Thirty-Eight Witnesses* (1964), 16.

45. William Glaberson. "Chilled by Violence, New Yorkers Are Questioning Life in Their City," *New York Times*, September 16, 1990 http://www.nytimes.com/1990/09/16/nyregion/ chilled-by-violence-new-y . . . ning-life-in-their-city.html (accessed January 25, 2014).

46. Steven Malanga, "Why Queens Matters," *City Journal*, 2004, http://www.city-journal.org/ html/14_3_why_queens_matters.html (accessed January 31, 2014).

47. A. M. Rosenthal. "The Way She Died," *New York Times*, March 15, 1994, A23.

48. Michael Cooper, "Homicides Decline below 1964 Level in New York City," *New York Times*, December 24, 1998, B7.

49. Marilynn S. Johnson, *Street Justice: A History of Police Violence in New York City* (Boston: Beacon Press, 2003), 291–92.

50. James Q. Wilson and George Kelling, "Broken Windows," *The Atlantic*, February 1982 http://www.theatlantic.com/magazine/archive/1982/03/broken-windows/304465/ (accessed February 1, 2014); Johnson, *Street Justice*, 291–92.

51. Johnson, *Street Justice*, 286.

52. Ibid., 292. See also Tanya Erzen, "Turnstile Jumpers and Broken Windows," in *Zero Tolerance: Quality of Life and the New Police Brutality in New York City*, ed. Andrea McArdle and Tanya Erzen (New York: New York University Press, 2001), 19–49 and Aaron S. Lorenz, "The Windows Remain Broken: How Zero Tolerance Destroyed Due Process," *Public Integrity* 12, no. 3 (Summer 2010): 247–59. In 2013 New York federal court judge Shira Scheindlin declared stop-and-frisk policies unconstitutional because of racially discriminatory application. *Floyd v. City of New York*, 813 F.Supp.2d 457 (2013).

53. Cooper, "Homicides Decline below 1964 Level in New York City," B7.

54. Karmen quoted ibid.

55. Jonathan Simon, "Consuming Obsessions: Housing, Homicide, and Mass Incarceration since 1950," *University of Chicago Legal Forum* (2010): 165, http://scholarship.law.berkeley.edu/ facpubs/436 (accessed November 22, 2013).

### 7. Challenging the Story of Urban Apathy

1. New York Crime Rates, 1960–2012, the Disaster Center (Sources: Federal Bureau of Investigation, Uniform Crime Reports), http://www.disastercenter.com/crime/nycrime.html (accessed January 18, 2014).

2. Martin Gansberg, "Kew Gardens Slaying: A Look Back," *New York Times*, March 17, 1974, BQLI 1, 15.

3. Glenn Collins, "Heroism in Modern Times," *New York Times*, May 3, 1982, http://www.ny times.com/1982/05/03/style/relationships-heroism-in-modern-times.html (accessed February 23, 2013).

4. Kenneth Gross, "Neighborhood Wound That Refuses to Heal," *New York Newsday*, March 11, 1984, 4.

5. Ibid., 17.

6. Ibid.

7. John Melia and Don Singleton, "Kitty's Death Still Haunts Us," *New York Daily News*, March 11, 1984, 23.

8. Maureen Dowd, "20 Years after the Murder of Kitty Genovese, the Question Remains: Why?" *New York Times*, March 12, 1984, B1, B4.

9. Ibid., B4.

10. "The Night That 38 Stood By as a Life Was Lost," *New York Times*, March 12, 1984, B1.

11. Ibid.

12. John Melia, "Stigma Remains from Genovese Case," *New York Daily News*, March 11, 1984.

13. Ibid.

14. Ibid.

15. Joseph De May, "Kitty Genovese: What You Think You Know about The Case May Not Be True," A Picture History of Old Kew Gardens, http://web.archive.org/web/20060616232708/http://oldkewgardens (accessed March 6, 2007).

16. Brooke Gladstone, interview with Joseph De May, "The Witnesses That Didn't," *On The Media with Brooke Gladstone*, WNYC, March 27, 2009, http://www.onthemedia.org/story/131359-the-witnesses-that-didnt/transcript/ (accessed March 27, 2009).

17. Jim Rasenberger, "Why Does Her Tragedy Touch Us So Deeply?" remarks at "Remembering Catherine 'Kitty' Genovese 40 Years Later: A Public Forum," Fordham University, New York, March 9, 2004, DVD in author's possession.

18. Ibid., emphasis added.

19. Rasenberger, "Kitty—40 Years Later," *New York Times*, February 8, 2004, CY 1, 14; Rasenberger, "Why Does Her Tragedy Touch Us So Deeply?"

20. A. M. Rosenthal, comments at "Remembering Catherine 'Kitty' Genovese 40 Years Later."

21. Ibid.

22. Ibid.

23. To my knowledge, Rosenthal's disavowal of the number of witnesses to the Genovese murder was never reported. It is not part of the printed summaries of presentations at the 2004 Fordham University commemorative forum, although his comments are included in the filmed record of the event. At the Fordham commemoration, Rosenthal appeared physically debilitated and used a cane to walk; he died two years later, on May 10, 2006. He had stepped down as executive editor of the *New York Times* in 1987, but he published three separate articles substantially about or referring to the Kitty Genovese murder in his weekly column, "On My Mind," in the *Times*: "The 39th Witness," February 12, 1987; "Question to a Judge," November 27, 1987; and "The Way She Died," March 15, 1994. In each of them he adhered to the "thirty-eight witnesses" theme of the *Times'* original 1964 front-page report of the crime.

24. Steven D. Levitt and Stephen J. Dubner, *SuperFreakonomics: Global Cooling, Patriotic Prostitutes and Why Suicide Bombers Should Buy Life Insurance* (New York: HarperCollins, 2009), 98; James Altucher, "The Secrets of SuperFreakonomics," *Wall Street Journal*, October 22, 2009, http://blogs.wsj.com/wealth-manager/2009/10/22/the-secrets-of-superfreakonomics (accessed February 23, 2013).

25. Levitt and Dubner, *SuperFreakonomics,* 104, 124–28.

26. Ibid., 129–30.

27. Ibid.

28. Rachel Manning, Mark Levine, and Alan Collins, "The Kitty Genovese Murder and the Social Psychology of Helping: The Parable of the 38 Witnesses," *American Psychologist* 62, no. 6 (September 2007): 555 .

29. Ibid., 556.

30. Ibid. 557. The textbooks they listed were authored by Aronson, 1988; Aronson, Wilson, and Akert, 2005; Baron and Byrne, 2003; Brehm, Kassim, and Fein, 2002; Brown, 1986; Franzoi, 2003; Hogg and Vaughan, 2005; Moghaddam, 1998; Myers, 2005; and Sabini, 1995.

31. Ibid., 559, 560.

32. Rachel Manning, Mark Levine, and Alan Collins, "The Legacy of the 38 Witnesses and the Importance of Getting History Right," *American Psychologist* 63, no. 6 (September 2008): 561.

33. Susan Krauss Whitbourne, "Fulfillment at Any Age: Why and How Do We Help?" *Psychology Today Online*, September 28, 2010, http://www.psychologytoday.com/blog/fulfillment-any-age/201009/why-and-how-do-we-help (accessed July 10, 2013).

34. Claude Brodesser-Akner, "Innocent Bystanders: 'Genovese Syndrome,' Amended," *New York Magazine*, http://nymag.com/news/intelligencer/catherine-susan-genovese-2011-10/ (accessed July 5, 2012).

35. Leslie Kaufman, "Timeless Book May Require Some Timely Fact Checking," *New York Times*, January 30, 2013, http://www.nytimes.com/2013/01/31/books/releasing-old-nonfiction-books-when-facts-have-changed.html?emc=etal&_r=0 (accessed January 31, 2013).

36. Ibid.; Bill Conlin, "When I'm King of the World . . . ," *Philadelphia Daily News*, November 11, 2011, www.philly.com (accessed July 11, 2012).

37. Kaufman, "Timeless Book May Require Some Timely Fact Checking."

38. David J. Krajicek, "38 Witnesses: Another Look at the Murder of Kitty Genovese," Good Reads blog, http://www.goodreads.com/author_blog_posts/3645531-38-witnesses (accessed July 11, 2013); David J. Krajicek, "A Random Murder: The Killing of Kitty Genovese," *New York Daily News*, March 13, 2011, 51.

39. Karen Matthews, "50 Years Later, New York Murder Still Fascinates," Associated Press, March 11, 2014, http://hosted.ap.org/dynamic/stories/U/US/KITTY_GENOVESE (accessed March 18, 2014).

40. Ruschell Boone, "Residents, New Book Challenge Controversy Surrounding Kitty Genovese's Death," NY1, March 13, 2014, http://www.ny1.com/content/news/205181/residents–new-book-challenge-controversy-surrounding-kitty-genovese-s-death (accessed March 18, 2014).

### Epilogue: Kitty, Fifty Years Later

1. Emmylou Harris, "Lost Unto This World," *Stumble Into Grace,* DVD (Nonesuch Records, 2003). For Harris's comments, see http://www.emmylou.net/ehsongs.html (accessed March 18, 2014).

2. Maureen Doallas, "Kitty Genovese," Writing Without Paper blog, posted March 20, 2012, http://writingwithoutpaper.blogspot.com/2012/03/kitty-genovese-poem.html (accessed January 23, 2013).

3. William (Bill) Genovese, comments at "Kitty Genovese Memorial Conference," Fordham University, New York, March 8, 2014, notes in author's possession. See also Abbe Smith, "The 'Monster' in All of Us: When Victims Become Perpetrators," *Suffolk University Law Review* 38 (2005): 367–94.

4. Rosenthal, *Thirty-Eight Witnesses* (1964, 1999), 77; Nicholas Lemann, "A Call for Help," *The New Yorker*, March 10, 2014, 74.

5. Nancy Dillon, "Brother of Kitty Genovese to Release Documentary about Sister's 1964 Murder, Which Prompted 'Genovese Syndrome' Research," *New York Daily News*, March 10, 2014, http://www.nydailynews.com/news/crime/murder-prompted-genovese-syndrome-research-approaches-50-years-article-1.1715424 (accessed March 18, 2014).

6. Kevin Cook, *Kitty Genovese: The Murder, the Bystanders, the Crime That Changed America* (New York: W. W. Norton, 2014); Catherine Pelonero, *Kitty Genovese: A True Account of a Public Murder and Its Private Consequences* (New York: Skyhorse Publishing, 2014); Lemann, "A Call for Help," 74.

7. Lemann, "A Call for Help," 74.

8. Ibid., 76.

9. Bibb Latané, letter to the editor, *The New Yorker*, April 7, 2014, 3.

10. Lemann, "A Call for Help," 75.

11. Charles Kaiser, "When the *New York Times* Came Out of the Closet," *New York Review of Books*, September 25, 2012, http://www.nybooks.com/blogs/nyrblog/2012/sep/25/when-new-york-times-came-out-closet/ (accessed June 25, 2013); Rosenthal, *Thirty-Eight Witnesses* (1999), vii.

12. Angelo Lanzone, Las Vegas, March 1, 2014, notes in author's possession; Jim Rasenberger, comments at "Kitty Genovese Memorial Conference."

13. Peter Hellman, who coauthored the 1974 book *Chief!* with former New York chief of detectives Albert Seedman, published an e-book in 2014 titled *Fifty Years after Kitty Genovese: Inside the Case That Rocked Our Faith in Each Other* (New York: The Experiment). In it Hellman reiterates the 1974 version of the Johnson-Genovese story that he and Seedman published and provides a great deal of information about Anna Mae Johnson's life and death, including the racist remark of a Queens neighbor who was questioned during the investigation of the Johnson murder: "The druggist at the corner where Annie May [*sic*] sometimes used the pay telephone shrugged at her photo and said, 'They all look the same to me.'" Hellman does not discuss why Moseley was prosecuted only for Genovese's murder.

14. Peter C. Baker, "Missing the Story," *The Nation*, April 8, 2014, http://www.thenation.com/article/179250/missing-story (accessed April 13, 2014).

15. PAVE: Shattering the Silence of Sexual Violence, http://pavingtheway.net/word press/2013/07/the-reauthorization-of-vawa/ (accessed January 19, 2014).

16. Lemann, "A Call for Help," 77.

# Selected Bibliography

## Primary Sources

### Archives and Special Collections

*Film and Television Archive, University of California, Los Angeles*

*Lesbian Herstory Archives, Brooklyn, New York*
Lesbian bars in New York City, 1950s and 1960s Files

*Rare Book and Manuscript Library, Columbia University, New York*
Cecile Starr Papers, Series III

*Rare Books and Manuscript Collections, New York Public Library, New York*
A. M. Rosenthal Papers
Adolph Ochs Sulzberger Papers
New York Times Papers

*Benjamin Rosenthal Library, Special Collections and Archives, Queens College, City University of New York*
Civil Rights Archives

*Arthur and Elizabeth Schlesinger Library on the History of Women in America, Radcliffe Institute for Advanced Study, Harvard University, Cambridge*
Boston Women's Health Collective Book Collection

*Special Collections and Archives, Kent State University, Kent, Ohio*
Jean-Claude van Itallie and Open Theater Collections

*Special Collections and Archives, Michigan State University, East Lansing*
American Radicalism Collection

## Legal Documents

Appellant's Brief, *People of the State of New York v. Winston Moseley*, Court of Appeals, State of New York (March 1965).

Indictment, *People of the State of New York v. Winston Moseley*. Indictment no. 542–64, March 23, 1964. Queens County Supreme Court, Criminal Term.

Memorandum of Law, Respondent's Brief. *People of the State of New York v. Winston Moseley*. Indictment no. 542–64. Queens County Criminal Term (June 1964).

New York State Department of Corrections and Community Supervision, Board of Parole. Parole Board Hearing: *In the Matter of Winston Moseley*. Reappearance, Clinton Correction Facility, New York, November 1, 2011.

Report, Investigation Bureau, District Attorney, Queens County, New York, March 20, 1964. Defendant: Winston Moseley. Arresting Officer: Mitchell Sanz, Shield 70, 102nd Squad. Detective Assigned: John Carroll. ADA: Phillip J. Chetta.

## Periodicals

*Chicago Defender*
*Chicago Tribune*
*Ebony*
*Life*
*Long Island Press*
*Los Angeles Times*
*The Nation*
*New York Amsterdam News*
*New York Daily News*
*New York Newsday*
*New York Times*
*New York Times Magazine*
*New Yorker*
*Queens Courier*

*Queens Tribune*
*Washington Post*


## Selected Periodical Articles

Dowd, Maureen. "20 Years after the Murder of Kitty Genovese, the Question Remains: Why?" *New York Times*, March 12, 1984.

Gansberg, Martin. "37 Who Saw Murder Didn't Call the Police." *New York Times*, March 27, 1964.

Latané, Bibb, and John Darley. "Bystander 'Apathy.'" *American Scientist* 57, no. 2 (1969): 244–68.

Manning, Rachel, Mark Levine, and Alan Collins. "The Kitty Genovese Murder and the Social Psychology of Helping: The Parable of the 38 Witnesses." *American Psychologist* 62, no. 6 (September 2007): 555–62.

Rasenberger, Jim. "Kitty, 40 Years Later." *New York Times*, February 8, 2004.

———. "Nightmare on Austin Street." *American Heritage*, October 2006.

Rosenthal, A. M. "Study of the Sickness Called Apathy." *New York Times Magazine*, May 3, 1964.

———. "There Is No News from Auschwitz." *New York Times Magazine*, August 31, 1958.

———. "The 39th Witness." *New York Times*, February 12, 1987.

Wainwright, Loudon. "The Dying Girl That No One Helped." *Life*, April 10, 1964.

Weiland, Edward. "Kitty Worshipped Life in the City, and Died in Its Lonely Streets." *Long Island Press*, March 14, 1964.


## Interviews

De May, Joseph. Interview by author, March 13, 2009 (telephone); July 20, 2013 (telephone).

Lanzone, Angelo. Interview by author, July 6, 2010 (e-mail); September 19, 2010 (telephone); September 26, 2010 (telephone); December 20, 2011, Las Vegas; March 1, 2014, Las Vegas.

LoLo, LuLu (Lois Pascale Evans). Interview by author, July 17, 2011, New York.

Melia, John. Interview by author, August 25, 2013 (e-mail and telephone).

Rasenberger, Jim. Interview by author, July 28, 2013 (telephone).

Zielonko, Mary Ann. Interview by author, July 16, 2009 (telephone); August 18, 2013 (telephone).


## Audio and Visual Sources

Belvaux, Lucas. *One Night* (original title "38 témoins"). Agat Films, 2012.

"Catherine Genovese Memorial Conference on Bad Samaritanism," Fordham University, March 9-11, 1984; DVD.

Chase, Sylvia. "Do You Remember Kitty Genovese?" ABC News, *20/20*. Produced by Aram Boyajian. March 21, 1979.

De May, "The Witnesses That Didn't." WNYC radio, *On The Media*. Interview by Brooke Gladstone. March 27, 2009.

Duffy, Troy. *The Boondock Saints*. Indican Pictures, 1999.

*History's Mysteries,* "Silent Witnesses: The Kitty Genovese Murder." A&E Television Networks, 1999.

LoLo, LuLu. *38 Witnessed Her Death, I Witnessed Her Love: The Lonely Secret of Mary Ann Zielonko*. New York, 2009. DVD of live performance.

Rebeck, Theresa. WNYC radio, *Ten After Eleven*. Produced and directed by Brian Smith. April 15, 2005.

"Remembering Catherine 'Kitty' Genovese 40 Years Later: A Public Forum." Fordham University, March 9, 2004. DVD.

"Remembering Kitty Genovese: 45 Years Later," Fordham University, March 12, 2009; DVD.

Silliphant, Stirling. *Death Scream* (original title *Streetkill*). Directed by Richard T. Heffron. American Broadcasting Company, 1975.

Wallace, Mike. *The Apathetic American*. CBS, August 1964.

Zielonko, Mary Ann. "Remembering Kitty Genovese." National Public Radio, *Weekend Edition Saturday*. Sound Portraits Productions. Produced by Matthew Ozug. March 13, 2004.

## Books

Arendt, Hannah. *Eichmann in Jerusalem: A Report on the Banality of Evil*. Viking Press, 1963; Penguin Books, 1977, 2006.

Baldwin, James. *Nobody Knows My Name: More Notes of a Native Son*. Dell Publishing Co., 1961.

Brownmiller, Susan. *Against Our Will: Men, Women, and Rape*. Fawcett Columbine, 1975.

Davis, Angela. *Women, Race, and Class*. Random House, 1981; Vintage, 1983.

Decoin, Didier. *Est-ce que meurent les femmes?* (*Is This How Women Die?*). Grasset, 2009.

Duberman, Martin. *Midlife Queer: Autobiography of a Decade, 1971–1981*. Scribner, 1996.

Ellison, Harlan. "The Whimper of Whipped Dogs." 1973. In *Deathbird Stories*. Kilimanjaro Corporation, 2001.

Friedan, Betty. *The Feminine Mystique*. W. W. Norton, 1963.

Glazer, Nathan, and Daniel P. Moynihan. *Beyond the Melting Pot: The Negroes, Puerto Ricans, Jews, Italians, and Irish of New York City*. Joint Center for Urban Studies, Massachusetts Institute of Technology and Harvard University, 1963; 2nd ed., 1970.

Gottlieb, Barry, ed. *New York City in Crisis*. Pocket Books, 1965.

Jacobs, Jane. *The Death and Life of Great American Cities*. Random House, 1961.

Jahn, Ryan David. *Good Neighbors*. Penguin Books, 2009.

Lefkowitz, Bernard, and Kenneth G. Gross. *The Victims*. Dell, 1969.

May, Rollo. *Love and Will*. W. W. Norton, 1969.

Moore, Alan, and Dave Gibbons. *Watchmen*. DC Comics, 1986.

Rosenthal, A. M. *Thirty-Eight Witnesses: The Kitty Genovese Case*. McGraw-Hill, 1964; University of California Press, 1999; Melville House, 2012.

Sayre, Wallace S., and Herbert Kaufman. *Governing New York City: Politics in the Metropolis*. Russell Sage Foundation, 1960; 2nd ed., 1965.

Seedman, Albert A., and Peter Hellman. *Chief! Classic Cases from the Files of the Chief of Detectives*. Arthur Fields Books, 1974.

Stearn, Jess. *The Grapevine*. MacFadden-Bartell, 1965.

Uhnak, Dorothy. *Victims*. Simon and Schuster, 1985.

## Secondary Sources

Abraham, Julie. *Metropolitan Lovers: The Homosexuality of Cities*. University of Minnesota Press, 2006.

Baatz, Simon. *For the Thrill of It: Leopold, Loeb, and the Murder That Shocked Chicago*. HarperCollins, 2008.

Banes, Sally. *Greenwich Village 1963: Avant-Garde Performance and the Effervescent Body*. Duke University Press, 1993.

Benedict, Helen. *Virgin or Vamp: How the Press Covers Sex Crimes*. Oxford University Press, 1992.

Bevacqua, Maria. *Rape on the Public Agenda: Feminism and the Politics of Sexual Assault*. Northeastern University Press, 2000.

Biondi, Martha. "How New York Changes the Civil Rights Movement." In *Afro-Americans in New York Life and History: An Interdisciplinary Journal*, July 1, 2007. Reprinted at Fighting for Justice: New York Voices of the Civil Rights Movement, http://www.nyc.gov/html/cchr/justice/html/research/research.shtml (accessed June 10, 2013).

——. *To Stand and Fight: The Struggle for Civil Rights in Postwar New York City*. Harvard University Press, 2003.

Breitman, George, ed., *Malcolm X Speaks: Selected Speeches and Statements*. Grove Press, 1990.

Brier, Jennifer. *Infectious Ideas: U.S. Political Responses to the AIDS Crisis*. University of North Carolina Press, 2009.

Burns, Sarah. *The Central Park Five: A Chronicle of a City Wilding*. Knopf, 2011.

Caro, Robert A. *The Power Broker: Robert Moses and the Fall of New York*. Vintage Books, 1975.

Catledge, Turner. *My Life and the Times*. Harper & Row, 1971.

Cherry, Frances. *The Stubborn Particulars of Social Psychology*. Routledge, 1995.

Cohen, Deborah. *Family Secrets: Shame and Privacy in Modern Britain*. Oxford University Press, 2013.

Cohen, Miriam. *Workshop to Office: Two Generations of Italian Women in New York City, 1900–1950*. Cornell University Press, 1992.

Cohen, Patricia Cline. *The Murder of Helen Jewett*. Random House, 1998.

Cook, Kevin. *Kitty Genovese: The Murder, the Bystanders, the Crime That Changed America*. W. W. Norton & Co., 2014.

Copquin, Claudia Gryvatz. "Kew Gardens." In *The Neighborhoods of Queens*. Citizens Committee for New York City and Yale University Press, 2007. 115–17.

Curry, Michael R., David J. Phillips, and Priscilla M. Regan. "Emergency Response Systems and the Creeping Legibility of People and Places." *The Information Society* 20, no. 5 (November–December 2004): 357–69.

Davis, Angela Y. *Women, Race, and Class*. Random House, 1981.

D'Emilio, John. *Lost Prophet: The Life and Times of Bayard Rustin*. University of Chicago Press, 2004.

Diamond, Edwin. *Behind* The Times: *Inside the New* New York Times. Random House, 1993.

di Prima, Diane. *Recollections of My Life as a Woman: The New York Years*. Penguin Books, 2001.

Duberman, Martin. *Hold Tight Gently: Michael Callen, Essex Hemphill, and the Battlefield of AIDS*. New Press, 2014.

Duggan, Lisa. *Sapphic Slashers: Sex, Violence, and American Modernity*. Duke University Press, 2000.

English, T. J. *The Savage City: Race, Murder, and a Generation on the Edge*. HarperCollins, 2011.

Einstadter, Werner J. "Citizen Patrols: Prevention or Control?" *Crime and Social Justice*, no. 21 (January 1984): 200–212.

Eisenstadt, Peter. "Rochdale Village and the Rise and Fall of Integrated Housing in New York City." In *Civil Rights in New York City: From World War II to the Giuliani Era*. Ed. Clarence Taylor. Fordham University Press, 2011.

——. *Rochdale Village: Robert Moses, 6,000 Families, and New York City's Great Experiment in Integrated Housing*. Cornell University Press, 2010.

Ethier, Bryan. *True Crime: New York City*. Stackpole Books, 2010.

Flamm, Michael. *Law and Order: Street Crime, Civil Unrest, and the Crisis of Liberalism in the 1960s*. Columbia University Press, 2005.

Fletcher, Laurel E., and Harvey M. Weinstein, "Violence and Social Repair: Rethinking the Contribution of Justice to Reconciliation." *Human Rights Quarterly* 24, no. 3 (August 2002): 573–639.

Freedman, Estelle. *Redefining Rape: Sexual Violence in the Era of Suffrage and Segregation*. Harvard University Press, 2013.

Freeman, Joshua B. *Working-Class New York: Life and Labor since World War II*. New Press, 2000.

Gallo, Marcia M. *Different Daughters: A History of the Daughters of Bilitis and the Rise of the Lesbian Rights Movement*. Carroll & Graf, 2006; Seal Press, 2007.

Gallo, Pat, ed. *The Urban Experience of Italian-Americans*. American Italian Historical Association, City University of New York, 1977.

Gelb, Arthur. *City Room*. Penguin Group, 2003.

Gilfoyle, Timothy. *A Pickpocket's Tale: The Underworld of Nineteenth-Century New York*. W. W. Norton, 2006.

Gladwell, Malcolm. *The Tipping Point: How Little Things Can Made a Big Difference.* Little, Brown, 2000.

Goulden, Joseph C. *Fit to Print: A. M. Rosenthal and His Times.* Lyle Stuart, 1988.

Greer, Chris. *NewsMedia, Victims, and Crime.* Sage, 2007.

Halttunen, Karen. *Murder Most Foul: The Killer and the American Gothic Imagination.* Harvard University Press, 1998.

Hanhardt, Christina B. "Butterflies, Whistles, and Fists: Gay Safe Streets Patrols and the New Gay Ghetto, 1976–1981." *Radical History Review*, no. 100 (Winter 2008): 61–85.

Hardie, Melissa Jane. "Dead Spots in the Case of Kitty Genovese." *Australian Feminist Studies* 25, no. 65 (September 2010): 337–51.

Innes, Martin. "Signal Crimes and Signal Disorders: Notes on Deviance as Communicative Action." *British Journal of Sociology* 55, no. 3 (September 2004): 335–55.

Jackson, Kenneth T., ed. *The Encyclopedia of New York City.* Yale University Press, 1995.

Johns, Michael. *Moment of Grace: The American City in the 1950s.* University of California Press, 2003.

Johnson, Marilynn S. *Street Justice: A History of Police Violence in New York City.* Beacon Press, 2003.

Jones-Correa, Michael. *Between Two Nations: The Political Predicament of Latinos in New York City.* Cornell University Press, 1998.

Karmen, Andrew. *Crime Victims: An Introduction to Victimology.* Wadsworth Cengage, 2007.

——. *New York Murder Mystery: The True Story behind the Crime Crash of the 1990s.* New York University Press, 2000.

Kinsella, James. *Covering the Plague: AIDS and the American Media.* Rutgers University Press, 1989.

Lanson, Gerald, and Mitchell Stephens. "Abe Rosenthal: The Man and His Times." *Washington Journalism Review* (July–August 1983).

Levitt, Steven D., and Stephen J. Dubner. *SuperFreakonomics: Global Cooling, Patriotic Prostitutes, and Why Suicide Bombers Should Buy Life Insurance.* HarperCollins, 2009.

Lipsitz, George. *Time Passages: Collective Memory and American Popular Culture.* University of Minnesota Press, 1990.

Long, Kat. *The Forbidden Apple: A Century of Sex and Sin in New York City.* Ig Publishing, 2009.

Lopate, Phillip, ed. *Writing New York: A Literary Anthology.* Library of America, 1998.

Lorde, Audre. *Zami: A New Spelling of My Name.* Persephone Press, 1982.

Lui, Mary Ting Yi. *The Chinatown Trunk Mystery: Murder, Miscegenation, and Other Dangerous Encounters in Turn-of-the-Century New York.* Princeton University Press, 2005.

Manning, Rachel, Mark Levine, and Alan Collins. "The Kitty Genovese Murder and the Social Psychology of Helping: The Parable of the 38 Witnesses." *American Psychologist* 62, no. 6 (September 2007): 555–62.

——. "The Legacy of the 38 Witnesses and the Importance of Getting History Right." *American Psychologist* 63, no. 6 (September 2008): 562–63.

Martin, Del. *Battered Wives.* Volcano Press, 1976.

May, Elaine Tyler. "Security against Democracy: The Legacy of the Cold War at Home." *Journal of American History* 97, no. 4 (March 2011): 939–57.

McGuire, Danielle L. *At the Dark End of the Street: Black Women, Rape, and Resistance— A New History of the Civil Rights Movement from Rosa Parks to the Rise of Black Power.* Knopf, 2010.

Meyers, Marian. *News Coverage of Violence against Women: Engendering Blame.* Sage Publications, 1997.

Miller, Gale, and James Holstein, eds. *Constructionist Controversies: Issues in Social Problems Theory.* Aldine De Gruyter, 1990.

Monkkonen, Erich. *Murder in New York City.* University of California Press, 2001.

Muhammad, Khalil Gibran. *The Condemnation of Blackness: Race, Crime, and the Making of Modern Urban America.* Harvard University Press, 2010.

Murray, Sylvie. *The Progressive Housewife: Community Activism in Suburban Queens, 1945–1965.* University of Pennsylvania Press, 2003.

Nestle, Joan. "Restriction and Reclamation." In *Queers in Space: Communities, Public Places, Sites of Resistance.* Ed. Yolanda Retter, Anne-Marie Bouthillette, and Gordon Brent Ingram. Bay Press, 1997.

Pelonero, Catherine. *Kitty Genovese: A True Account of a Public Murder and Its Private Consequences.* Skyhorse Publishing, 2014.

Perkins, Douglas D., Paul Florin, Richard C. Rich, Abraham Wandersman, and David M. Chavis. "Participation and the Social and Physical Environment of Residential Blocks: Crime and Community Context." *American Journal of Community Psychology* 18, no. 1 (February 1990): 83–115.

Plunka, Gene A. *Jean Claude van Itallie and the Off-Broadway Theater.* University of Delaware Press, 1999.

Podair, Jerald E. *The Strike That Changed New York: Blacks, Whites, and the Ocean Hill–Brownsville Crisis.* Yale University Press, 2002.

Reitano, Joanne. *The Restless City: A Short History of New York from Colonial Times to the Present.* Routledge, 2006; Taylor and Francis e-Library, 2010.

Rentschler, Carrie. *Second Wounds: Victims' Rights and the Media in the U.S.* Duke University Press, 2011.

———. "An Urban Physiognomy of the 1964 Kitty Genovese Murder." *Space and Culture* 14, no. 3 (August 2011): 310–29.

Roberts, Sam, ed. *America's Mayor: John V. Lindsay and the Reinvention of New York.* Museum of the City of New York and Columbia University Press, 2010.

Rotolo, Suze. *A Freewheelin' Time: A Memoir of Greenwich Village in the Sixties.* Broadway Books, 2008.

Salisbury, Harrison. *Without Fear or Favor.* Times Books, 1980.

Samuel, Lawrence R. *The End of the Innocence: The 1964–1965 New York World's Fair.* Syracuse University Press, 2007.

Schneider, Eric C. *Vampires, Dragons, and Egyptian Kings: Youth Gangs in Postwar New York.* Princeton University Press, 1999.

Seedman, Albert A., and Peter Hellman. *Fifty Years after Kitty Genovese: Inside the Case That Rocked Our Faith in Each Other.* The Experiment, 2014.

Sen, Amartya. "Elements of a Theory of Human Rights." *Philosophy and Public Affairs* 32, no. 4 (Autumn 2004): 315–56.

Simon, Jonathan. "Governing through Crime Metaphors." *Brooklyn Law Review* 67 (2001–2): 1035.

Skoller, Charles E. *Twisted Confessions: The True Story behind the Kitty Genovese and Barbara Kralik Murder Trials.* Bridgeway Books, 2008; AuthorHouse, 2013.

Soothill, Keith, and Sylvia Walby, *Sex Crimes in the News.* Routledge, 1991.

Sotomayor, Sonia. *My Beloved World.* Knopf, 2013.

Srebnick, Amy Gilman. *The Mysterious Death of Mary Rogers: Sex and Culture in Nineteenth-Century New York.* Oxford University Press, 1995.

Stashower, Daniel. *The Beautiful Cigar Girl: Mary Rogers, Edgar Allan Poe, and the Invention of Murder.* Penguin Group, 2006.

Steinberg, Nicole, ed. *Forgotten Borough: Writers Come to Terms with Queens.* State University of New York Press, 2011.

Takooshian, Harold. "The 1964 Kitty Genovese Tragedy: Still a Valuable Parable." *PsycCritiques, Contemporary Psychology: APA Review of Books* 54, release 10, article 2 (March 11 2009).

Takooshian, Harold, and Herzel Bodiner. "Bystander Indifference to Street Crime." In *Contemporary Criminology.* Ed. Leonard D. Savitz and Norman Johnston. Wiley, 1982.

Talese, Gay. *The Kingdom and the Power.* World NAL, 1969.

Taylor, Clarence, ed. *Civil Rights in New York City: From World War II to the Giuliani Era.* Fordham University Press, 2011.

Thabit, Walter. *How East New York Became a Ghetto.* New York University Press, 2003.

Theoharis, Jeanne, and Komozi Woodard. *Groundwork: Local Black Freedom Movements in America.* New York University Press, 2005.

Tongson, Karen. *Relocations: Queer Suburban Imaginaries.* New York University Press, 2011.

van Itallie, Jean Claude. "The Open Theater (1963–1973): Looking Back." *Performing Arts Journal* 7, no. 3 (1983): 25–48.

von Hoffman, Alexander. *House by House, Block by Block: The Rebirth of America's Urban Neighborhoods.* Oxford University Press, 2003.

Walkowitz, Judith. *City of Dreadful Delight: Narratives of Sexual Danger in Late-Victorian London.* University of Chicago Press, 1992.

Wiese, Andrew. *Places of Their Own: African American Suburbanization in the Twentieth Century.* University of Chicago Press, 2004.

Wood, Jennifer K. "In Whose Name? Crime Victim Policy and the Punishing Power of Protection." *NWSA Journal* 17, no. 3 (Fall 2005): 1–17.

Zimring, Franklin. *The City That Became Safe: New York's Lessons for Urban Crime and Its Control.* Oxford University Press, 2012.

Zipp, Samuel. *Manhattan Projects: The Rise and Fall of Urban Renewal in Cold War New York.* Oxford University Press, 2010.

# Index